PASSIVE PROFITS

THE TURNKEY RENTAL INVESTOR'S GUIDE

*Business plans and systems to
build a profitable turnkey rental business*

SCOTT A. STANFIELD, PhD

Tuxedo Press

Copyright © 2024 by Scott A. Stanfield, II

All rights reserved. This book or any portion thereof may not be reproduced or used in any manner whatsoever without the express written permission of the publisher, except for the use of brief quotations in a book review.

ISBN (Paperback): 979-8-9888467-0-3
ISBN (eBook): 979-8-9888467-1-0

Cover Design and Interior Formatting by Aaxel Author Services

Printed in the United States of America

This book is sold with the understanding that the author is not engaged in rendering legal, accounting, tax, or other professional advice by publishing this book. Each individual situation is unique, and the contents of this book are broad in scope and are intended to assist in financial organization and decision-making. Your personal financial, legal, and tax situation is unique, and any information from the contents of this book may not be appropriate for your situation. Thus, if legal, tax, or financial advice or other expert assistance is required for your specific situation, the services of a competent professional should be sought to ensure that your situation has been evaluated carefully and appropriately. The author disclaims any liability, loss, or risk resulting directly or indirectly from the use or application of any of the contents of this book.

This book is dedicated to my family and friends. It only seems appropriate as this book would not have been written without their support and help. Thank you for always being there for me.

CONTENTS

Introduction 1

Part One: Getting Started as a Turnkey Investor

Chapter 1 Why Choose Turnkey Rental Investing? 9

Chapter 2 The Master Checklist for Turnkey Investing ... 13

Chapter 3 Turnkey Investor vs Turnkey Providers 23

Chapter 4 Setting Up Your New Turnkey Rental Business 29
- How to Determine Your Startup Costs 29
- Determining Your Business Structure 31
  - The Limited Liability Company 32
  - Real Estate Trust 34
- Title Transfers 35

Chapter 5 Financial Bookkeeping 37
- Separate Your Personal Finances from Your Business Finances 37
- Select a Bank 38
- Meet with Your Tax Professional 39
- Track Expenses and Revenue Streams 40

Part Two: The Fundamentals of Turnkey Rental Investing

Chapter 6 The Return on Investment 45

Chapter 7 The Four Returns of a Turnkey Investment Property 53
- Return 1: Cash Flow 54
- Return 2: Loan Paydown 54
- Return 3: Appreciation 57
- Return 4: The Return from Depreciation 59

Chapter 8 Accessing Equity Gains — 61
    Selling the Property — 61
    Refinancing the Property — 62
    Getting a HELOC for the Property — 62

Chapter 9 The Importance of the Mortgage: Leverage and Inflation — 65
    Leverage — 65
    The Interaction between Inflation and a Mortgage — 66

Chapter 10 The Real Estate Market Cycle — 69
    The Recovery Phase — 70
    The Expansion Phase — 71
    The Hyper Supply Phase — 73
    The Recession Phase — 73
    Putting it All Together — 75

Chapter 11 Crowd Psychology, Market Participants, and Establishing Market Trends — 79
    My Market Theory — 80

Part Three: Establishing Purchase Criteria and How to Evaluate a Market

Chapter 12 Personal Financials, Objectives, and Goals — 85
    Total Gross Income — 85
    Total Expenses — 86
    Total Debt — 87
        Personal Residence Debt — 87
        Rental Property Debt — 87
        Other Debt — 87
    Total Assets — 88
        Cash Assets — 88
        Asset Value of Rental Portfolio — 89
        Asset Value of Personal Residence — 89
        Asset Value of Retirement Accounts — 89
        Value of Everything Else — 89
    Setting Objectives and Goals — 90

Chapter 13 Cash Flow vs Appreciation Properties   93

Example 13.3 Cash Flow Properties versus
     Appreciation Properties   94
     Comparing Purchasing Requirements   94
     Appreciation Rates   95
     Monthly Fixed Expenses Comparison   95
     Projections of Returns   96
     Appreciation and ROI Analysis   97
     Tax Implications   98
     Carryover Losses   98
     Revisiting Definitions   99
     Portfolio Building   100
     Key Takeaways for This Chapter: 100

Chapter 14 How to Evaluate a Market   103

How to Select Cash Flow Markets   104
     Population and Population Dynamics   105
     Percentage of Renters   107
     The Housing Affordability Index   108
     Rent-to-Price Ratio   110
     Recent and Future Job Growth   111
     Gross Domestic Product   113
     Further Considerations   115
Selecting a Market Based on Appreciation   116
     Population and Population Dynamics   116
     Percentage of Renters, Housing Affordability Ratio, and
         Rent-to-Price Ratio   117
     Recent and Future Job Growth   118
     Gross Domestic Product   118
     Further Considerations   118
     Where to Invest—Metros that Meet the Criteria   119

Chapter 15 How to Find Good Turnkey Operators   123

How to Check the Quality of the Renovations   125
The Appraisal Problem   125
How to Handle the Appraisal Problem   127
The Value of a Good Turnkey Provider   129
Selecting a Turnkey Provider Using the Questionnaire   130

Part Four: Purchasing a Turnkey Property

Chapter 16 The Preapproval Process — 141
- Beginning the Purchasing Process — 141
- Preapproval Process and the Prequalification Process — 142
  - The Preapproval Process — 142
  - A Final Note About the Preapproval Process — 145

Chapter 17 How to Evaluate Properties — 147
- Evaluating Curb Appeal — 149
- Evaluating Property Specs — 149
- Review the Scope of Work — 150
- Estimate the Appraised Value — 152
  - Sales Comparison Method — 152
  - The Replacement Cost Method — 153
  - Income Method — 153
- Evaluate the Property Tax — 153
- Estimate the Financial Performance — 155
  - Compute the Cash Flow — 157
  - Compute the Cash-on-Cash ROI — 158
  - Estimate Appreciation — 159
- Strategically Schedule Your Closing — 160
- Determine Your Exit Plan — 161
- Putting Everything Together: My Purchasing Criteria — 162

Chapter 18 Purchase and Sales Agreement — 165
- The Inspection Contingency — 166
- The Appraisal Contingency — 166
- The Financing Contingency — 167
- The Title Contingency — 167
- The Property Disclosure — 167
  - Record Key Data — 167
  - Other Aspects to Watch Out For — 168

Part Five: After You Sign the Purchase and Sales Agreement

Chapter 19 Earnest Deposit — 173

Chapter 20 Property Insurance — 175

Chapter 21 Due Diligence and the Inspection Process   181
    Title Inspection   182
        Title Insurance   183
    Documentation Inspection   183
    The Physical Inspection   184
    The Appraisal Process   185

Chapter 22 The Closing Process   187

Chapter 23 What to Expect Going Forward   189

Chapter 24 Replacing or Finding Property Management   191

Part Six: Exit and Long-Term Strategies

Chapter 25 Long-Term Rental Performance   201
    Example 25.4 Financial Performance and Scaling for Cash Flow and Appreciation Properties   201
        Assumptions   202
        Scaling Results for Cash Flow Properties   204
        Scaling Results for Appreciation Properties   207
        A Note About Maintenance and Repairs   210
    A Summary of the Key Findings   211

Chapter 26 Lending Products   213
    Refinancing   214
    Cash-Out Refinance   214
    Refinance   216
    Home Equity Loan   217
    Home Equity Line of Credit (HELOC)   219
    HELOC Example   220
    Is a HELOC Right for You?   221

Chapter 27 Selling Properties   225
    Selling Option #1: Selling with a Real Estate Agent   227
    Selling Option #2: Selling Directly to an Investor   230
        Is It Worth It?   232

Selling Option #3: Selling Directly to your Tenant ... 232
Selling Option #4: Selling Using a Lease Option ... 235
Selling Option #5: Selling Using Seller Financing ... 238
Summary of the Different Selling Options ... 241

Part Seven: Long-Term Strategies

Chapter 28 Maximizing Cash Flow ... 245

Snowball Effect ... 246
Arbitrage Strategies ... 248
  Escrow Arbitrage ... 248
  Credit Card Arbitrage Strategy ... 250
  In Summary ... 252

Chapter 29 How to Scale Your Turnkey Business ... 253

Example 29.5 Executing the Business Scaling Action Items ... 255
  Option 1: Refinancing without Purchasing Any New Properties ... 262
  Option 2: Refinancing and Purchasing One New Property ... 263
  Option 3: Cash-Out Refinance without Buying a New Property ... 265
  Option 4: Cash-Out Refinance and Purchase Two New Properties ... 266
  Option 5: Home Equity Loan Without Purchasing New Properties ... 268
  Option 6: Home Equity Loan and Purchasing Two New Properties ... 269
  Option 7: Home Equity Line of Credit Without Purchasing New Properties ... 270
  Option 8: HELOC with Three New Purchases ... 272

Chapter 30 Succession Plans ... 281

Passing To Heirs ... 281
  Selling the Business Off One Property at a Time ... 282

Part Eight: Taxes and Retirement Accounts

Chapter 31 Real Estate Taxes	**287**
The Tax Benefits of Rental Property Investing	288
Annual Taxes	288
Annual Tax Example	289
Depreciation	291
Expenses for Real Estate Professionals vs. Non-Real Estate Professionals	295
Adjusting the Cost Basis	296
How to Include the Depreciation Return in Your Business Plan	297
For Real Estate Professionals	297
For Non-Real Estate Professionals	298
Tax Example for Real Estate Professional	298
1031 Tax Exchange	300
What is the 1031 Tax Exchange?	300
How to Perform a 1031 Tax Exchange	301
Depreciation Reset	303
Capital Gain Tax	303
How to Calculate Capital Gain Tax	304
Chapter 32 Retirement Accounts	**307**
Self-Directed IRA	**307**
Disadvantages of Rental Investing in a Self-Directed IRA	308
Unfavorable Loan Products	308
Rental Property Tax Advantages are Nullified.	309
Expenses Must be Paid from the IRA	310
401k Retirement Account Plan	311
401k from Your Employer	311
401k from Your Own Company	312
Putting it All Together	313

Part Nine: Beyond Turnkey Rental Investing

Chapter 33 Complementary Real Estate Investing Strategies	**317**
Converting Personal Residences into Rentals	318
Buying, Renovating, and Leveraging Your Network	322

Wrapping Up	**325**
Appendix A: Checklists	**327**
Master Checklist	328
Due Diligence Checklist	329
Establish a Purchase Criteria Checklist	332
Loan Preapproval Checklist	335
Market Evaluation Checklist	337
Monthly Business Management Checklist	339
New Business Setup Checklist	342
Post-Purchase Checklist	343
Property Evaluation Checklist	344
Purchase and Sales Agreement Checklist	347
Appendix B: Questionnaires	**349**
Business Bank Account Questionnaire	350
Certified Public Accountant Questionnaire	352
Inspector Questionnaire	354
Insurance Broker Questionnaire	356
Lawyer Questionnaire	357
Property Management Questionnaire	360
Questionnaire for Finding Good Turnkey Partners	362
Real Estate Agent Questionnaire	366
Appendix C: Mathematics for Loan Products	**371**
Appendix D: Mathematics for the Examples	**385**
Example 3.1 Turnkey Investor versus Turnkey Provider	387
Example 10.2 Market Cycle Analysis for Atlanta, GA	401
Example 13.3 Cash Flow Properties vs Appreciation Properties	407
Example 25.4 Projected Financial Performance and Scaling for Cash Flow and Appreciation Properties	416
Example 29.5 Executing the Business Scaling Action Items	422
Glossary	**445**

INTRODUCTION

Turnkey rentals are single and multifamily rental properties that have been newly built or fully renovated and then tenanted, with professional property management in place, and are then sold to an investor. Hence, all aspects of the rental property business are neatly outsourced in one simple purchase, which is the defining characteristic of a turnkey rental business.

Businesses that specialize in selling turnkey rentals to investors, known as turnkey providers, can be found operating in every major metropolitan area in the United States, which is one of the many advantages of turnkey property investing. At first glance, turnkey rentals may seem like a fairly straightforward and simple investment vehicle; however, like all worthwhile endeavors, there are many subtle details that you must understand and properly implement in order to lower your risks and increase your profits.

Before I get into the details about turnkey rental investing, let me talk about my experiences and portfolio. I completed my PhD in engineering in 2009 and worked as a research scientist in the Air Force Research Laboratory at Wright-Patterson Air Force Base in Dayton, Ohio. My real estate investment journey began in 2013 when I purchased two luxury condos in downtown Cincinnati, Ohio. I self-managed them for a while but quickly discovered that I was working too many hours for the small profits I generated. I eventually sold both condos and made a small profit; in fact, if you were to determine my hourly rate—that is, the total profit I made divided by the total number of hours I spent working on those properties—it would have been less than $10 an hour.

Operating those condos, which included tenant screening and placement, answering late-night emergency calls, and handling leases, repairs, maintenance, rent collection, and all the other aspects of operating a rental, proved to be an excellent learning experience. For example, I learned that I never wanted to manage property again, though I still wanted the benefits of rentals. I also realized that I wanted an investment vehicle more suitable for my busy professional work schedule. This insight led me down the path toward turnkey rentals, and, after spending a lot of time researching, I purchased my first turnkey rental property in Memphis, Tennessee, in 2017.

The purchase price was $119,000, with a down payment of just under $24,000. I was all in at just over $30,000, which included all the expenses associated with buying the property. That property produced a profit of $334.64 per month after paying the fixed expenses: the property management fee, property tax, property insurance, and the mortgage. More importantly, I spent less than one hour per month working on anything related to the property.

Fast-forward five years, and the property has increased in value to $192,000 with a monthly profit of $685.88. This growth in property value and rental rate throughout this time proved to be much faster than its average historic growth. Based on the average historical rates in the United States, the value of the house would have been around $142,000 after five years, with a monthly profit from the rent of around $460 per month after fixed expenses. In my opinion, that is still very good, especially when the other benefits, such as the loan paydown and taxes, are accounted for.

INTRODUCTION

As of this writing, my turnkey rental business contains twelve rentals (I sold three), produces a cash flow of $5,450 per month, and has a total appraised value of just under $3 million with $1.3 million in equity. I still spend less than two hours per month working on my turnkey rental business. That time involves reading monthly statements, reviewing the business checking account, and making sure all the automatic payments are processed correctly.

For many, the idea of having a large portfolio of income-producing investment properties that require very little time sounds too good to be true. For the naysayers, I know it can be done because I have done it, and I know others can too. I have helped them do it. It is certainly true that you need some funds to begin a turnkey rental business, and while the speed at which your business grows will depend on how much money you can invest, your business will still increase once you own at least one property.

I have encountered many who've shown interest in owning and operating a turnkey rental business. The main hurdle preventing a lot of these people from moving forward is a lack of guidance. That guidance is the main focus of this book.

In *Passive Profits*, I define all the processes required to operate a turnkey rental business. Each process is broken down into a list of action items, presented as a checklist. Every detail and nuance in these lists are thoroughly discussed. I've included them to help guide you on exactly how to begin, manage, and grow a turnkey rental business.

With proper execution of the business processes provided in this book, you can enjoy substantial income while spending no more than two hours a month working. Perhaps more importantly, a well-honed business plan with excellent business processes will help you scale your turnkey rental business to as many properties as you desire while maintaining low working hours. For example, my business portfolio grew to twelve rental properties in a short period even as my time spent working on my business has remained at less than two hours a month.

Having a clearly defined path forward is just one advantage of reading the checklists in this book. Other key advantages of using the checklists include

- lower risks because you are leveraging my experience and the lessons I learned,
- rapid acceleration of your business,
- an agile business that does not rely on one person,
- the ability to outsource business activities, thereby removing you from your business,
- the seamless ability to pass your business to your heir or heirs, and
- the ability to sell your business.

To the best of my knowledge, at the time this book was printed, no other book provided checklists for the different business processes of a turnkey rental business. It is worth noting that the checklists in my book *Passive Profits*, which include my purchasing criteria, were developed for my goals, objectives, and resources. The tools and specific examples I discuss in this book offer specific instructions on how to modify or redevelop my criteria based on your goals, objectives, and resources, at least within the realm of turnkey rental investing.

Not only does this book provide checklists for you to use to help streamline the process but it also provides a very different and complimentary perspective. This is one of the first books published by a dedicated turnkey investor. A few other books are out there on turnkey rental investing, but those were written and published by turnkey rental providers, not investors.

That said, many rental investment books are certainly available, and while turnkey rental investing overlaps with many topics from other real estate investment strategies, it is a unique strategy that requires special treatment to capture the specific nuances.

Due to the ever-changing nature of the professionals in this industry, such as turnkey providers, CPAs, and property management companies, this book will not include referral information. For those who would like up-to-date referral information or to share experiences and feedback, you are welcome to email me at:

scott@scottastanfield.com

I would be more than happy to share who I use for my business, and feedback about the book is always welcome.

Additionally, apps such as a purchase calculator or market evaluation tool and new information about turnkey rental investing, which can be found in quarterly market reports, are provided for free at my website:

https://scottastanfield.com.

I encourage you to visit my website regularly as I am constantly adding new resources.

My website also includes a blog and videos, all of which are designed to (1) educate, and (2) provide up-to-date information about turnkey rental investing. In this regard, I can provide up-to-date information for any section of this book that becomes antiquated. The videos are also available at https://www.youtube.com at the channel:

TheTurnkeyRentalGuide.

To summarize, I have been very pleased with my decision to invest in turnkey rentals. It has proven an excellent strategy and as close to a perfect fit for my busy schedule as I think I could have found. It's also been an excellent strategy for building supplemental income, and, as I alluded to above, the income can grow over time and eventually surpass your main source of income. For these reasons and many more (to be identified in this book), I think turnkey rental investments are an excellent fit for busy professionals or people with busy schedules. With that, it is time to dive into Part One of this book.

PART ONE: GETTING STARTED AS A TURNKEY INVESTOR

CHAPTER 1

WHY CHOOSE TURNKEY RENTAL INVESTING?

Turnkey rental investing is a good choice for many reasons. For one, it can provide you with significant passive income every month when properly executed. While the norm is to work around one hour or less per month on your turnkey rental business, times will arise when you must put in more work such as when you purchase a new property. Regardless, your hourly rate will be extremely high, and the work can be performed from anywhere. That is why the income is passive, i.e., income earned while you spend your time on other activities.

More importantly, the time you spend managing your business will not increase if you add more properties, at least not significantly. It should only result in your hourly rate increasing. Additionally, many turnkey providers can provide properties on demand. Hence, a turnkey rental business is scalable; your hourly rate, and therefore, your earnings, will continue to increase as your business matures. For these reasons and others I will go into later in this chapter, turnkey rental investing is a great investment vehicle for working professionals or individuals who can leverage their time to generate other income-producing streams while focusing on their careers or on other callings in life.

While the gains from turnkey rentals may not be as large as the potential gains earned by purchasing, renovating, and managing investment properties, for individuals who have never managed property, your risk and losses are more likely to be lower with turnkey rentals. For example, consider the process involved when purchasing an investment property. You will almost certainly spend a fair amount of time looking for the ideal property. Once found, you will need to walk the property and estimate the renovation budget, determine what the property is worth once fixed, and decide on an offer. This process is labor intensive and requires not only some experience and know-how but also a dependable and experienced contractor or team of contractors to get the work done in a competitive market.

Moreover, the financial model your offer is based on will need to include projections for how long the property will sit vacant so that property tax, insurance, and utilities are accounted for prior to receiving income from a renter. Once the renovation begins, unforeseen problems might be uncovered that can cost you thousands of dollars and delays. You might think the inspection process will uncover these problems, and it likely will, but not always.

Now, assume the property is ready for rent. A lot of time and knowledge is required to find a potentially good tenant. You will need to market the property and determine how to accept applications, what you will use for your screening criteria, and how to run a credit report and a criminal report, as well as keep a flexible schedule for showing the property. Don't forget, you must also look into the various federal, state, and local laws for operating rental properties. Next, you will need to determine how you will accept rental payments as well as create a system to document the rental income and deposits. On top of all of that will be the evictions, twenty-four seven phone calls, scheduled maintenance and repairs, and tenant move-ins and move-outs that you'll have to handle. Lastly, you will be constrained to living near the property, and forget about going out of town unless you have someone to help with emergency phone calls.

Clearly, the process of operating a real estate investment business requires more time than operating a turnkey rental one. Moreover, the property you purchase from a turnkey provider will have already been renovated and the work described above already completed. Hence, the probability of unexpected expenses is lower, thus lowering your risk.

When you build your rental portfolio through a turnkey provider, you are leveraging the turnkey's renovation and management teams. By doing so, building a rental property portfolio becomes a possibility for more than just real estate professionals or individuals with a significant amount of time and dedication.

You can see through the examples I've provided so far that deciding between turnkey rental investing and operating a real estate investment business comes down to individual preference, available resources, knowledge, and goals. Turnkey investments also provide other excellent opportunities that might not be possible for you otherwise. For example, a good turnkey provider operates in specific neighborhoods that maximize profits for their clients, based on their research, market knowledge, and experience. By renovating many properties in the same neighborhoods, turnkey providers can force appreciation beyond the rate one would expect or predict, thus increasing returns.

Turnkey companies can be found operating in every major city. This provides opportunities to own property outside of your local city. By diversifying your portfolio to include multiple markets, your risk decreases. Investors living in cities with pro-tenant laws, high property tax, or high purchase prices will likely find opportunities with a turnkey provider they would not have otherwise. Though such opportunities can be achieved without a turnkey provider, they are significantly more difficult and time-consuming to find that way.

In summary, the many excellent qualities offered by turnkey investing align well with the goals and resources of many. To take full advantage of this opportunity, you'll need to develop a plan and execute it accordingly. Within this book is a plan tailored to my resources that you can easily customize to meet your goals, objectives, and own resources. For example, the purchase price and number of properties I initially targeted were selected to fit my funds. Your resources may allow for or require you to develop a different startup process for your business.

CHAPTER 2

THE MASTER CHECKLIST FOR TURNKEY INVESTING

To achieve your turnkey rental investing goals, you will need a plan. That's why I included my Master Checklist in this book. When followed correctly, executing the Master Checklist—a list of processes that I've ordered logically and chronologically based on my experiences and lessons learned—will result in successfully beginning, managing, and growing a turnkey rental business.

Each chapter begins with a resources box indicating which step of the Master Checklist is covered, as well as the associated checklists and questionnaires available within the appendices at the end of the book. These individual checklists are designed to help guide you through each step of the Master Checklist; the questionnaires included are comprised of questions I recommend you use when interviewing the different professionals you'll need in your business such as turnkey providers, property managers, insurance brokers, lawyers, and certified public accounts (CPAs).

All checklists and questionnaires mentioned throughout this book are available in printable form in **Appendix A: Checklists** and **Appendix B: Questionnaires**.

The processes listed in the Master Checklist are:

- ☐ Begin your business using the **New Business Setup Checklist**.
- ☐ Select the metropolitan area or areas you want to invest in by using the **Market Evaluation Checklist**.
- ☐ Select a turnkey provider using the **Questionnaire for Finding Good Turnkey Partners**.
- ☐ Establish your purchase criteria using the **Establish a Purchase Criteria Checklist**.
- ☐ Interview and select your property inspector using the **Inspector Questionnaire**.
- ☐ Complete the preapproval process with a lender using the **Loan Preapproval Checklist**.
- ☐ Evaluate potential turnkey rental properties using the **Property Evaluation Checklist**.
- ☐ Put a property under contract using the **Purchase and Sales Agreement Checklist**.
- ☐ Use the **Due Diligence Checklist** to complete the due diligence process.
- ☐ Use the **Post-Purchase Checklist** to set up your monthly management for a new property purchase.
- ☐ Use the **Monthly Business Management Checklist** to manage your ongoing business.

The Master Checklist, which includes eleven processes, can be further broken down into sixteen steps that loosely describe the day-to-day business processes. For each step, I included the criteria I used and am still using to create and grow my turnkey rental investment business. One important aspect discussed in this book is how I established my criteria. That way, you can more easily understand my process and then change it as needed to better fit your goals and resources.

Do not get overwhelmed with the number of steps. Purchasing a property will be the most time-intensive process, but the steps involved are typically spread out over a two-to-three-month period. Otherwise, many of these steps require only a few minutes to one hour at most.

Step 1. Determine the funds you have available to invest.

These funds represent your maximum purchase price for a turnkey property, which you should never exceed. The investment funds need to cover the down payment, closing costs, and reserve fund.

Checklist for Step 1: **New Business Setup Checklist**

Step 2. Determine how to title the property.

The title for a property shows who owns it. The primary purpose of having some sort of business structure, defined in this book as how your rental properties are titled, is to provide asset protection. Some of your options include titling in your personal name, an LLC, or a trust—all of which have advantages and disadvantages. Seek guidance from an asset protection lawyer and your tax preparer. These professionals will set up a plan for you.

Checklists for Step 2: **Lawyer Questionnaire** and **Certified Public Accountant Questionnaire**

Step 3. Set up your financial system for your business.

I recommend separating your personal finances from your rental business even if you plan to title the properties in your name instead of that of a company. This will require setting up a separate checking account with a linked credit card for your rental business.

Checklist for Step 3: **Business Bank Account Questionnaire**

Step 4. Set your investment criteria.

Investment criteria is an all-encompassing term that describes everything related to a rental property. These criteria include some of the more commonly thought-of parameters such as price, the size of the property, and its number of bedrooms and bathrooms. It also includes the age of the HVAC, the roof, and other components with various life expectancies. The investment criteria you set will vary due to changes in the area you choose to buy within as well as what is needed in your rental portfolio. The nature of your criteria can also change due to the variability of the tenants that you are trying to cater to.

Checklist for Step 4: **Establish a Purchase Criteria Checklist**

Step 5. Select the metropolitan area where you want to invest.

Rental turnkey providers can be found in just about every major city. This fact allows you to determine which cities you want to invest in based on economic and demographic criteria coupled with your goals, investment criteria, and portfolio needs.

Checklist for Step 5: **Market Evaluation Checklist**

Step 6. Interview and select a turnkey provider.

My recommendation is to use or adapt the questionnaire provided later in this book to complete this step.

Checklist for Step 6: **Questionnaire for Finding Good Turnkey Partners**

Step 7. Get pre-approved for a loan unless you are planning to purchase with cash.

Your turnkey provider will almost certainly require you to get pre-approved for a mortgage. Fortunately, these providers work with several lending institutions, any of which they can recommend to you. Select a lender and complete the pre-approval process.

Checklist for Step 7: **Loan Preapproval Checklist**

Step 8. Request properties from the turnkey provider.

At this stage, I always communicate my purchase criteria with the turnkey provider. The provider will send you property brochures that typically include a financial model with projections for income, expenses, and profit. Make sure you perform your own analysis; do not select a property unless it meets the criteria you established in Step 4.

Checklist for Step 8: **Property Evaluation Checklist**

Step 9. Commit and sign the purchase and sales contract.

The purchase and sales agreement is a legally binding contract that lists all the terms and conditions between the seller and the buyer of the property.

Checklist for Step 9: **Purchase and Sales Agreement Checklist**

Step 10. Hire an inspector and select property insurance.

For each property purchased, you should have an inspection done. A closing coordinator or closing liaison from the turnkey provider will reach out and offer multiple inspectors. Review the inspectors presented and either select one or find an inspector independently. I would advise you to do your own research and hire an inspector independently.

It is very important that property insurance be in place before closing. Otherwise, you could lose your entire investment should a fire or some other disaster occur while you own the property before your insurance is in place.

Your turnkey liaison will likely provide a quote for insurance, and the coverage and price will likely be very good. You should still compare insurance policies; check the coverage provided and the premiums charged.

Questionnaire and Checklists for Step 10: **Inspector Questionnaire**, **Due Diligence Checklist**, and **Insurance Broker Questionnaire**

Step 11. Prepare and deliver financial documents to the bank.

The bank will reach out and request many documents during the underwriting process, including checking and savings account statements, retirement account statements, and paystubs. Save the documents to a separate folder to help you reference which documents will be needed for future purchases.

During this time, the bank will order the appraisal of the property. Even if you decide to purchase the property with cash, you should still have the property appraised. The appraisal process protects the buyer and lender. It is advised that you delay any major purchases during this time to prevent other delays or complications.

Step 12. Evaluate the inspection and appraisal reports.

You and the turnkey liaison will receive a copy of the inspection and appraisal reports when they are ready.

Checklist for Step 12: **Due Diligence Checklist**

Step 13. Schedule the closing.

Closing, the process during which you complete the purchase of the property, requires a third party to witness that you are the one purchasing and signing the documents. To complete the closing, the liaison will reach out to schedule a traveling notary. Make sure to have a copy of your driver's license handy.

Step 14. Set up your portal account.

Your portal account, which is your personal account with your turnkey provider, is a browser-based program accessible online from anywhere. The in-house property management team or outsourced management team will reach out to help you set up your portal account.

The portal will include the current status of your property, answering such questions as whether the property has a tenant or is vacant and the status of rent. You can also find important documentation in the portal such as proof of insurance, the property management agreement, the lease, and current and past monthly financial statements.

Checklist for Step 14: **Post-Purchase Checklist**

Step 15. Set up automatic payment for the mortgage.

Log into the business checking account (see Step 3) and set up an automatic payment for the mortgage. The mortgage payment will include the property tax and property insurance unless you have waived the escrow account.

Checklist for Step 15: **Post-Purchase Checklist**

Step 16. Block time each month to manage the business.

I block one hour on the twenty-fifth of every month (one day before the automatic payment is scheduled). In the beginning, you may need more time, so plan accordingly.

Checklist and Questionnaires for Step 16: **Monthly Business Management Checklist**, **Property Management Questionnaire**, and **Real Estate Agent Questionnaire**

These are the same sixteen steps I use to purchase and manage my turnkey rental properties. It is also worth noting,

- starting a new business will require completing the sixteen steps listed,

- more time will be needed to complete the steps listed when you start the business than when repeating those steps for additional purchases, and
- monthly management of the business is handled only in Step 16, which requires one to two hours of work per month.

These steps should provide you with a good idea of the work and time required to operate your own turnkey rental business, along with the advantages that come with it. Moreover, this introduction provides an idea of the profits and the required startup funds involved.

At this stage, it is worth summarizing the information presented thus far so that you can decide if turnkey rental investing is right for you.

- At the time of this writing, purchasing a turnkey rental property requires between $40,000 to $50,000 for the properties I target.
- The monthly profits (cash flow) are on the order of $300 per month and increase on average by $25 per month each year (historical rental growth rate).
- There are other monetary benefits, including tax savings, loan paydown, and appreciation. The typical return on investment for the properties I target is between 20 and 25 percent annually when all these monetary benefits are taken into consideration.
- It takes around fifteen to twenty hours of work to purchase your first property.
- It takes around eight to ten hours of work to purchase additional properties.
- It takes around one to two hours of work per month to manage your business.
- You can invest in any metropolitan area you want.
- You can perform the work from anywhere.

- The time you spend managing your business will not increase by adding more properties.
- Many turnkey providers can provide properties on demand; hence, the turnkey rental business is scalable.
- For many, turnkey rentals offer lower risk and lower barrier to entry than other buy-and-hold real estate investment strategies.
- Good turnkey providers bring value such as professional services and knowledge about the neighborhoods in their markets that you can leverage by partnering with them.

Some of the cons to turnkey rental investing are:

- Rental properties can require a lot of time to sell.
- Liability protection requires help from other professionals to properly set up.
- Income taxes become more complicated.

You should spend some time reviewing the pros and cons of turnkey rental investing before launching your business. The strategy provided in this book fits well for my needs, but it isn't for everyone. Now that you have an overall picture of a turnkey rental business, I will go into how the turnkey business operates by looking at the activities of turnkey providers, turnkey investors, and the more typical buy-and-hold rental investor in Chapter 3.

CHAPTER 3

TURNKEY INVESTOR VS TURNKEY PROVIDERS

Whenever I begin something new, I like to understand how all the different players operate and compare. As for turnkey rental investing, I wanted to know not just the monetary compensation for turnkey providers and the more traditional buy-and-hold rental investors but also how their businesses compared with my turnkey rental business. I felt the best way to do this was through a side-by-side comparison. Below, I list the total returns and time spent on an investment property for:

- **The turnkey rental investor**: An investor who builds their portfolio through turnkey providers.
- **The turnkey provider**: A business that specializes in buying, renovating, selling, and managing properties.
- **The traditional rental investor**: An investor that buys, renovates, rents out, and manages a property.

My financial calculations for this example can be found in **Appendix D: Mathematics for the Examples** as **Example 3.1 Turnkey Investor versus Turnkey Provider**. The discussion below provides a summarized version of the key findings.

Before we begin, bear in mind that the results in this example are not guaranteed. If you purchase a similar property, you may not necessarily achieve the same results. Your results could be significantly better, or they could be worse. This example uses the financial data for the first turnkey rental property I purchased. Hence, much of the financial data is well-established.

The timeline is fairly straightforward; the turnkey provider or the traditional rental investor purchased the property, renovated the property, and found a tenant. The invested funds for the turnkey provider and traditional rental investor were $99,700. It is assumed that this process took three months. At the three-month mark, the turnkey provider sold the property to me, the turnkey investor, whereas the traditional rental investor continued to self-manage the property. A visual illustration of the timeline is shown below in Table 1.

Table 1. Timeline of events for the turnkey provider, traditional investor, and turnkey investor.

	Turnkey Provider	**Traditional Investor**	**Turnkey Investor**
0-3 Months	Purchased a property	Purchased a property	
0-3 Months	Renovated the property	Renovated the property	
3 Months	Tenanted the property	Tenanted the property	
3 Months	Sold property to turnkey investor	Manages property	Purchased property from turnkey provider
Funds Invested	$99,700	$99,700	$28,980

The funds I invested in the property were initially much lower than the other two investors at $28,980. These funds represent my down payment; the remaining balance owed was covered by a mortgage. I assumed the turnkey provider and traditional rental investor purchased the property in cash, a fairly common occurrence when purchasing investment properties due to deferred maintenance. The total profit shown below in Table 2 is the sum of all the returns produced by the rental property after one year of ownership.

Table 2. Comparison of Year 1 financial summary

Performance Comparison	Turnkey Provider	Traditional Investor	Turnkey Investor
Total Profit	$23,038	$33,282	$9,414
ROI	23.1%	33.4%	32.5%
Hours Worked	480	480	20
Hourly Rate	$48	$69	$471

Clearly, the total profits earned are greater for the turnkey provider and traditional rental investor at the cost of more risk; however, the ROI and hours worked by a turnkey investor do provide some advantages.

My total profit, the turnkey provider's profit, and the traditional rental investor's profit were estimated at $9,414, $23,038, and $33,282, respectively. At a glance, it appears that the traditional rental investor has the largest return. However, in order to make a fair comparison, we need to

- utilize the return on investment, which illustrates the annual return as a percentage of the funds invested, and
- calculate the hourly rate of our effort as an investor.

The return on investment (ROI) is defined below in Equation 3.1 as the annualized return divided by the invested funds or

$$ROI = \frac{Annual\ Return}{Invested\ Funds} \times 100$$

As shown above in Table 2, my ROI is 32.5 percent, which is greater than the 23.1 percent of the turnkey provider. You'll note that the ROI for the traditional rental investor is similar to mine but will likely be much greater in Year 2, or as soon as they are eligible to refinance the property.

One of the key advantages of the turnkey provider is, selling the property at the three-month mark returns their investment funds, along with some profits. Opening up these funds means they can be used to secure a new property, which can then be sold again to me or another turnkey rental investor once the property is ready.

If the turnkey provider can maintain the pace of buying, renovating, tenanting, and selling a property every three months, they can potentially sell four properties in one year. Their ROI would increase by as much as a factor of four to 92.4 percent, but understand—this business plan carries more risk than mine. Also note: The ROI is 92.4 percent, much higher than what the provider will net after they pay their capital gain taxes.

Regarding the hourly rate, purchasing and renovating the property is a full-time effort. I assumed in my calculations that 480 man-hours of work were required by the turnkey provider and traditional rental investor, whereas I worked about twenty hours. As shown in Table 2, my hourly rate was approximately $471 per hour. The turnkey provider's and traditional rental investor's rates were estimated at $48 and $69 per hour, respectively.

While all three investors made a decent return, note these important points:

- The turnkey provider can make a much larger return on investment than the other two investors if they can continuously find below-market deals and buyers without

missing a major monetary setback from an unforeseen rehab expense.
- The turnkey provider absorbs a lot of the risk and then sells the property to the turnkey investor.
- The hourly rate of the turnkey investor is significantly greater than that of the other two investors in the beginning, and it would take time for the turnkey provider and traditional rental investor to outsource the work to increase their hourly rates.

Now you should have a good sense of what turnkey rental investing is and how it varies from traditional rental investments. I've provided the basics regarding the time, resources, and monetary commitments required for you to determine whether turnkey rentals are the right business strategy for you. Just like with any venture, the first step is always the hardest. The next chapter, geared toward starting up your turnkey rental business, is all about taking that first step.

CHAPTER 4

SETTING UP YOUR NEW TURNKEY RENTAL BUSINESS

> Where We Are At: Master Checklist Steps 1 and 2
> - **New Business Setup Checklist**
> - **Lawyer Questionnaire**

Starting a turnkey rental business requires (1) determining the startup costs needed to begin, and (2) determining your business structure.

How to Determine Your Startup Costs

Your initial startup costs or investment funds include

- the down payment to buy a property,
- the closing costs, and
- the reserve fund.

The down payment is determined as 20 percent of the purchase price of the property. For example, the down payment for a $200,000 property is $40,000:

$$20\% \times \$200{,}000 = \$40{,}000.$$

The criteria I provide in this book target turnkey rentals with a purchase price between $150,000 and $250,000, which means the down payment will range between $30,000 and $50,000.

$$20\% \times \$150,000 = \$30,000.$$

$$20\% \times \$250,000 = \$50,000.$$

Next, we'll determine the closing costs, which are the expenses accrued by your business when purchasing properties. The fees pay the lender, title company, inspector, and appraiser. The closing cost is typically around 3 percent of the purchase price. That means, the closing costs for a $150,000 purchase price is $4,500:

$$3\% \times \$150,000 = \$4,500.$$

Hence, the closing costs will range between $4,500 and $7,500 for properties priced between $150,000 and $250,000.

The reserve fund is intended to cover any unexpected expenses associated with the property. I recommend a reserve fund of $5,000 for the first property and an additional $2,000 for each additional property for the turnkey rental properties targeted by the business plan in this book. Later, when you understand more about accessing your risk in the market, you can adjust the reserve fund accordingly.

Your total startup funds are, again, the sum of the down payment, closing costs, and the reserve fund. For a $150,000 property, your startup funds are estimated at $39,500:

$$\$30,000 + \$4,500 + \$5,000 = \$39,500.$$

Similarly, the startup funds for a $200,000 property are estimated at $67,500:

$$\$55,000 + \$7,500 + \$5,000 = \$67,500.$$

Hence, the startup funds needed to execute the business plan in this book and purchase your first turnkey rental property, valued between $150,000 and $250,000, would be $39,500 and $67,500, respectively. If you choose to target properties outside of the price range given, you can use the same process above to determine your startup funds.

Determining Your Business Structure

When setting up your business, it is important to hire an asset protection lawyer to help with the process. To that end, I included the questionnaire in the resources box at the beginning of this chapter to help you interview different lawyers. That being said, setting up a business refers to how your business is structured, defined here as how you plan to title your properties. As previously mentioned, the title for a property shows who owns that property, which is recorded by the county and is publicly available. There are many ways to title a property. The most common ones are

- in your personal name,
- in a Limited Liability Company (LLC), or
- in a trust.

Fannie Mae guidelines—the regulations used by underwriters for conventional mortgages—require the property to initially be titled in your personal name. In general, however, I do not recommend keeping the title in your name. If a rental property is kept titled in your personal name, it won't be possible to separate your personal assets from your business assets. To give yourself a layer of protection and reduce liability, you must keep the two separate. So, although the property is titled in your name at the time of purchase, you can transfer the title to your business or trust afterward. Note: You can finish the transfer from your personal name into your business well after the closing date if you choose.

The primary purpose of having some sort of business structure is to provide asset protection. There are also tax implications with each business structure, a topic that is beyond the scope of this book. Seek professional guidance with your CPA regarding such tax matters.

The Limited Liability Company

The idea behind the LLC is to separate your personal assets from your business assets. If a tenant were to sue and win, they would, in theory, be able to receive a settlement up to the monetary value of the assets in the LLC but not the assets held in other LLCs or your personal assets.

While the use of LLCs for liability protection may seem convoluted, it can be illustrated with a simple example. Envision a messy room and multiple empty containers. The messy room represents everything you own, which includes your personal assets and rental properties. Each container represents an LLC or your personal assets. It would be difficult for a court to sort through your messy room to decide which assets belong to your business and which belong to you personally.

The solution is simple: Sort the messy room (assets) into different empty containers. Make sure to document exactly what is in each container, how the containers are structured (personal, LLC 1, LLC 2, etc.), and exactly how the assets are stored. At any rate, your personal assets will be stored in one container, and your business assets will be stored in another. This concise structure is needed for a legal interpretation. If the need to go to court ever arose, you could grab the container required, allowing the rest to go untouched. If you do not keep your assets separate, the courts have to look through everything, and your personal assets could be affected.

You can further partition the assets of the business. For example, maybe you would like to have a designated container for each property. Once the assets have been separated and properly stored, it is easy for a third party to review your assets and determine which assets belong to you and which belong to your businesses.

Further, legally, these different containers are treated as different people or entities. If a person had an issue with McDonald's, they would not file a lawsuit against Burger King. Similarly, if a tenant had a problem with 123 Main Street, LLC, they would not file a lawsuit against 456 Cemetery Street, LLC. Hence, your money in 456 Cemetery Street, LLC would, in theory, be protected from the lawsuit. Obviously, the analogy presented is a simplistic point of view, and, as with all legal instruments, the details are extremely important, thus making it imperative to seek the professional services of a qualified attorney.

To achieve asset protection using an LLC, you must adhere to certain business practices. For example,

- do not comingle funds,
- keep your business up to date with regulations so that it is compliant, and
- keep your business in good standing.

Comingling funds happens when you remove the assets from one storage container and place them in another container without proper documentation. Again, an asset protection attorney can help with setting up your business structure and educate you on how to maintain compliance. Failure to remain compliant could lead to what is known as piercing the corporate veil. This veil refers to the legal distinction between you and your LLC. When the corporate veil is pierced, the court considers the assets in the LLC and your personal assets; that is, the assets are no longer separated for litigation. Remember, I am not a lawyer and am not giving advice on how to structure your business and achieve asset protection; instead, I am pointing out things you should discuss with your attorney and your CPA. It is also important to note that laws vary from state to state; so, always consult with a licensed professional.

Since the laws do vary by state, it is important to take into consideration the states in which you choose to form an LLC. The laws in some states protect the business owner better than in others. That is why so many large businesses are incorporated in Delaware, and so many small companies are incorporated in Nevada and Wyoming. Another important consideration is that each state has different charges for setting up and maintaining an LLC. These costs are not insignificant and should be taken into consideration when setting up your structure.

Realize that incorporating in one state and then operating your business in another will require filing the appropriate forms with the states you plan to operate in. The form is called Registration of a Foreign Limited Liability Company. One thing to take note of is that you do not have to live in either the state in which your LLC is formed in or the state(s) in which you have turnkey rentals.

Real Estate Trust

A real estate trust is another legal instrument that can help you with asset protection. Going forward, I will refer to the real estate trust as a trust. The idea behind a trust is to appoint a trustee who will essentially act as your liaison or point of contact for any business-related activities. Tax documents and other business-related documents will be mailed to the address of the trustee instead of your personal address. The result: your contact information and name are not publicly known and are therefore difficult to find.

How a trust can help with liability is simple. It is difficult to sue someone if you do not know who they are. While this sounds good, it only works under certain conditions. A trust can work extremely well if the property is purchased in cash or if you use a nonconforming loan.

Nonconforming loans are the type that do not meet the Fannie Mae or Freddie Mac lending regulations. As such, the mortgage (note) cannot be sold to Fannie Mae or Freddie Mac. The lender for the nonconforming loan is more likely to let you take title to the property in a trust. The key here is that the title is never in your personal name.

The interest rates for nonconforming loans are typically 1 to 2 percent higher than conventional loans. Closing costs are also more expensive. These types of loans do, however, offer some other advantages. For example, refinancing under Fannie Mae guidelines (for a conventional loan) requires the property to be titled back into your name, which defeats the purpose of a trust. To complete this process costs money for the title transfer and takes some time. The title transfer can also be complicated, depending on the structure of your business. When refinancing with a nonconforming loan, however, no title transfer is needed.

Another advantage of nonconforming loans is that you are no longer bound to ten mortgages—the current cap for conventional personal loans. The number of nonconforming loans a person can have in their name is dependent on the lending institution underwriting the loans. In general, the cap will be significantly higher than what is allowed under Fannie Mae guidelines (often totaling fifty mortgages or more). Some investors purchase the first ten properties using conventional mortgages because it is cheaper money (a lower interest rate) and then switch to nonconforming loans.

Title Transfers

As alluded to in the previous section, a title transfer or change of title is required to complete some of the business operations of the turnkey rental business. Specifically, at the time of this writing, if you are using real estate trusts and/or LLCs to hold the title, you will need to change the title to your personal name whenever you seek any personal lending products (per Fannie Mae or Freddie Mac lending regulations).

There are three methods you can use to change the title, namely, through a:

- General Warranty Deed: usually used when you purchase a property.
- Quit Claim Deed: used during ownership, usually to move a property from your personal name to an LLC.
- Special Warranty Deed: typically not used with turnkey rental properties.

*Note: The transfer of a title isn't always straightforward and, depending on the structure of your business, may require steps beyond simply filing a Quit Claim Deed.

For a turnkey rental business, the plan to transfer a title is simple. Let's assume you have decided to refinance. First, contact the bank and begin the process. After you let the bank know how the property is titled, the bank will let you know if you need to title differently. If so, simply call your attorney and have them take care of the title transfer. Another possibility is to have the title company or the closing attorney handling the refinance complete the title transfer for you, but you will need to discuss this with that attorney at the beginning of the process.

The last title transfer I performed in my business was in 2021; the legal expenses totaled around $500. Your attorney may charge a different rate, but this at least gives you some idea of the costs. You can classify this as a business expense for tax purposes, so keep the invoice for your CPA.

The key information you need from this chapter:

- Consider the startup funds you will need. For example, startup funds for your first purchase of a property priced at $150,000 to $250,000 will be approximately $39,500 to $67,500.
- Talk to an attorney to help you set up your business structure.
- Hire a CPA who can help you optimize and adjust your business structure each year to minimize your taxes.

I provided a lot of general information in this chapter but take care to not overthink things. Focus instead on hiring the right attorney and CPA. Let the professionals handle the setup and paperwork for your business. Your time is better spent on other business activities such as financial bookkeeping, the topic of the next chapter.

CHAPTER 5

FINANCIAL BOOKKEEPING

> Where We Are At: Master Checklist Step 3
> - **Monthly Business Management Checklist**
> - **Business Bank Account Questionnaire**
> - **Certified Public Accountant Questionnaire**

For Step 3 of the Master Checklist, you will need to set up a financial system for your business. The financial health of your rental property or portfolio of properties should be your top priority. It is imperative to develop financial tracking and monitoring systems during the initial setup of your turnkey rental property business. If you are already operating your business, prioritize setup as soon as possible. Establishing your accounting systems in the beginning will provide a huge time savings going forward.

Separate Your Personal Finances from Your Business Finances

I recommend separating your personal finances from your rental business even if you plan to title the properties in your name instead of that of a company. Separating those finances will require opening a checking account for your portfolio of properties.

Once that account is opened, deposit the reserve fund into it. Later, this account will be linked to your—the turnkey provider's—browser-based portal. This portal will become the centralized location for everything about your property such as financial statements, property leases, and distribution of your profits.

Open a credit card. For the sake of convenience, make sure the card is linked to the business checking account. Be sure to only use the card to pay for business-related expenses. This will offer the added benefit of building business credit, something that will prove useful as your business matures.

Select a Bank

Finding a bank that provides the appropriate banking solutions is not difficult; follow the questionnaire in the appendix under **Business Bank Account Questionnaire**. When opening an account for your business, make sure that the account will work (is business-friendly) for your specific business plan. Some questions you want to ask include:

1. Is the bank insured by the Federal Deposit Insurance Corporation (FDIC)?
2. Are there any recurring or initial fees, and, if so, are the fees waived if the account balance is above a certain value?
3. Are any fees charged after a certain number of monthly transactions, and, if so, what is the threshold?
4. Does the bank have any promotional offers?
5. Does the bank offer online wire transfer options? (A limit of at least $5,000 is needed for the earnest deposit. Ideally, you want the limit to be high enough to handle the down payment.)
6. Are any physical locations nearby? (A requirement if you need to complete a wire transfer in person.)
7. What online services does the bank offer?

- ◊ Automatic bill pay is a must.
- ◊ Automated messaging for whenever an automatic payment is scheduled, processed, or returned is also crucial.
8. What mobile apps does the bank offer?
9. Can the account transaction history be downloaded in Excel or whatever software package you've chosen for financial monitoring?
10. What other services or options are available?

These features will greatly reduce the time you spend balancing the books each month. I also recommend setting automatic payments for the linked credit card and for recurring bills such as the mortgage payment.

The mortgage payment is typically due on the first of the month. In my case, because the turnkey providers I use disperse funds on or around the fifteenth of each month, I've set up automatic recurring payments for the 26th. I make sure to select email notifications so that I receive a notification when the payment is scheduled and goes/does not go through.

Meet with Your Tax Professional

Start by meeting with your tax professional, or if you do not have one, make it a priority to find a CPA (certified public accountant) to handle your taxes. To help you select the CPA best suited to your needs, I've included the **Certified Public Accountant Questionnaire**. Once you find a CPA, ask how they would prefer you track the revenue and expenses of your turnkey rental business. They may have a specific program they refer to their clients and other useful information.

Track Expenses and Revenue Streams

At this point, all your expenses and revenue streams should be documented in the business account; however, it is important to utilize a spreadsheet program such as Excel or Google Sheets or an accounting software such as QuickBooks to determine your monthly profit. Each accounting program listed has pros and cons. For example, QuickBooks costs money to purchase and requires time to learn, but it can be linked with your checking and credit card accounts to auto-populate all your monthly transactions. It is also very good at scaling as you add in more properties.

Excel and Google Sheets are very similar in that both are spreadsheet programs. The biggest difference is that Excel costs the initial license fee or a monthly subscription fee, whereas Google Sheets does not. Both programs require you to begin with a blank spreadsheet to build your tracking system. The spreadsheet I use to track expenses and revenue is shown below in Figure 1. A Google Sheets version of the spreadsheet is available for free on my website: https://scottastanfield.com/

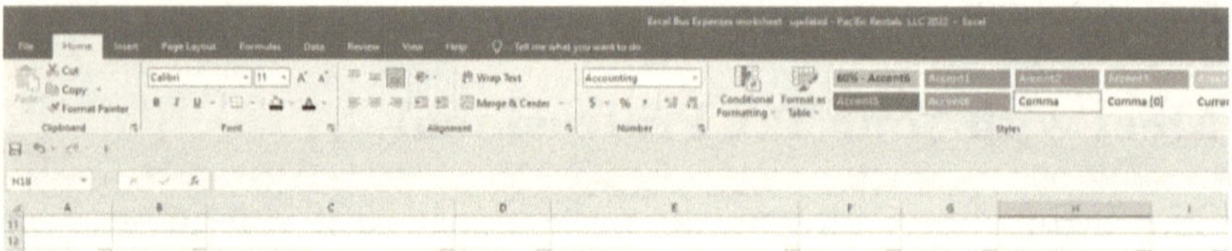

Figure 1. Example spreadsheet to track revenue and expenses.

As shown in the spreadsheet, all transactions are listed and include the date, the property address, the vendor, a description, the amount of the transaction, and an expense category. All these transactions are tied to the appropriate business account. I add all expenses and revenue to my spreadsheet once per month using the financial monitoring system given in the **Monthly Business**

Management Checklist.

To summarize, maintaining an organized approach and utilizing automation for your finances will

- greatly reduce the time required to complete your taxes— the second most time-consuming activity of the turnkey rental business,
- improve the accuracy of your financial reporting to help avoid IRS audits and enhance your CPA's ability to reduce your income taxes,
- help reduce the time you need each month to manage your business, and
- keep you on top of the financial performance of your business.

Now that we've finished Part One Getting Started, we'll move on to Part Two in which we will discuss the fundamentals of turnkey rentals.

PART TWO:
THE FUNDAMENTALS OF TURNKEY RENTAL INVESTING

CHAPTER 6

THE RETURN ON INVESTMENT

The concept of return on investment (often abbreviated in the business world as ROI, as I will call it for the remainder of this book) is fundamental to all investing and is one of the main parameters used to make financial decisions and comparisons between investment vehicles. The ROI, previously defined for you in Equation 3.1, is the annualized return divided by the invested funds. But what does it actually mean? In traditional terms, the ROI represents the return in dollars the investor receives for every dollar invested. For example, a $100 investment that returns $7 has an ROI of 7 percent:

$$\$7 \, / \, \$100 = 0.07.$$

The ROI is typically expressed as a percentage by multiplying by 100. For the example given, the ROI is 7 percent.

ROI can be used to compare any investment or purchase. When investing, the objective is to look at your specific portfolio, decide on investments that are useful for that portfolio, gauge the risk, and then compare the ROIs for each potential investment. In general, you want the ROI to be as high as possible while maintaining as low of a risk as you can for the investments that fit your specific portfolio needs.

It is not always obvious, but the ROI can be calculated for every purchase or use of money. Let me illustrate with an example that relates back to turnkey rental investing.

Let's assume you own two properties with mortgages. The first mortgage is a thirty-year fixed (meaning it requires 360 monthly payments), with an initial outstanding balance of $160,000 and an interest rate of 3.5 percent, and you are getting ready to make the first payment. The second mortgage is a thirty-year fixed with an initial outstanding balance of $160,000 and an interest rate of 4.5 percent, and you are getting ready to pay payment number 265. I've noted all these parameters below in Table 3.

Table 3. Summary of example parameters for an ROI example.

	Mortgage 1	Mortgage 2
Initial Outstanding Balance	$160,000	$160,000
Interest Rate	3.5%	4.5%
Total Payments	360	360
Payment Number	1	265
Remaining Payments	359	94

You currently have $200, which you would like to apply to either Mortgage 1 or Mortgage 2. The question is, which mortgage should you pay that additional $200 toward? Most people would answer the mortgage with the higher interest rate. Let's see if this is correct. The equations used to model this example are out of the scope needed for this discussion. Only the results are mentioned below, along with a brief discussion of how they were determined. For those wanting the mathematics needed to model this example, they can be found in **Appendix C: Mathematics for Loan Products**.

Step 1: Calculate the total interest you will pay over the lifetime of each mortgage.

$$\text{Total interest for Mortgage 1} = \$98{,}650$$
$$\text{Total interest for Mortgage 2} = \$131{,}851$$

The total interest paid was determined by computing the amortization table and then summing the interest paid each month over the remaining life of each loan.

Step 2: Determine the total interest you will pay over the lifetime of the mortgage with the additional $200 payment.

Mortgage 1: total interest with extra payment = $98,281
Mortgage 2: total interest with extra payment = $131,765

To compute Step 2, the mortgage balance after the first payment is reduced by $200, the amortization table is updated, and then the monthly interest is summed. A similar computation was used to determine the interest you would pay for Mortgage 2 after an extra payment of $200 was made for payment number 265.

The next step would be to subtract the total found in Step 2 (total interest with the extra payment) from the total in Step 1 (the total interest).

Step 3: Compute how much the extra payment will save with each mortgage.

Mortgage 1: savings: $98,650 - $98,281 = $369.00
Mortgage 2: savings: $131,851 - $131,765 = $85.40

The savings from the extra payment is determined by subtracting the results from Step 2 from Step 1. For Mortgage 1, these savings of $369 are slowly realized over the 359 remaining payments or months, and for Mortgage 2, the savings of $85.40 are realized over the ninety-four remaining payments or months.

Step 4: Determine the total ROI for each.

The total ROI for mortgages 1 and 2 are 184.5 percent and 42.7 percent, respectively:

$$ROI_1 = \frac{\$369}{\$200} = 184.5\%;$$

$$ROI_2 = \frac{\$85.4}{\$200} = 42.7\%.$$

Step 5: Determine the annualized ROI.

To truly compare the returns, it is necessary to compute the annualized ROI, which is simply the ROI for one year and is given as:

$$Average\ Annual\ ROI = 12 \times \frac{Total\ ROI\ (\%)}{Remaining\ payment\ number}$$

For mortgages 1 and 2, the average annual ROI is 6.17 percent and 5.45 percent, respectively:

$$ROI_1 = 12 \times \frac{184.5\%}{359} = 6.17\%;$$

$$ROI_2 = 12 \times \frac{42.7\%}{94} = 5.45\%.$$

The results are summarized below in Table 4.

Table 4. Summary of the results for the ROI example.

	Mortgage 1	Mortgage 2
Interest Paid over the Life of the Loan	$98,650	$131,851
Interest Paid with Extra Payment	$98,281	$131,765
Money Saved	$369	$85
ROI	184.5%	42.7%
Annualized ROI	6.17%	5.45%

The answer to the initial question in this example is: You should determine the annualized ROI and allocate your extra funds toward the option with the higher ROI. In this example, making an extra payment toward Mortgage 1, even though the interest rate is lower, gives you the better return.

Now, what if you were making the first payment for both mortgages? Which mortgage should you pay off first? In this scenario, you should use your additional funds toward Mortgage 2, the higher-interest-rate mortgage. The reason is simple: the annualized ROI is higher.

This example kept the options simple; namely, two properties and a onetime additional payment. What if the same question was applied to a portfolio of twenty properties with different start dates, interest rates, and initial balances? What if your extra funds could be applied to an additional payment each month, and the amount of the additional payment varied? Again, the ROI should be computed each month and the funds distributed accordingly.

Let's consider another example, this time for a depreciating asset, i.e., one with the expectation of decreasing in value. For this example, we will use one of the most infamous depreciating assets: the purchase of a new car. For the most part, as soon as you purchase a car and drive it off the lot, the vehicle starts to lose value immediately. Using a car purchase for this example should also reinforce the idea that the ROI can and should be used for any asset.

Let's say you plan to purchase a car for $20,000 and then sell it for $10,000 after five years. In this scenario, the total return is -$10,000:

$$\$10,000 - \$20,000 = -\$10,000.$$

The annualized return would be -$2,000:

$$\frac{-\$10,000}{5} = -\$2,000.$$

The resulting annualized ROI is -10 percent:

$$ROI = \frac{-\$2,000}{\$20,000} \times 100\% = -10\%.$$

In this example, a loss of 10 percent per year occurs.

The example illustrates how to compute an ROI for the purchase of a depreciating asset. Moreover, if you had to choose between buying a car with a -10 percent ROI and a different asset with a 10 percent ROI, you might choose to delay purchasing the vehicle. While this is clearly contingent on the age and condition of your existing vehicle, it does illustrate how the ROI can be used for financial decisions.

To summarize, the key takeaways of this chapter are

- the ROI is a fundamental parameter used to compare different investment vehicles,
- the ROI is a nondimensional value expressed as a percentage and is determined by dividing your annual monetary return by the invested funds, and
- making decisions on how to deploy your money should incorporate the ROI in addition to other factors such as your assessment of the risk.

The ROI is fundamental to both evaluating the assets you own or want to purchase and the performance of potential investments, including rental properties, as we will discuss in the next chapter.

CHAPTER 7

THE FOUR RETURNS OF A TURNKEY INVESTMENT PROPERTY

Turnkey investment properties generate a total return from four distinct sources, namely,

- cash flow,
- loan paydown,
- appreciation, and
- tax savings from a depreciation expense.

Going forward, the tax savings from a depreciation expense will be referenced as depreciation and these four distinct profit sources listed above as the four returns.

You might think it odd to break the return from a rental property into distinct categories, but as will be discussed here, understanding the details about each will influence your purchasing criteria, the amount you choose to hold as a reserve fund, and how you view and evaluate markets. Moreover, the IRS views each differently by levying different tax laws, which is extremely important since your annual tax *bill* is likely your largest expense.

Return 1: Cash Flow

Your cash flow is your income achieved as you operate the property, which is realized every month after all operating expenses have been covered, including the mortgage, or as shown in this equation:

$$Cash\ Flow = Sum\ Revenue - Sum\ Expenses.$$

Typical cash flow returns for single-family turnkey rentals are initially between 5 and 15 percent. For the properties I target, the initial cash flow is around $300 per month. Cash flow is a realized gain (money you get now) under normal operations. These funds are available to reinvest in other investments on a monthly basis. That means you can earn a compounded return on cash flow. However, this does require you to identify other opportunities more suitable for the approximate $300 a month generated from cash flow. Over time, that return will increase because, for a typical rental property, the rent will increase at a faster rate than the expenses.

Return 2: Loan Paydown

When you take out a mortgage, you are borrowing money from a lender, and as you may know, for that lender to make a profit, they charge interest on the money you borrow. Your payment can be broken down into two parts: the interest and the principal. The principal reduces the amount of money you owe to the lender and is the loan paydown.

As you make mortgage payments each month, the principal will decrease monthly; hence, you get a return from the loan paydown twelve times a year. The return occurs because the principal part of the mortgage payment decreases the outstanding balance of the mortgage, thereby increasing property equity. This equity is simply the difference between the appraised value of your property and the outstanding mortgage balance. Though this return occurs monthly, it is not a realized monetary return until you release the equity by selling the property, refinancing the property, or acquiring a home equity line of credit (HELOC) or some other loan product.

To better understand the breakdown of the mortgage payment, consider the following example. If a mortgage has an annual interest rate of 5 percent, you would first need to determine the monthly interest rate, which is simply 0.416 percent:

$$5\% / 12 \text{ months} = 0.416\%.$$

If the current mortgage balance owed is $100,000, the interest portion of your first mortgage payment is $416:

$$0.416\% \times \$100,000 = \$416.$$

The principal portion of the mortgage payment is the difference between the mortgage payment and the interest payment. For this example, let's assume the mortgage payment is $550 per month. The principal of the first mortgage payment is then $134:

$$\$550 - \$416 = \$134.$$

The amount you owe the lender, which is the outstanding balance, is reduced from $100,000 to $99,866:

$$\$100,000 - \$134 = \$99,866.$$

Since the outstanding balance is lower at $99,866, the interest portion of your next mortgage payment decreases to $415.44, and the principal portion increases slightly.

$$\text{Interest portion: } 0.416\% \times \$99,866 = \$415.44$$
$$\text{Principal portion: } \$550 - \$415.44 = \$134.56$$

The mortgage payment of $550 per month does not change throughout the life of the loan; however, the principal and interest components are different for every payment.

The $134 that reduced the mortgage balance in the example above represents the return from the loan paydown, which is nothing more than an increase in equity. Further, if you were to sell the property, the amount earned from the sale would have increased by $134 if we ignore selling-related expenses.

There are dependent variables associated with mortgages that affect how much of a return you receive from the loan paydown. These variables include the amount of your down payment, the interest rate at which your lender is charging, and the term (number of years to repay the loan). To determine how each variable affects your return, let's go back to a concept discussed earlier. As mentioned, all investment vehicles or uses of money can be viewed as an ROI, including the loan paydown. Using the ROI can help you develop a general understanding of how the dependent variables affect your return. To summarize the key results:

- The ROI from a loan paydown is dependent on the down payment, the interest rate, and the term (the number of years to repay the loan).
- A lower interest rate (cheaper money) lowers the interest expense, which increases the loan paydown, resulting in a higher ROI.
- A smaller down payment results in lower invested funds and a higher ROI.
- A shorter term, for example, twenty years instead of thirty, results in a higher ROI.

Table 5 tabulates the ROI for the loan paydown of the first three different scenarios. As shown in the table, the ROI, which ranges from 4 to 7 percent for a thirty-year term, is greater for the lower down payment and lower interest rate loan.

Table 5. ROI for loan paydown of different loan terms.

Purchase Price	$100,000	$100,000	$100,000
Loan to Value	75%	80%	80%
Interest Rate	5%	5%	4%
Invested Funds	$25,000	$20,000	$20,000
Loan Paydown	$1,107	$1,180	$1,409
ROI	4.43%	5.90%	7.04%

Results shown are to illustrate the difference in ROI for the different loan parameters. Higher loan-to-value ratios and lower interest rates increase the ROI.

Return 3: Appreciation

The third return listed, appreciation, occurs when the property value increases. Similar to a loan paydown, the result is an increase in equity, which is, again, not liquid and not realized until you sell, refinance, or get a HELOC for the property.

The gains from appreciation can be significantly greater than the other three returns combined, especially with a leveraged position using a mortgage; however, buying for appreciation usually involves a lot of speculation. That said, my preference is to buy based on cash flow, but I still make sure to evaluate the appreciation. I should also mention that many investors choose to invest in properties based on the expected appreciation; you should evaluate what works best for you based on your personal goals and personal finances.

The average historical appreciation rate for single-family homes in the United States is between 3.5 and 3.8 percent annually. To get a feel of your leveraged ROI, simply divide the purchase price of the property by your down payment, which we will refer to as "the lever", and then multiply this ratio (the lever) by the historical appreciation rate. The equation is given below:

$$ROI = \frac{purchase\ price}{down\ payment} \times historical\ appreciation\ rate.$$

To illustrate, let's assume you are purchasing a property for $100,000, and the loan-to-value ratio is 80 percent. Therefore, the borrowed balance from the lender is $80,000:

$$80\% \times \$100,000 = \$80,000.$$

The corresponding down payment is $20,000:

$$\$100,000 - \$80,000 = \$20,000.$$

Your leverage is given by dividing the purchase price by the down payment, which, for this example, equals 5:

$$\$100,000 / \$20,000 = 5.$$

Your leveraged ROI for a 3.5 percent appreciation rate is then 17.5 percent:

$$5 \times 3.5\% = 17.5\%.$$

The 17.5 percent ROI is, in my opinion, impressive and highlights the power of leverage. That said, for my criteria, I still prefer to purchase rental properties based on cash flow requirements that correspond to appreciation rates at or are slightly below the national average. My reason has to do with minimizing risk and my personal risk tolerance. Properties with appreciation rates above the national average usually correspond to properties with lower or even negative cash flow.

Although I do not purchase for appreciation, many scenarios exist in which buying for appreciation is preferred. It depends on personal financials, market conditions, and goals. For example, some investors already have a lot of income and can handle the higher risks of owning a property that may operate at a negative or breakeven annual cash flow. Different scenarios in which such situations might be favorable will be discussed in detail later in this book.

Return 4: The Return from Depreciation

The fourth and final return is from depreciation. Depreciation does not directly put money into your pocket. Instead, it lowers your income tax expense as a business-allowed deduction realized each year when you file taxes. Businesses are allowed to deduct the assets they purchase. For low-cost items or expendable items such as office supplies, the deduction occurs all at once; however, for assets that last a long time, such as a property, the deduction occurs incrementally annually over a predetermined number of years.

The IRS defines the depreciable lifetime of a single-family rental property as 27.5 years. That is, you can claim depreciation every year for 27.5 years. Note that the building is viewed as having a useful lifetime of 27.5 years, but the land is considered to last forever. For this reason, the purchase price of your rental property is separated into the cost of the land and of the building. Your cost basis, the cost used to determine taxes, is set equal to the cost of the building and can include the closing costs.

The concept of depreciation plays a large factor when determining the four returns. The main concept to keep in mind is that taxes are one of the larger expenses for a turnkey rental business, and that depreciation, though not technically an expense, can be used to offset taxes. In my opinion, depreciation is one of the best tax advantages available to rental properties.

To conclude, four main concepts within your turnkey rental business will control how much money you will receive from your investment properties. These four returns come from the monthly cash flow, loan paydown, appreciation, and a tax savings from depreciation. Monthly cash flow refers to the money that comes in each month from your business. Tax savings from depreciation will help reduce what will become one of your greatest expenses—

taxes—and that means more money in your pocket at tax time. Loan paydown refers to your return in equity, received monthly, and appreciation is an equity return from an increase in the value of your properties. Equity returns require some work from the start of the process to the point that the money hits your bank account. Those processes will be discussed in the next chapter.

CHAPTER 8

ACCESSING EQUITY GAINS

One of the disadvantages of loan paydown and appreciation is that neither is a realized monetary gain and, thus, is not readily available for reinvestment. Regarding loan paydown, think of your property as a battery that stores money (equity) instead of electricity. The monthly payments you make slowly charge your property with money. When the loan is paid off, your property is fully charged; yet, just like a battery, you do not have to wait for it to be fully charged to utilize the stored funds. The stored funds in your property can be accessed in a variety of ways such as:

- Selling the property
- Refinancing the property
- Getting a HELOC for the property

Selling the Property

When you sell your property, it releases the stored funds, but note that selling will also trigger capital gain tax. Fortunately, this tax can be postponed indefinitely using a tax strategy called a 1031 exchange.

In a 1031 exchange, you sell the property and then purchase

one or more properties with a sum value equal to or greater than the value of the sold property. Strict regulations must be followed to execute a 1031 exchange; so, seek professional guidance before starting the process.

Refinancing the Property

Another way to release the stored funds is to refinance the property, which means replacing the original mortgage with a new mortgage. A good time to use this option is when interest rates are lower than your current rates. At closing, the title company or closing attorney will issue a check or wire transfer in the amount of your equity gains after paying the costs for their services. Since the property was not sold, the capital gain tax is not triggered.

Note: You have already paid taxes for the loan paydown because the principal is not an expense that can be deducted for tax purposes. Though the principal is not considered an expense for tax purposes, it does reduce the monthly cash flow.

Getting a HELOC for the Property

A third option for gaining access to the stored funds is to get a HELOC, a home equity line of credit. HELOCs have some clear advantages over selling and refinancing, but they also have disadvantages. An investor needs to carefully consider the pros and cons before pursuing a HELOC.

To illustrate one advantage, let's assume the existing mortgage rate is really low at 3 percent, and the current rates are really high at 7 percent. As discussed earlier, an increased interest rate affects the ROI. Refinancing your property will be hard to justify in this situation because the ROI from the loan paydown will drop significantly. Moreover, your cash flow will be significantly lower due to the higher interest portion of the mortgage payment and the increase in the borrowed funds. This is one scenario in which a HELOC can be useful because it will grant access to the equity without replacing the lower interest rate mortgage.

Unfortunately, HELOCs are challenging to get for a rental property. For those interested in acquiring one, from my experience, smaller local lending institutions are more likely to offer them. The terms for HELOCs tend to vary significantly from lender to lender; so, it is worth shopping around.

To summarize, several options can be explored when looking to access the equity in your properties, including selling, refinancing, and acquiring a HELOC. Each option has advantages and disadvantages. If it's a seller's market, selling the property might be the best choice. If the current interest rates are lower than the interest rate you have, refinancing might be best. If the current interest rate is higher than that of your current mortgage, a HELOC might be the right choice. In general, refinancing is the more common approach, but it requires you to use a mortgage. While receiving equity from refinancing can be a huge advantage, there are other advantages to using a mortgage. We'll explore these advantages in the next chapter.

CHAPTER 9

THE IMPORTANCE OF THE MORTGAGE: LEVERAGE AND INFLATION

Receiving equity gains from the loan paydown requires a mortgage, as does accessing the equity gains from the loan paydown and appreciation. While nice to build equity from the paydown, there are other important reasons to purchase with a mortgage.

1. The interest payment of the mortgage is an expense that lowers your taxable income by reducing your cash flow, thereby reducing your tax bill.
2. Leverage is a vital concept that can greatly enhance your returns.
3. The interaction between inflation and a mortgage is a very important concept.

Leverage

The concept of leverage, defined as the enhanced ROI achieved from an investment purchased with borrowed money, is best understood with the following example. If you purchase a home for $100,000 using a mortgage with a 75 percent loan-to-value ratio, the borrowed balance will be $75,000:

$$\$100{,}000 \times 75\% = \$75{,}000.$$

Your down payment will be $25,000 because the bank will only loan up to $75,000, which leaves you the difference. For this example, let's assume your property appreciates at an appreciation rate of 3 percent, resulting in the value of your property increasing to $103,000:

$$1.03\% \times \$100{,}000 = \$103{,}000.$$

If you had purchased the property in cash, the ROI would be 3 percent:

$$\$3{,}000 / \$100{,}000 = 3\%.$$

But because you purchased the property with a mortgage, the ROI is 12 percent:

$$\$3{,}000 / \$25{,}000 = 12\%.$$

Note that the larger return, or leveraged return, is greater by a factor of four than the unleveraged return. Properly using leverage is one of the best approaches to generate substantial wealth.

The Interaction between Inflation and a Mortgage

A mortgage is a short position on the US dollar. That is, you will experience a gain if the dollar drops in value and similarly, a loss occurs if the value of the dollar goes up.

Let's illustrate with a quick example. The dollar in 1990 had an equivalent purchasing power of almost two dollars in 2020 (an average annual inflation rate of 2.25 percent). Thus, the buying power for the last mortgage payment for a thirty-year term loan would have been about half of the buying power of the borrowed money.

Where this becomes powerful is when inflation is high or projected to be high. Under such conditions, it may be advantageous to borrow money, especially if the interest rates are low and the borrowed funds are used to purchase income-producing assets expected to appreciate in value.

Chapters 7, 8, and 9 include a lot of key concepts worth highlighting before moving on to the next chapter, which is dedicated to the real estate market cycle. To review, the key takeaways from this section are:

- Turnkey rentals provide a total return from cash flow, the loan paydown, appreciation, and a tax savings from depreciation.
- Cash flow is your monthly profit after servicing all expenses.
- Loan paydown is the monthly increase in equity from paying the mortgage.
- Appreciation is the increase in equity when the property increases in value.
- Depreciation is the reduction in your taxes from a non-monetary expense.
- Accessing your equity gains requires selling or utilizing mortgage products.
- A mortgage provides leveraged returns, which can, if used properly, greatly enhance the growth of your net worth.
- A mortgage tied to an income-producing asset with the expectation of appreciating in value is one of the best hedges against inflation.

Next up, we'll discuss the market cycle!

CHAPTER 10

THE REAL ESTATE MARKET CYCLE

A discussion about investment fundamentals for any real estate investment strategy would not be complete without bringing up the real estate market cycle—known as the boom-and-bust cycle that the real estate market cycles through over and over again.

The time between the start and end of the cycle is, on average, 18.6 years. Even more interesting, the cycle has never been shorter than seventeen years or longer than twenty-one. While this alone is intriguing, it must be mentioned that these values represent the mean and variance of a time series that began in 1800; hence, the numbers represent a series with twelve market cycles. I personally find it fascinating that the economic reasons for the different market recessions have been different for each cycle and yet the mean and variance are so tight.

In 2006, before the market recession, many had thought the market could not go down, and yet it did. Why mention this? In 2021 and early 2022, a lot of people asserted that the economic factors were very different from past recessions and that properties at that point could only go up in value. In October 2022, federal interest rate increases resulted in lower values for properties, and the housing market was in or near a recession. This recession, though very different than 2007, was still a deleveraging period.

It behooves you, as the investor, to monitor the market for yourself and ignore the outside noise. Understand what is best for the real estate agent, the turnkey provider, and any other professional you work with. Remember, it is your money on the line, and many who claim to be experts have their own reasons for wanting the market to perform a certain way. That's not to say all resources are untrustworthy. Some are excellent sources of information and try to truly help their clients, but not all of them.

My advice: Listen to the experts but **verify all the information for yourself** so that the noise does not push you into a bad decision. Do not ignore history, and remember, no one can actually predict with any real certainty when the next recession will occur or why. That said, this chapter describes the different market cycle phases and concludes with a case study illustrating how to include the market cycle into your turnkey investment plans.

The market cycle has four distinct phases, namely,

- recovery,
- expansion,
- hyper supply, and
- recession.

The Recovery Phase

The recovery phase begins when the real estate market is at its lowest point (the end of the recession). In general, rental growth is stagnant, meaning you can expect little to no new construction. Typically, the unemployment rate is high but begins to improve. The vacancy rates start to decline, and, at some point, new construction begins slowly.

The recovery phase can be brief, transitioning to expansion

quickly, or it can last for years. In general, an excellent time to buy turnkey single-family rental properties is during the recovery period because the property values are a bargain, and, if properly selected, their value will increase during the expansion phase. This is also easily the best time to purchase appreciation properties—properties in which the total return is dominated by appreciation.

The Expansion Phase

During the expansion phase, which follows the recovery phase, the economy is growing, and the number of jobs increases. The demand for housing begins to rise, which, after some time, will push property values and rental rates up while the vacancy rate decreases.

During this phase, investors make money by redeveloping properties to the current trends and then selling for more than market value. Remember, people's emotions play a role when they purchase homes; because the supply is low, buyers have this perceived notion that they need to offer more so that they do not lose out. Regardless of the buyer's psychology, the result is appreciation, which a well-positioned turnkey rental property can take advantage of.

My buying criteria, per the **Establish a Purchase Criteria Checklist** includes action items based on the market cycle. You will notice that I have broken the expansion phase into its early, middle, and last quarters. The plan I use is simple:

- Early Expansion Phase: Look to purchase cash flow or appreciation properties.
- Middle Expansion Phase: Look to purchase cash flow or appreciation properties with two-year leases.
- Last Quarter Expansion Phase: Do not purchase properties in the last quarter of the expansion phase. Instead, focus on financing and selling options that increase cash flow, reduce debt, and increase reserve fund.

To ease into the concept of what a cash flow market is, a loose definition is provided here. In later sections, we will build upon this base. Cash flow properties are rentals in which the return is dominated by cash flow, which, as previously mentioned, is any profit from rent that is sufficient to cover the expenses while enabling you to put some money into your pocket, at least when compared with appreciation properties. Recall that appreciation properties are properties that are increasing in value or speculated to increase in value. Appreciation rates for cash flow properties tend to be just at or slightly below the national average appreciation rate.

In the last quarter of the expansion phase, I sell properties that fail to produce enough cash flow, which I loosely define as greater than 20 to 30 percent of the gross rent. My goal here is to decrease the loan-to-value ratio of my portfolio to below 60 percent in preparation for the upcoming recession. The loan-to-value ratio (LTV) for your portfolio is determined by summing together the outstanding debt for all your mortgages and then dividing by the sum of the appraised value of all your properties. The equation is below:

$$LTV = \frac{Total\ Outstanding\ Debt}{Total\ Appraised\ Value}$$

As for increasing cash flow, cash flow properties tend to cost less, making them ideal for a 1031 tax exchange, which allows you to sell some of your higher-end appreciation properties and purchase two or even three cash flow properties. Trimming your amount of appreciation properties for additional cash flow properties might appeal to you for multiple reasons such as:

1. The value of cash flow properties tends to decrease less than appreciation properties during a recession.
2. Cash flow properties tend to command decent rental rates and low vacancy rates during a recession.
3. Depending on the profits from the sale, you can exchange for two properties with a loan-to-value ratio much lower

than the typical 75 to 80 percent, which will increase your cash flow and lower your debt-to-value ratio.

As mentioned, it is never my plan to purchase new properties toward the end of an expansion phase, but remember, no one can predict a recession. My criteria, which are conservative, could result in waiting multiple years. For some, your financials and risk tolerance may allow you to purchase properties when I wouldn't. This is absolutely fine, as long as you have a plan.

The Hyper Supply Phase

The hyper supply phase follows the expansion phase. At the end of the expansion phase, the demand for housing peaks. Developers and redevelopers work very hard to provide housing during this phase.

The demand will continue until either too much inventory hits the market or there is a pullback in demand. Such a pullback could be caused by many factors, including rising interest rates or some other economic event(s). At any rate, eventually, demand decreases, resulting in an increase in vacancy while the rental rates decrease.

The hyper supply phase can last a long time and represents a challenging leasing and investing market. I do not recommend purchasing properties during the hyper supply phase. If you choose to, look to purchase at the end of this phase. The objective would be to buy properties well-positioned to benefit during the next cycle. It is important to maintain higher cash reserves if you decide to purchase at this time.

My purchasing criteria for the hyper supply phase are identical to my criteria for the fourth quarter of the expansion phase. Again, try to increase cash flow and lower your debt.

The Recession Phase

Eventually, the supply greatly exceeds demand, and the hyper supply phase gives way to the recession phase. During this phase, rentals tend to have a high vacancy rate, resulting in stagnant or reduced rental rates. The number of foreclosures will increase, and, generally speaking, it becomes a good time to purchase turnkey properties as long as you have sufficient cash reserves—since home prices are likely to decrease during this period. So, selling during this phase is not a good option.

When buying, make sure to budget for higher vacancies and look for properties that are already tenanted with long leases. Specifically, look to purchase either cash flow or appreciation properties with two-year leases after the market has bottomed out. The goal is to purchase near the bottom since it's hard, if not impossible, to determine if and when the market has completely bottomed. A summary of what typically occurs during each cycle is shown below in Table 6.

Table 6. Market Cycle Summary

	Recovery Phase	Expansion	Hyper Supply	Recession
Rental Growth		+	+	−
New Construction		+	+	−
Unemployment		−	−	+
Vacancy Rates		−	−	+
Rental Rates		+	+	−
Demand for Houses		+	+	−

| No Growth | + Increasing | − Decreasing |

Putting it All Together

The descriptions provided for each phase include a bunch of generalized statements of what typically occurs. The market will certainly not evolve exactly as the generalized descriptions provided suggest. Every market is different, and, as such, nuances will occur that result in smaller perturbations of what typically emerges. It is important to understand how the various dependent variables are likely to affect the profits of your turnkey rental business. For example, inflation was a key player in the real estate market in 2022.

Starting in 2022, the Federal Reserve raised rates in an attempt to combat inflation. The result has been less buying pressure (lower demand), but this is not the only important ramification. By increasing the rate, the cost to purchase is significantly more, which, historically, has resulted in an increase in demand for rentals and higher rental rates, even during the recession phase. This direct correlation between interest rates and rental rates is clearly shown below in Figure 2.

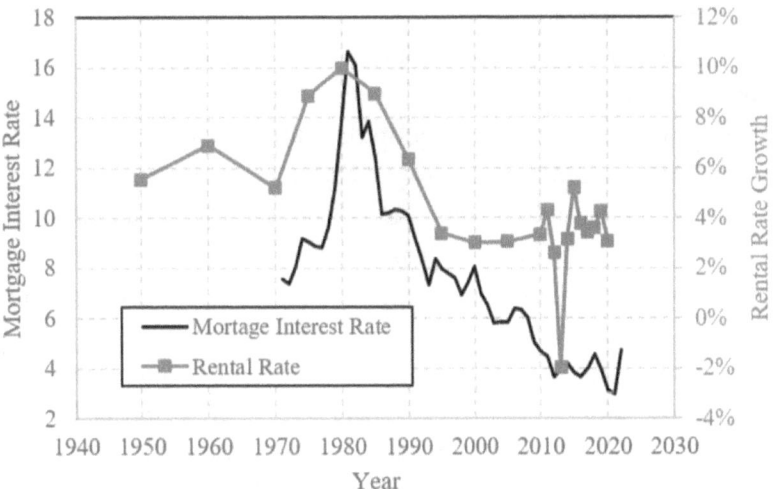

Figure 2. Comparison between mortgage interest rate and rental rate growth. (https://fred.stlouisfed.org)

As shown, the mortgage rates increased to almost 20 percent in the 1980s to combat inflation. The rental rate increases were greatest when the mortgage rate was highest. Note: This does not match the generalized description provided about the recession phase, but it may be a key player in the turnkey rental business in the coming years.

As described, there are multiple parameters that are dependent on the market cycle, including rental growth, new construction, unemployment rate, vacancy rate, economic growth, number of jobs, housing supply and demand, crowd psychology, and property prices. One of the best approaches to understanding how these parameters might change during the market cycle is to look at historical data.

An analysis showing how the dependent variables fluctuate with the real estate market cycle for the Atlanta metropolitan area is given in **Example 10.2 Market Cycle Analysis for Atlanta, GA** located in **Appendix D**. While the analysis given is for the Atlanta metropolitan area, the analysis can be put together for any metropolitan region.

If you were to compare metropolitan areas, the results would show that some markets would be at different phases of the market cycle. In general, some of the higher appreciation markets, such as San Francisco and New York City, tend to lead the rest of the country. That is, they hit the end of the market cycle before other metropolitan areas; for this reason, savvy investors and real estate professionals monitor these markets for an early warning of cycle changes.

In general, monitoring the markets you are invested in is beneficial because investment opportunities will present themselves. Knowing where the market is can be tricky. The worst-case scenario is that you may purchase a property at the wrong time. If this happens, property values over time still tend to slowly increase in value, so a setback is likely temporary (on the order of multiple years). Moreover, the property will produce income if you purchase using the cash flow criteria in the business plan.

One final note regarding the real estate market cycle: The criteria in the **Establish a Purchase Criteria Checklist** were derived from market-generated data. I am a firm believer in establishing investment plans based on this kind of data instead of listening to noise. By establishing criteria in advance, it is easier for you to not get emotionally wrapped up in a purchase. Moreover, the probability of investing at the right time and for the right reasons increases significantly.

To summarize, the key concepts from this chapter include the following:

- The real estate market is cyclical.
- Each cycle lasts an average of 18.6 years with a tight variance.
- The cycle has four phases: recovery, expansion, hyper supply, and recession.
- Monitoring the housing market can help determine the phase of the market cycle.
- Including the market cycle in your purchasing criteria is useful.

The market cycle is a fundamental phenomenon. The changes that take place occur because of the collective decision-making of market participants, which is the subject of the next chapter.

CHAPTER 11

CROWD PSYCHOLOGY, MARKET PARTICIPANTS, AND ESTABLISHING MARKET TRENDS

The previous chapter listed psychology as a dependent variable of the housing supply and, in general, one of many market drivers. Markets change because people participate in them. If a single person, such as myself, makes a purchase, it does not change the market overly much; however, when large groups of people with a similar agenda begin to participate in the market in a similar fashion, the market will begin to shift into something that looks very different.

Crowd psychology is defined here simply as how large groups of people or different generations view and respond to market conditions, environmental factors, and government policy. In general, it is not something that can be quantified easily. As such, my preference is to maintain a working theory, i.e., a theory that I am constantly evaluating and updating to describe the market. My goal is to include the major events that have impacted the viewpoint of many people (generations). The main objective of the exercise is to build a theory for where the housing market has been, is at, and is heading. The theory is just that—a theory—but I have found it useful and so have included it here.

My current theory is below; I do include some market-generated data, but at the end of the day, I recommend that you still view it as noise because it is, after all, simply a theory. I briefly mentioned noise in Chapter 10, and it is worth reiterating here that noise is simply someone's opinion or hypothesis and not necessarily based on market-generated data. I am sharing this as an example, but by no means is it all-inclusive; there are certainly going to be inaccuracies. Remember, no one (not me or anyone else) can consistently make accurate market predictions.

My Market Theory

My theory is as follows. In the 2000s, prior to the real estate crash in 2007, home ownership was desired by the vast majority of adults, and plenty of builders were available to satisfy those desires. There was a lot of speculation from investors, and the number of real estate investors grew significantly during this period. I think some of this growth was from investors who switched from stock investing to real estate investing after the.com bubble burst. Regardless of where the investors came from, during this timeframe, the real estate market expanded rapidly and went into hyper supply. Another contributing factor was the lending policies of the early 2000s, during which subprime mortgages became the norm. Subprime mortgages refer to loans offered to individuals who do not qualify for a prime-rate loan.

In 2007, the housing market crashed. Many homeowners lost their houses and became renters. The impact of this event shaped the generation born in the 1990s. Statistically speaking, this group preferred to rent instead of purchase a home after watching their parents lose theirs. The market finally bottomed sometime between 2009 to early 2010, and the result was the loss of individual wealth and many builders. The key takeaway is that a large, nationwide event shifted the ideals of an entire generation from homeownership to renting. Note: A shift from homeownership to renting by a large population will certainly affect the supply and demand of housing as this group participates in the market.

Market recovery began somewhere around 2011 to 2012, and property values grew slowly for the rest of the decade. During the recovery and expansion period (up to 2020), very few rental (multifamily) or single-family units were built. For comparison, there were 14.6 million homes built between 2000 and 2010 but only 6.9 million homes between 2010 to 2020. From 2010 to 2020, the population grew by 22.7 million.

What's interesting is that property values did not grow much from 2010 to 2020 because inventory held around five to seven months (it was starting to increase at a higher rate in 2018 but not significantly). In general, an inventory below six-months supply results in appreciation, and an inventory greater than six-months supply results in lower property values. The slow appreciation rate during recovery and expansion had a lot to do with how many people preferred to rent. Again, this preference to rent was a lasting effect of the housing recession.

In 2020, the COVID-19 pandemic occurred, and people were forced to stay in their small rentals and were unable (or unwilling) to venture out. As the market reopened, many employers continued to accommodate remote work. A large portion of the adult population began to gravitate toward home ownership instead of renting because of pandemic-related living conditions. The ensuing buying pressure, coupled with historically low interest rates, resulted in unheard-of appreciation rates (15 to 20 percent) as demand for housing increased.

Typically, you would expect builders to begin building houses once the value of a house increases so that building is profitable. Unfortunately, with increasing inflation, the replacement cost for housing increased significantly, slowing the construction of new properties. Going forward, I would expect replacement cost to likely play a key role in the next recession, recovery, and expansion phases.

Currently, mortgage rates have increased sufficiently to slow the market. Unfortunately, the reduction in demand occurred before builder participation increased the supply. This dynamic could result in a push-pull, which could, in turn, create a long hyper supply phase. Moreover, the market will ultimately go through a deleveraging or recession. The next recession is going to look much differently than it did in 2007, however, because

- housing inventory is low,
- people still want to own homes,
- people are still working remotely, and
- inflation will keep the replacement costs for homes high.

Again, this is a working theory that I continually update as time goes on and new information becomes available. Certainly, events can occur that I did not foresee, and some of the events I expected to arise never may. The purpose of maintaining this theory is to keep me thinking about how different, large, and important events may impact the housing market by influencing market participants.

Let's review the key takeaways from this chapter, which are

- market dynamics establish market trends when large groups of people begin to make similar decisions;
- large shifts caused by market participants can have a profound and long-lasting market impact, even decades later; and
- the initial effect on the market will, over time, affect other components of the market, which is exceedingly hard to predict with any accuracy.

Next up is Part Three, wherein we will discuss some of the more practical aspects of the turnkey business: evaluating markets and evaluating and buying properties.

PART THREE:
ESTABLISHING PURCHASE CRITERIA AND HOW TO EVALUATE A MARKET

CHAPTER 12

PERSONAL FINANCIALS, OBJECTIVES, AND GOALS

> Where We Are At: Master Checklist Step 4
> - **Establish a Purchase Criteria Checklist**

Your personal financials will play a crucial role in how you build and modify your business plan. Your net income, expenses, savings rate, debt, and net assets should be monitored so that your buying criteria can be carefully selected to best leverage your resources to accomplish your goals. These financials make up your financial state. Regardless of how complicated your financials are, you can reduce them into four separate figures, which are

- total gross income,
- total expenses,
- total debt, and
- total assets.

Total Gross Income

Your total gross income, which can be broken down into the different revenue streams that make up your income, is what you make prior to paying your expenses. For most, this will include a salary from a job but could also include rental income, dividend income, and royalties. Obviously, this is not an exhaustive list.

Your net income is the amount leftover after all your expenses are taken care of. Your net income can be determined quickly by subtracting the total gross income from your total expenses.

Net Income = Total Gross Income - Total Expenses

Total Expenses

Your total expenses can be broken into expense categories such as

- income tax,
- housing,
- transportation,
- food,
- utilities,
- clothing,
- medical,
- personal, and
- entertainment.

This is not an exhaustive list. For most, taxes will easily be your largest expense. By breaking expenses into categories, you can more easily label these as fixed expenses and discretionary spending. For many, discretionary spending can be reduced to enhance saving funds for investing.

Dependence on a job for income ends as soon as your gross income from passive revenue streams is greater than your expenses. I mention this because the vast majority of financial planners recommend saving and investing to build a nest egg to retire. While many problems exist with the nest egg approach, I will focus on the obvious—a person retires based on income, not net worth.

Total Debt

Your total debt, which is simply the money you owe to banks, credit cards, people, or businesses, can also be broken down into bad debt and good debt. Bad debt is debt tied to a depreciating asset while good debt is tied to an appreciating asset or an income-producing asset.

For tracking purposes, I separate my debt into several categories, namely,

- the debt of my personal residence,
- the debt of my rental properties, and
- all my other debt.

Personal Residence Debt

I track the debt attached to my personal residence separately because lending products that provide access to my equity have much more favorable terms than lending products for rental properties. For example, the interest rate may be lower, and you will likely be eligible for a better loan-to-value ratio. That said, you must be very careful if you decide to leverage your personal residence because it does increase your risk.

Rental Property Debt

Similarly, I track the debt of my rental properties separately so that I can leverage the equity when appropriate. If you do not monitor your debt once per month, you will almost certainly fail to notice when the equity becomes sufficient to reinvest, which is exactly why my business plan includes monthly monitoring.

Other Debt

My "other debt" category includes how much I owe for my vehicle and my student loans. For some, credit card debt may be included in this category. If it does, and you are making high-interest payments each month, consider paying this off before investing. In general, you can prioritize your bad debt using the interest rate. Higher interest rate debt should be dealt with first, and then other debt, and so on.

Total Assets

Your total assets refer to the monetary value of your belongings, which could include

- cash,
- properties,
- stock,
- retirement accounts,
- cars,
- jewelry, and
- collectables.

Assets can further be characterized as appreciating or depreciating assets. To review, an appreciating asset is an asset that has the expectation of increasing in value. Similarly, a depreciating asset has the expectation of decreasing in value.

When I track my total assets, I separate my assets into the following five categories:

- cash,
- the value of my rental portfolio,
- the value of my personal residence,
- the value of my retirement accounts, and
- the value of everything else.

Cash Assets

Cash assets are liquid and represent my reserve fund and investment fund. I like to maintain a one-year reserve in cash. That way, I have enough cash to cover my bills for one year. I use any additional cash for investments. One year is likely too conservative for most, but it is always a good idea to maintain a reserve.

Asset Value of Rental Portfolio

I track the value of my rental portfolio separately to better monitor it and review it monthly to check how it is performing and determine when and if I need to make changes.

Asset Value of Personal Residence

Your personal residence is just that—a personal residence. It is always a good idea to keep your personal separate from the business. For asset monitoring, I keep it separate for the same reasons mentioned during the discussion on debt.

Asset Value of Retirement Accounts

I track my retirement accounts separately from everything else because I can borrow up to $50,000 at a low interest rate. The funds I borrow can be used to purchase rental properties.

The repayment of the loan goes back into my retirement account; hence, the interest I pay is not lost. I like to borrow from my retirement account, especially a 401k tied to an employer because the performance is not very good, especially after fees. For example, the ROI of my retirement account (ignoring the matched funds) is around 7 percent annually for a good year, which is significantly lower than the 20 to 25 percent I make from a turnkey rental property. The funds from your retirement account can also be used to meet a traditional bank's reserve fund requirements when applying for a loan.

Value of Everything Else

The reason I track my total assets, which includes all the assets that can be listed, is so I can calculate my net worth, defined simply as the difference between your total assets and total debt:

Net Worth = Total Assets - Total Debt.

I track my net worth as I have other investment ventures that require me to be an accredited investor.

The requirements for an accredited investor are (1) a net worth greater than $1,000,000 or (2) an annual income greater than $200,000 if you are single or $300,000 if you are married, with the expectation of maintaining this income. Although I track my personal residence, I do not include it when I compute my net worth since it does not count toward the requirements of an accredited investor. For turnkey rental investing, you do not need to be an accredited investor.

Setting Objectives and Goals

Setting objectives and goals should be based on what you are trying to accomplish, which can then be tied to your business plan. Your business plan will look to adjust your revenue, expenses, debt, and assets to meet your goals. For example, if your goal is to become a full-time turnkey rental investor, you will need to increase cash flow by increasing revenue, decreasing expenses, or both until the cash flow from your properties exceeds your expenses.

My first objective was to increase cash flow by reducing expenses to accumulate more money for investment. My plan was to increase my good debt to maximize leverage, which would increase my assets and increase my cash flow as quickly as possible. My long-term goal was to replace my salary from my job with rental income.

Another objective I had when I began investing in turnkey rentals was to balance the total expenses of my first turnkey rental property with my net W-2 income. That is, I wanted my net income (savings) from my employer to be at least the same or more than the total expenses of the property. My reasoning was as follows: I would be able to cover my expenses even without a tenant. This turned out

PERSONAL FINANCIALS, OBJECTIVES, AND GOALS

to be excessive, but it gave me peace of mind by reducing my risk.

I know the discussion thus far may seem obvious, but in practice, your plan to accomplish your goals may not be so clear. For example, your goal may be to achieve maximum cash flow from your turnkey rental business at the end of ten years. The plan you craft to achieve this goal could be to

- purchase and operate multiple appreciation properties for ten years, which will LOWER your cash flow, and then
- utilize a 1031 tax exchange to exchange each appreciation property for multiple cash flow properties after the ten-year mark.

This plan is not likely the first plan you were thinking of, but it could be the correct course to achieve your goal.

To recap, the key concepts for this chapter are as follows:

- You should track your finances every month and record:
    - ◊ Your revenue from your job, properties, and other revenue sources.
    - ◊ Your expenses.
    - ◊ Your assets—I recommend tracking the value of your cash, personal residence, rental properties, retirement account, and everything else.
    - ◊ Your debts—I would track the debt of your personal residence and rental properties separately.
- Your financial state is fully defined once you have reduced your finances into revenue, expenses, assets, and debt.
- Building a plan to meet your goals comes down to making decisions that change one of the four parameters of your financial state.

We will discuss changing your financial state, i.e., changing your revenue, expenses, assets, and debt using turnkey rental properties, in the next chapter.

CHAPTER 13

CASH FLOW VS APPRECIATION PROPERTIES

At this point, it is probably clear that the only way to assemble and modify a plan that incorporates turnkey rental properties is to have a better understanding of how the different types of property, i.e., cash flow and appreciation properties, will modify your financial state. To facilitate your reading, I am providing the financial-based definitions below:

A cash flow property is defined in this book as:

- a property with a total leveraged ROI greater than 20 percent and,
- taxable income greater than $0.

An appreciation property is defined as:

- a rental property with a total leveraged ROI greater than 20 percent and,
- taxable income less than $0.

The following example is intended to provide you with how the two property types perform financially in the first year of service and where the criteria for the above definitions come from.

Example 13.3 Cash Flow Properties versus Appreciation Properties

For in-depth financial calculations related to this discussion, please refer to **Appendix D: Mathematics for the Examples**, under **Example 13.3: Cash Flow Properties versus Appreciation Properties.** For those who prefer digital access, these calculations are also available as a spreadsheet and reference article, without charge, on my website. The discussion below provides a summarized version of the key findings.

Comparing Purchasing Requirements

The purchasing requirements for a cash flow and appreciation property are compared below in **Table 7**.

Table 7. Comparison of the purchase requirements between a cash flow property and an appreciation property.

	Cash Flow Property	Appreciation Property
Purchase Price	$150,000	$350,000
Investment Funds	$34,500	$80,500
Rental Rate	$1,300	$2,300
Appreciation Rate	2%	5%

For this example, the purchase prices for the cash flow and appreciation properties are $150,000 and $350,000, respectively. As shown, the typical appreciation property is significantly more expensive than the typical cash flow property. The numbers will fluctuate depending on the market cycle and the market but provide an idea of what to expect. In addition to market variance, there will be variance in the financial performance of cash flow or appreciation properties.

Appreciation Rates

The appreciation rates of 2 and 5 percent for the cash flow and appreciation properties were selected respectively to represent numbers below and above the national historical average of 3.5 percent. Again, the appreciation rate will fluctuate significantly with the real estate market cycle, where, historically, most of the appreciation occurs during the end of the expansion phase and the hyper supply phase.

Monthly Fixed Expenses Comparison

The monthly fixed expenses for a cash flow property and an appreciation property are compared below in **Table 8**.

Table 8. Comparison of the monthly fixed expenses for a cash flow property and an appreciation property.

	Cash Flow Property	Appreciation Property
Mortgage	$644	$1,503
Insurance	$65	$128
Management	$104	$184
Property Tax	$200	$513
Total	**$1,013**	**$2,328**

The fixed expenses for appreciation properties tend to be greater than cash flow properties because they have a higher price point.

As shown, the total monthly expenses for the appreciation and cash flow properties are $2,328 and $1,013 per month, respectively. As you would expect, the fixed expenses for the appreciation property are significantly greater than those for the cash flow property. Although the mortgage principal is not technically an expense, I included it in the above table because it lowers the cash flow.

The total allowable expenses for tax purposes for the cash flow and appreciation properties at the end of the first year of service are shown below in **Table 9**.

Table 9. Comparison of the tax allowable expenses for a cash flow property and an appreciation property after the first year of service.

	Cash Flow Property	Appreciation Property
Mortgage Interest	$5,960	$13,906
Insurance	$780	$1,540
Management	$1,248	$2,208
Property Tax	$2,400	$6,160
Depreciation	$4,495	$10,487
The total expenses include depreciation which is not an out-of-pocket expense.		

The year 1 out-of-pocket expenses are $10,388 and $23,814 for a cash flow and appreciation property, respectively. The total allowable tax expenses are $14,883 and $34,301, respectively. The difference between the out-of-pocket and total allowable tax expenses is the depreciation.

Projections of Returns

The projections of the four returns (cash flow, loan paydown, appreciation, and the tax savings from depreciation) produced by the cash flow and appreciation properties are shown below in **Table 10**.

Table 10. Comparison of the annualized four returns for a cash flow property and an appreciation property.

	Cash Flow Property		Appreciation Property	
	Dollars	ROI	Dollars	ROI
Cash flow	$3,442	10.0%	-$345	-0.4%
Loan Paydown	$1,770	5.1%	$4,131	5.1%
Appreciation	$3,000	8.7%	$17,500	21.8%
Total	$8,212	23.8%	$21,286	26.5%
Taxable Income	$717		-$6,701	
Effective Tax Rate	3.3%		0.0%	

As shown in the table, the appreciation property produces an annual cash flow of -$345 or -$29 every month, whereas the cash flow property produces $3,442 or $287 per month. The negative cash flow means that the investor of the appreciation property will need to provide an additional $29 every month to pay the expenses. Since the appreciation property is in the negative, any additional expenses, such as maintenance, repairs, and tenant turnover, will need to be paid out of pocket. The cash flow property, on the other hand, generates enough income to cover the typical additional expenses. This is to be expected in the first year of owning the property.

Appreciation and ROI Analysis

The value of the appreciation property increased by $17,500 in the first year from appreciation, whereas the cash flow property increased by $3,000. Again, the uncertainty of appreciation is much higher than the other profit returns. Your plan needs to include this uncertainty if appreciation is the main focus of your plan.

The ROI for the total returns for both properties are 23.8 and 26.5 percent and represent the leveraged return by purchasing with a mortgage at a loan-to-value ratio of 80 percent. Notice that the total ROI is greater than 20 percent for both properties even though the returns are distributed very differently in cash flow and equity gains.

Tax Implications

The return from depreciation results in lowering the tax rate by reducing the taxable income. What this means is you get to keep more of your profit. For the cash flow and appreciation properties, depreciation lowered the tax rate from 24 percent—which is the tax bracket I selected for the example—to 3.3 and 0.0 percent, respectively.

The cash flow property reported a gain of $717 for tax purposes (math is shown in the appendix). The tax liability is $172 (24 percent of $717), resulting in 3.3 percent of your earnings from the property being paid in taxes. All said, this is a very good, effective tax rate. The key points to remember about taxes for cash flow properties are:

- the effective tax rate is not 0 percent, and
- there are no carryover losses.

The appreciation property reported a loss of $6,701 for tax purposes (math is shown in the appendix) for the year due to depreciation, calculated by simply subtracting the total allowable expenses from the total rent. Because of this reported loss, the resulting tax liability was $0.

Carryover Losses

The losses that you cannot claim for tax purposes are known as carryover losses. The good news is that carryover losses can be used later to offset:

- capital gain tax if the property were sold at a higher price, and
- income tax during more profitable years.

In Example 13.3, some if not all of the reported loss for the appreciation property of -$6,701 will be a carryover loss. Unfortunately, you'll likely never be able to put these carryover losses to use to offset capital gains; it is almost always better to sell using a 1031 tax exchange. In regard to more profitable years, the revenue of a rental property tends to grow at a faster rate than the expenses, resulting in the taxable income increasing over time. Carryover losses from previous years can be applied in later years to reduce your taxable income.

Revisiting Definitions

A key distinction between cash flow and appreciation properties lies in the distribution of their total returns across the four returns (cash flow, loan paydown, appreciation, and a tax savings from depreciation). Appreciation properties generate a lot of equity and typically report a loss for tax purposes, whereas cash flow properties produce less equity but provide monthly income. I utilize total ROI and taxable income as the criteria for defining these property types because they are the most significant parameters when building and/or modifying my portfolio.

Recall that I defined a cash flow property as:

- a property with a total leveraged ROI greater than 20% and,
- taxable income greater than $0.

I defined the appreciation property as:

- a rental property with a total leveraged ROI greater than 20% and,
- taxable income less than $0.

Notice the definitions are independent of the purchase price and can be applied to generalize the performance of any single-family rental property. Also, you can adjust the ROI requirements for other loan-to-value ratios to accommodate different levels of leverage. The values shown are for an 80% loan-to-value ratio.

Portfolio Building

Cash flow and appreciation properties are the first two building blocks we are going to use to build our portfolios and alter our financial state. As I have mentioned, I almost always purchase cash flow properties because of my financial goals and risk tolerance. The exception is when I am projecting taxable income in my portfolio. I will purchase an appreciation property to reduce the taxable income of my portfolio. I do exercise caution because of the additional risk of appreciation properties.

Bear in mind, Example 13.3 from this chapter provided information on how cash flow and appreciation properties perform for the first year of ownership only. In later years, the performance of the properties will be similar but include some important differences. In later chapters, we will evaluate a model that predicts the financial state for later years and update our plan accordingly.

Key Takeaways for This Chapter:

- Our portfolios are built by purchasing cash flow and/or appreciation properties.
- Cash flow properties are defined as having taxable income with a total leveraged ROI greater than 20 percent.
- Appreciation properties are defined as having negative taxable income with a total leveraged ROI greater than 20 percent.
- Cash flow or appreciation properties offer different financial performance that can be used to alter our financial state.

In Chapter 13, we developed an understanding of how different property types perform financially in the first year of service. The next step is properly evaluating and selecting a market to find the turnkey properties you need to accomplish your goals. We'll explore all of this in the next chapter.

CHAPTER 14

HOW TO EVALUATE A MARKET

> Where We Are At: Master Checklist Step 5
> - **Market Evaluation Checklist**

Turnkey rental providers operate in almost every major city; for this reason, the initial selection of potential markets to invest in should be done without considering turnkey providers. Later on, when you have built relationships with such providers, you can put more weight toward investing in the cities your turnkey partners operate in. For now, determine which cities you want to invest in based on economic and demographic criteria combined with your goals, investment criteria, and portfolio needs.

Since I purchase properties based on cash flow, I look for metropolitan areas that are strong cash flow markets. This type of market refers to a metropolitan area with rental properties that produce above-average cash flow. For those wanting to build a turnkey business based upon appreciation, an appreciation market is considered a metropolitan area where above-average appreciation is expected. At the time of this writing, some examples of cash flow markets include Memphis, TN; Little Rock, AR; and Cleveland,

OH. Examples of appreciation markets: Austin, TX; Dallas, TX; and San Diego, CA. A more quantitative definition will be provided, along with a more comprehensive list of metropolitan areas, later in this book.

For the following analysis, keep in mind that the idea is to identify metropolitan areas with a higher probability of success, i.e., markets with rentals that perform similarly to your purchase criteria. If you do not have your own criteria yet, you can use my criteria in **Establish a Purchase Criteria Checklist** as a guide.

How to Select Cash Flow Markets

You'll find my process of selecting cash flow markets, presented as a checklist, in my **Market Evaluation Checklist**, found in the appendix section. Part of the market selection process involves reviewing national averages based on the criteria discussed below. My preference is to avoid metropolitan areas with extreme values, i.e., markets deemed too far from the mean. There will be good markets that do not meet all the criteria established later in this section. Remember, a turnkey rental business can operate anywhere. For this reason, you can be very selective about the markets you invest in.

To begin executing the Market Evaluation Checklist, we first must look at nine questions, the answers to which will be used to determine:

- The demographic health of a metropolitan area
- The economic health of the metropolitan area
- The strength of the rental market
- Whether the metropolitan area is a cash flow market, an appreciation market, or a market between these two extremes

Population and Population Dynamics

Question 1: What is the population of the metropolitan area?

In this book, a major metropolitan area is defined as a metropolitan area with a population of at least 500,000. The first criterion is to select a metropolis with a higher population than this. At the time of this writing, 109 metropolitan areas in the United States satisfy this criterion.

Questions 2 and 3: Is the population of the metropolitan area growing? Has the population of the metropolitan area been growing for multiple years?

While obvious, it is worth highlighting again that a turnkey rental business is a business that supplies housing. Therefore, the single most important parameter to evaluate is the demand for housing, which is directly related to population growth. For those not interested in performing a detailed analysis (about to be given below), the population should still be evaluated, and metropolises with growing populations considered. The relationship between population and demand is fairly straightforward—in the United States, approximately 2.6 people per house is the average, which means a new house is required for every 2.6 people who move into a metropolitan area.

Evaluating demand using only the dynamics of a metropolis' population is a simplistic approach, omitting any consideration regarding the existing housing inventory or newly arriving housing inventory. While it can be helpful to monitor the number of new building permits, this level of detail is not needed to successfully identify good metropolitan areas—though such information is useful for monitoring the real estate market cycle, as discussed in **Example 10.2 Market Cycle Analysis for Atlanta, GA**.

The histogram in Figure 3 shows the population growth of the

109 metropolitan areas in the United States with a current population of at least 500,000.

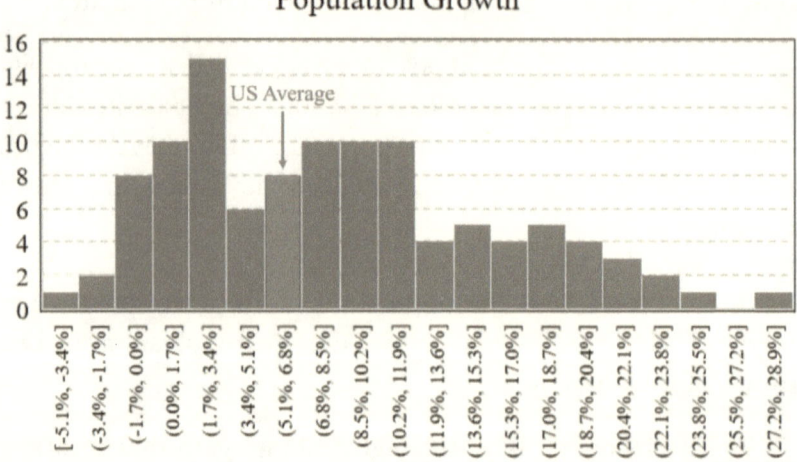

Figure 3. Population growth of the major metropolitan areas in the United States. (*Source: https://www.bestplaces.net*)

The figure above represents the percentage of population growth from 2010 to 2019. Regarding your selection of metropolitan areas, I prefer metropolitan areas that have population growths greater than the national average of 6.12 percent and that are actually above 7 percent.

The criteria I arrived at (greater than 7 percent) can change over time depending on how the histogram in Figure 3 changes. For this reason, it can be beneficial to evaluate markets annually. Also, there are likely plenty of opportunities to make money in metropolitan areas below the national average. I choose to let others work these metropolises. Again, the idea is to identify metropolitan areas with a high probability of success. Population data can be found at https://www.bestplaces.net or through a quick internet search.

A lot of the additional analysis described below is helpful, but population and population dynamics are the most important components, especially when coupled with a quick evaluation of the projected financial performance of a rental property. Look for large cities that everyone seems to want to move to and confirm their populations are growing. Most likely, these cities will have an excellent gross domestic product (GDP), which is increasing at an above-average rate. The financials for the properties located in these cities will quickly reveal whether the rental rates and purchase price ranges are suitable for your investment criteria and goals.

The demand ascertained from the population dynamics is generic since there is no way to differentiate whether the demand is weighted more toward home ownership or renting. Question 4, shown below, is intended to help identify demand for home ownership and for rentals.

Question 4: What is the percentage of renters, the housing affordability ratio, and the rent-to-price ratio?

To answer Question 4, it is worth first defining:

- Percentage of Renters
- Housing Affordability Index
- Rent-to-Price Ratio

Percentage of Renters

The percentage of renters, a measure of the number of renters in the existing population, does not represent the likelihood that new residents will also rent. That said, the dynamics of the city that created a rental-heavy environment, such as property prices, property tax, rental rates, median household salary, and other factors, will likely result in a similar percentage of renters for new residents.

The percentage of renters is also a measure of how much competition there is in the rental market. At the time of this writing, the percentage of renters in the United States was between 32 and 35 percent. A histogram of the percentage of renters in the 109 major metropolitan areas in the United States is shown below in Figure 4.

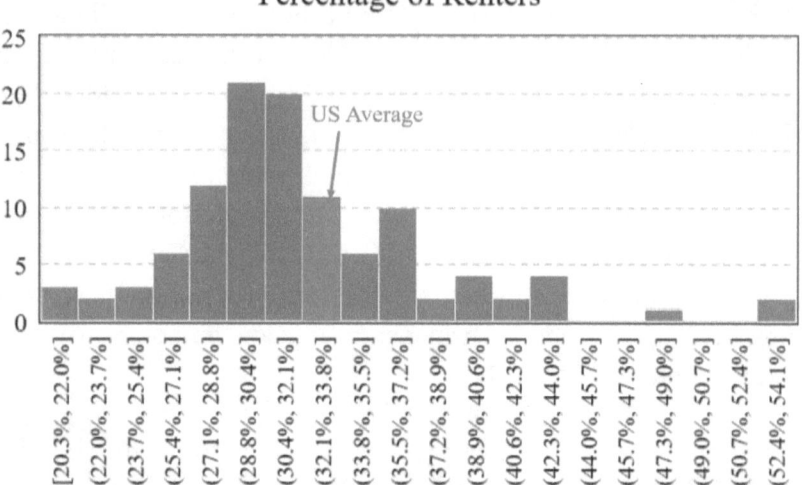

Figure 4. Percentage of renters within major metropolitan areas in the United States. (Source: *https://www.census.gov*)

Since I prefer to avoid the extremes, any metropolitan areas with renters above 40 or below 25 percent would be outside of the range I would consider. Data for percentages of renters can be found at https://www.census.gov and https://www.bestplaces.net. Another good source is https://www.nar.realtor.

The Housing Affordability Index

The housing affordability index is a measure of the likelihood that a household can afford to purchase a home. The calculation, which is dependent on the median household salary and median home price, determines how many people can qualify for a mortgage to purchase a home.

You'll find different calculations used to determine this such as simply using the median household salary and median home price or by using mortgage rates to determine a more accurate estimate of the cost of a home. My preference is to keep the calculation simple.

The housing affordability index (HAI) is given as:

$$HAI = \frac{Median\ home\ price}{Median\ household\ income}.$$

I prefer the simple method because it is fairly easy to find data and compute the housing affordability index. Also, the median household income and median home price are the only two dependent variables that vary between metropolitan areas since the interest rate is very similar. Moreover, the simple approach results in a national average and a distribution of values, which is all that is required. An example of a histogram for the housing affordability index is shown below in Figure 5 for the 109 major metropolitan areas in the United States.

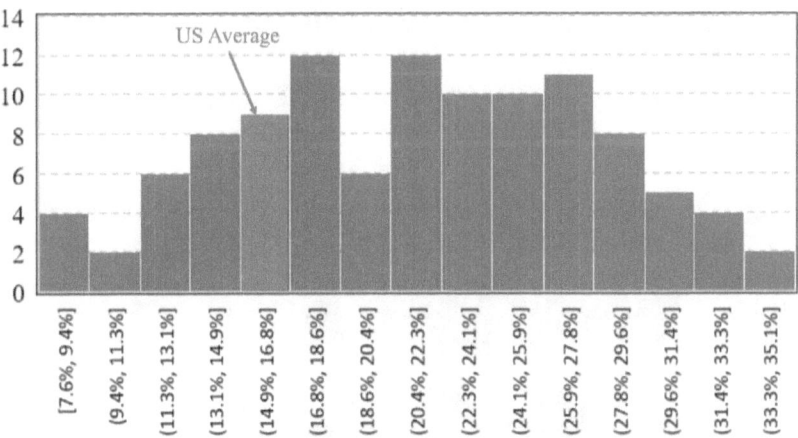

Figure 5. Housing affordability in US major metropolitan areas. (Source: *https://www.bestplaces.net*)

Again, the method you use may vary, but whatever calculation is used should still filter out extreme markets. The metropolitan areas with housing affordability between 11 and 30 percent are the cities I would consider investing in. Data relating to the housing affordability index can be found at https://www.census.gov and https://www.

bestplaces.net. Another website with good information: https://www.nar.realtor.

Rent-to-Price Ratio

Thus far, we've estimated through our analysis whether sufficient demand exists for rentals, but we still have not considered how profitable rental properties are likely to be. To determine this, we're going to look at the rent-to-price ratio, a simple calculation that looks at the ratio of the median rent of a property and the median price of a property. High rent-to-price markets represent markets with higher gross profits. A low rent-to-price ratio represents markets with low gross profit. In general, cash flow markets have higher rent-to-price ratios, and appreciation markets yield lower rent-to-price ratios. You can find data relating to rent-to-price ratios at https://www.census.gov. Many sources report the price-to-rent ratio, which is simply the inverse.

A histogram of the rent-to-price ratio is shown below in Figure 6.

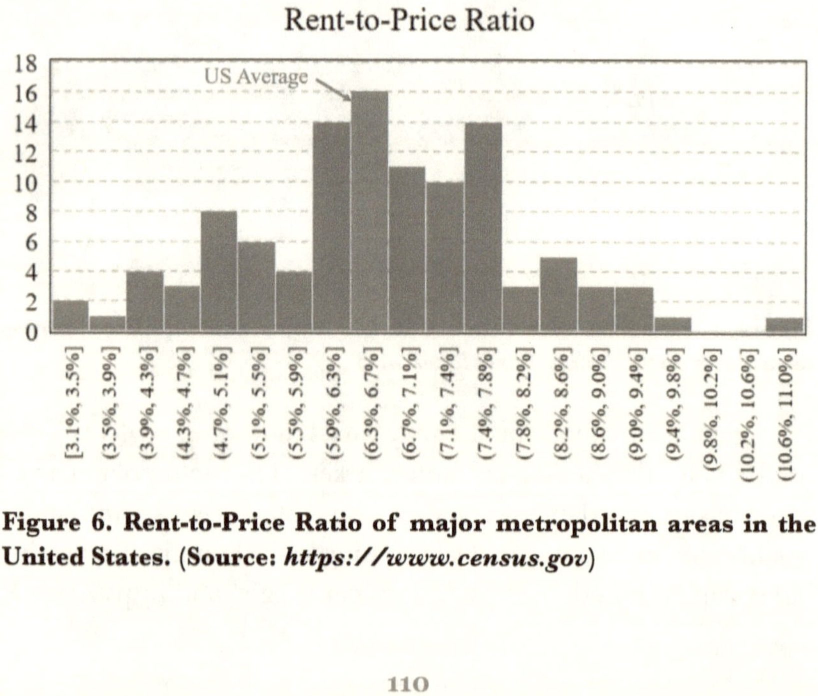

Figure 6. Rent-to-Price Ratio of major metropolitan areas in the United States. (Source: *https://www.census.gov*)

The rent-to-price ratio for the United States is around 6.4 percent, indicated with the arrow in this figure. Based on this histogram, I would look for metropolitan areas with a rent-to-price ratio above the national average of 6.4 percent but below 8 to 8.2 percent. Remember, selecting a suitable metropolitan area requires more than just the rent-to-price ratio. The other economic and population criteria need to also align.

A quick side note: Some readers at this point may be thinking that some of these markets will have pockets that meet the criteria. This is certainly true; however, finding pockets that may have a relatively small population is not necessarily advantageous. Instead, identifying large populations (such as the entire metropolitan area) with averages that fall into the range of the different metrics introduced in this section is more likely to produce lower-risk investment opportunities that produce a good return on investment.

Moreover, performing a complete top-down analysis in which the large metropolitan areas are first analyzed and then partitioned into their various neighborhoods, is very time-consuming. This level of analysis has its place but is not needed or necessarily wanted to achieve the objectives of this section.

Recent and Future Job Growth

Question 5: Is the city's job market growing?

Thus far, we've determined through our analysis in this chapter that the population is growing, as well as figured out the demand for rentals and the profitability of rentals. Population growth will likely correspond to a growth in jobs; hence, an increase in jobs is a good confirmation of the demand for housing.

An increase in jobs represents the likelihood that the population will continue growing. Population growth will lag job growth; hence, a change in job growth could be an important leading indicator for a change in population growth. It is also helpful to determine the types of jobs that are increasing and their salary ranges as both can help predict the likelihood that new residents will rent or buy.

For Question 5, my preference for evaluating job growth is to look at data for recent job growth, as shown below in Figure 7, and to look at projected future job growth, as illustrated below in Figure 8.

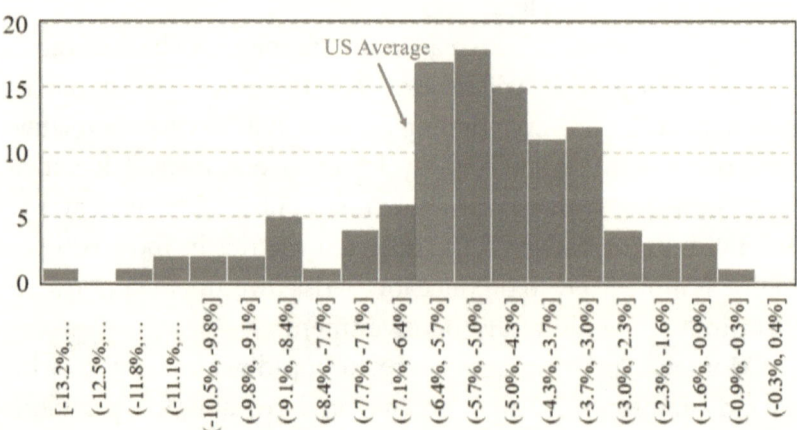

Figure 7. Recent job growth in major US metropolitan areas. (Source: *https://www.bestplaces.net*)

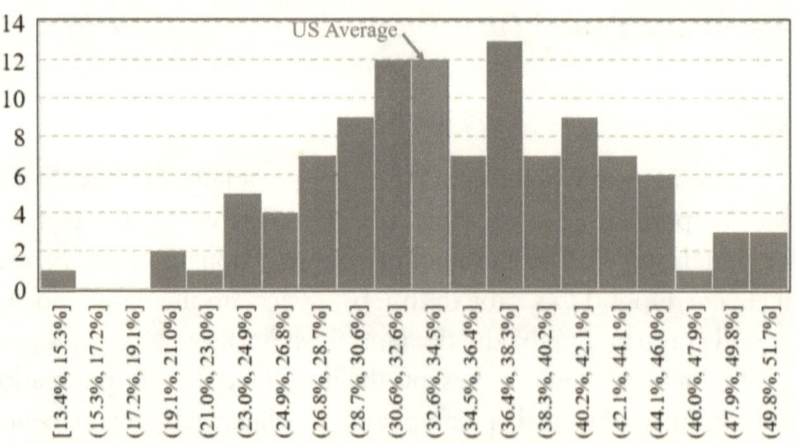

Figure 8. Future job growth in major US metropolitan areas. (Source: *https://www.bestplaces.net*)

At the time this data was pulled (August 2022), the economy in the United States was at the onset of a recession, resulting in recent job growth (see Figure 7) showing as negative for almost every major metropolitan area. As shown, the US median job growth is at -6.18 percent. In general, I would set certain criteria when conducting my search such as current job growth being greater than the US median job growth. US future job growth for the next ten years is 33.5 percent, as shown in Figure 8. Thus, I would select metropolitan areas greater than 33.5 percent.

Gross Domestic Product

The gross domestic product (GDP), reflects the monetary value of goods and services performed within a metropolitan area for a specified period. A growing GDP is a good indication that the city's economy is healthy.

Questions 6 and 7: Is the city's gross domestic product growing? Has it been growing for multiple years?

The job growth indicated should correspond to an increasing GDP, which is another verifying indicator. Data for the GDP and the different industries for metropolitan areas can be found at https://www.bea.gov/tools. The GDP for the 109 major metropolitan areas in the United States is shown in Figure 9.

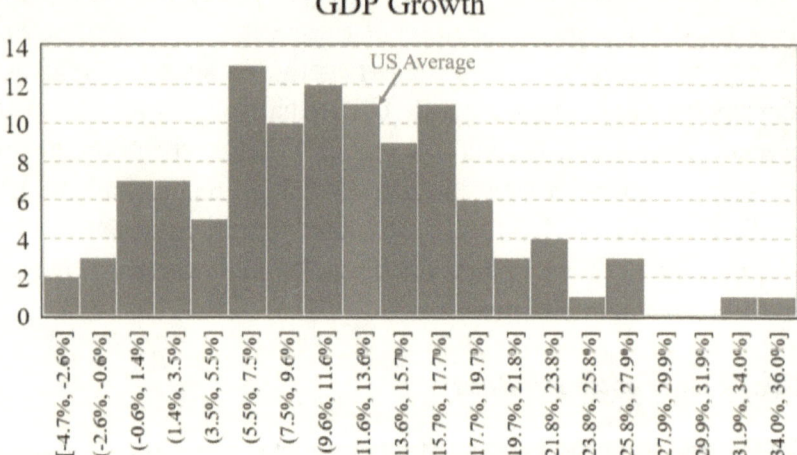

Figure 9. GDP growth of major metropolitan areas in the United States. (*Source: https://www.bea.gov/tools*)

The GDP growth in Figure 9 was computed from 2016 to 2020. During this time, GDP growth for the United States was calculated as 11.8 percent. Again, I recommend selecting metropolitan areas with a GDP growth that is greater than the US average.

Question 8: Which companies are the biggest employers in the city?

I included this question to help you pinpoint the large employers in the local economy. Here, be sure to select markets with multiple large employers in industries that are growing and that you think will continue to do so.

Question 9: Which industries do these companies operate in?

To answer this question, we'll identify the different industries that make up the local economy. Look for large employers with stable or growing businesses in industries that are also stable or growing. Ideally, you want cities that contain multiple industries, which typically means a more diverse and resilient economy. By diversified, I mean an economy with a significant number of jobs in multiple sectors and with industries such as healthcare, shipping, education, agriculture, etc. Select cities with different economies to further diversify your portfolio. For example, I would consider not selecting two cities with the same industries. Lastly, state capitals also provide stability due to government jobs stimulating their economies.

Further Considerations

Further diversify your portfolio by including several properties located in different cities that meet the above criteria. For example, if your portfolio contains ten properties, consider two to three houses located in four or five different cities. I tend to avoid cities susceptible to natural disasters such as hurricanes; however, plenty of excellent investments can be found in many of the coastal cities.

I also tend to avoid anti-landlord states. The reason is simple: I want the property manager to be able to evict someone who refuses to pay rent, and I want the eviction process to go swiftly. Determining which states are landlord-friendly requires nothing more than a quick online search. Some examples of landlord-friendly states: Alabama, Arkansas, Arizona, Florida, Georgia, Indiana, Michigan, North Carolina, Ohio, and Texas. States that are tenant-friendly include New York, California, Oregon, Washington, Maryland, Vermont, Nebraska, Rhode Island, Nevada, and Delaware.

I avoid metropolitan areas with extreme growth. Ideally, you want to get into such areas before the growth gets out of control. During extreme growth, the demand for properties skyrockets, and turnkey providers charge a premium for their product. Property pricing in such an environment starts to resemble an auction, with lots of bidders who are emotionally charged. These bidders do not want to be left out and are willing to pay huge premiums. The result: very high prices and properties that will not appraise anywhere near the asking price—and, since it is a seller's market, you likely won't be able to negotiate for better terms. Moreover, the cash flow will likely be negative, which means you are not really investing; you are speculating on appreciation. In addition, if the property does not appraise, you will need to bring additional funds to closing. Markets that rapidly appreciate tend to lose a lot of value if the market turns. Remember, no one can consistently or accurately predict when the market will tank. If the market turns for the worse, your property will be deeply underwater.

Selecting a Market Based on Appreciation

As mentioned, I purchase properties based on the cash flow, not appreciation. For many of you, your criteria might target appreciation properties, i.e., properties for which the return from appreciation is projected as greater than the national average. An outline is included that shows how I would go about beginning the process of selecting metropolitan areas based on appreciation. Again, this is intended only as a starting point.

Population and Population Dynamics

Question 1: What is the metropolitan area's population?

To begin the process, tabulate the appreciation rates for all metropolitan areas with a population of at least 500,000 people. Plot the histogram of this dataset; make sure to include the national average. Note: Different single-family properties will have different appreciation rates. For example, three-bedroom homes will likely have a lower appreciation rate than four-bedroom homes. Hence, I would recommend separating the analysis by property type.

For the metropolitan areas that look promising (those with appreciation rates above the national average), look at how the appreciation rate has changed over time by comparing the appreciation rates from previous years. The more conservative approach to buying for appreciation is to select markets that are appreciating and have been for multiple years. Identifying metropolitan areas likely to appreciate above the national average beforehand is more difficult and riskier.

Questions 2 and 3: Is the population of the metropolitan area growing? Has it been growing for multiple years?

Population growth will be the most important dependent variable for appreciation. Multiple approaches to evaluating population growth can be used for this purpose. Firstly, you could look for metropolitan areas already growing at a rapid rate by adjusting the criteria for population growth to metropolitan areas in the upper 75th percentile of the distribution, as shown earlier in this chapter in Figure 3. The upper 75th percentile would correspond to population growth above approximately 13.5 percent.

Secondly, you can try to anticipate population growth by monitoring projected job growth. Look for metropolitan areas where large companies have recently announced new expansions, and read through city planning minutes for information that might indicate population growth.

Percentage of Renters, Housing Affordability Ratio, and Rent-to-Price Ratio

Question 4: What is the percentage of renters, the housing affordability ratio, and the rent-to-price ratio?

I would not put much emphasis on the percentage of renters, the level of housing affordability, or the rent-to-price ratio when evaluating markets for appreciation. The data may provide some insight, but I would expect little return for the effort. In general, rent-to-price ratios will be lower for appreciation markets, likely below 6 percent.

Recent and Future Job Growth

Question 5: Is the city's job market growing?

I touched on job growth during our discussion on population growth. I would adjust the criteria for recent job growth and future job growth to include metropolitan areas in the upper 75th percentile of the distributions shown in Figure 7 and 8 earlier in this chapter. The upper 75th percentile would correspond to recent job growth and future job growth greater than approximately -4 and 40 percent, respectively.

If population growth is highly correlated to future job growth (meaning a high correlation coefficient), future job growth will lead to population growth, providing a leading indicator. Finding a metropolitan area ready to grow rapidly before the majority of the market participants (investors and future residents) discover it is likely to lead to excellent returns from appreciation but is challenging to accomplish.

Gross Domestic Product

Questions 6 and 7: Is the city's GDP growing? Has it been growing for multiple years?

Appreciation markets should be accompanied by a strong and growing economy, which is clearly evident in the GDP data. Adjust the criteria for GDP growth to include only the metropolitan areas that are in the 75th percentile or better for the distribution shown in Figure 9 earlier in this chapter. The upper 75th percentile would correspond to a GDP growth of greater than approximately 18 percent.

Further Considerations

Investing for appreciation requires significant analysis. The criterion for appreciation provided above should be treated as a starting point.

In this regard, think of it as an initial screening you can use to identify candidates for further review during round two of your process.

Once several metropolitan areas have been selected based on their appreciation rates and economic strength, review the different submarkets. Look for areas that are currently growing within the targeted metropolitan areas. Estimate the appreciation rates and use these values to estimate the appreciation of the properties sent to you by your turnkey provider.

Additionally, it is also worth reviewing city planning meeting notes. You are looking for areas that the city has plans to expand and develop. A new planned area, such as an older neighborhood that the city has designated to be renovated as an entertainment district, could be the equivalent of striking gold. At any rate, sifting through news and looking for anything that could be a stimulus for growth is key if your goal is to identify up-and-coming appreciation markets.

Where to Invest—Metros that Meet the Criteria

So far, in this chapter, we have established a method to determine investment criteria for selecting metropolitan areas. Now, let's highlight all the metropolitan areas that satisfied the criteria listed for cash flow markets in this book. These metropolitan areas were

- Atlanta, Sandy Springs, and Alpharetta, GA;
- Augusta, and Richmond County, GA;
- Dallas, Fort Worth, and Arlington, TX;
- Indianapolis, Carmel, and Anderson, IN;
- Jacksonville, FL;
- San Antonio and New Braunfels, TX; and
- Tampa, St. Petersburg, and Clearwater, FL.

Therefore, metropolitan areas that meet population growth but are outside of the established ranges for some of the other criteria can still, if desired, be included. Some of these "fringe" metropolitan areas include

- Little Rock, AR;
- Kansas City, MO;
- Oklahoma City, OK; and
- Tulsa, OK.

In the end, you will need to apply some common sense. For example, should you eliminate a metropolitan area that has met all your criteria except for current job growth, which is skewed negatively for all markets? Only you can decide. For myself, I would review the metropolitan area and likely include it.

Some examples of "appreciation markets" or an up-and-coming "appreciation market" include

- San Fransico, CA;
- New York, NY;
- Dallas and Houston, TX;
- Austin, TX;
- Atlanta, GA; and
- Huntsville, AL.

The Dallas, TX; Houston, TX; and Atlanta, GA metropolitan areas satisfied the criteria for a cash flow market but also show signs of soon becoming a high-priced housing market. The examples given are obviously not exhaustive. Below, I've included a list of metropolitan areas where I own or have owned rental property to give you some reference regarding my preferred cities and states:

- Cincinnati, OH
- Memphis, TN
- Little Rock, AR
- Tulsa, OK
- Kansas City, MO
- Montgomery, AL
- Atlanta, GA

A summary of the criteria above—which I use for an average

business plan—using 2022 data is given below. Remember, these criteria will change with time and should be evaluated yearly. You can always view my up-to-date criteria on my website:

https://scottastanfield.com

For cash flow markets, select metropolitan areas with

- a population above 500,000,
- population growth greater than 7 percent,
- a rent-to-price ratio between 6.4 to 8.2 percent,
- a housing affordability index between 11 and 30 percent,
- a percentage of renters between 25 to 40 percent,
- current job growth greater than -6 percent,
- future job growth greater than 33.5 percent, and
- a GDP greater than 11.8 percent.

For appreciation markets, select metropolitan areas with

- a population above 500,000,
- population growth approximately equal to 13.5 percent,
- current job growth greater than -4 percent,
- future job growth greater than 40.0 percent, and
- a GDP greater than 18 percent.

You should now have a clear idea of how to select markets for your plan. Again, the best approach is to begin by reducing a large list of potential cities to a smaller, more manageable list using market-generated data. Now that we have introduced some markets worth investing in, your next step will be to select a turnkey provider, a topic we'll explore in the next chapter.

CHAPTER 15

HOW TO FIND GOOD TURNKEY OPERATORS

> Where We Are At: Master Checklist Step 6
> - **Questionnaire for Finding Good Turnkey Partners**

Developing the kind of turnkey rental business described in this book requires, among other things, finding the right turnkey rental providers. To properly select and manage turnkey providers, you must understand their side of the business. Turnkey providers work with several goals in mind. In general, they seek to

- buy properties in decent areas at as low of a price as possible,
- renovate the properties while spending as little as possible while still maintaining a quality product attractive to tenants and investors,
- sell the property for top dollar to an investor, and
- continue to profit by managing the property.

Therefore, as an investor, you will want to

- make sure the renovations are not too cheap and are indeed worth buying,
- confirm the appraised value of the property, and
- confirm the management team is worth employing.

It is important to go further into understanding your role as an investor. When working with a turnkey provider, that provider will posture as having what you want; sometimes, the turnkey provider will try to exploit this by pushing the price as high as possible. This is especially true when there is high demand for rental properties. Your goal as an investor is to

- identify how to purchase properties that will appraise at the asking price,
- negotiate for a fair price, and
- optimize your approach to capitalize from the operations of the turnkey provider.

Remember, while turnkey providers may provide something investors want, investors definitely have what turnkey providers desire: our business. More specifically, turnkey providers want a reliable, long-term buyer who will purchase many properties and not badger them on how to manage rental properties.

Further, it is crucial to know that turnkey providers either partner with real estate agents or employ real estate agents to sell their properties. You will never be able to offer more value to an agent than the turnkey provider, even if you purchase ten or more properties per year. Most real estate agents adhere to an ethical code and thus will represent both parties accordingly, but it only takes one agent who does not abide to result in a loss of money. For this reason, assume the worst and represent yourself accordingly.

Let's look at the worst-case scenario: The agent, who is supposedly representing both parties, favors the turnkey provider. Remember, turnkey providers offer real estate agents ongoing transactions and both sides of the commission. This makes for an excellent arrangement for the real estate agent; so, do not expect them to have your best interests in mind. Instead, assume the agent will steer you toward what they want. Worst-case, the agent will maneuver you so that they can maintain their excellent arrangement and gain their commission.

Before my email blows up with messages from angry real estate agents, remember, I am describing the worst case, which only represents a small percentage of agents. Again, many operate their business with integrity. That said, you should follow your business plan, negotiate price and closing costs, and not let the agent or anyone else talk you into something you are unsure about.

How to Check the Quality of the Renovations

During the purchasing process, make sure to ask for a list of the renovations done to the property. In fact, I suggest you go a step further and ask for a list of materials. Review the list and remember, you can always reach out and ask the inspector whether the materials listed are of lower quality. If unsure where to turn, ask your turnkey provider if any warranties are available for maintenance. The turnkey provider might offer such a warranty throughout the first year. Instead of accepting, ask the provider whether they can cover the third year when maintenance issues are more likely to happen.

The Appraisal Problem

As far as the asking price is concerned, turnkey providers tend to ask for more than what their properties are worth. Let's assume the turnkey provider is selling a property that would appraise at $150,000. Some turnkey providers will ask for $160,000 or more. Worse, the contracts these turnkey providers use will contain language designed to contractually obligate the buyer as long as the appraisal is within $10,000 (sometimes more) of the asking price. The investor (buyer) will then be required to pay the difference at closing.

Turnkey providers are aware that

1. many investors will not negotiate the price because they fear the turnkey provider will choose not to do business with them, and
2. appraisers are likely to appraise the property closer to the asking price.

Remember, the appraiser does not work for you; they work for the lender who stands to make money from your purchase. Appraisers are not going to risk souring a business relationship over a few thousand dollars. Again, however, this is a worst-case scenario.

What does this mean for you, the investor? For one thing, you will notice an appraisal gap, which is the difference between the purchase price and the appraisal. The result: Your down payment will increase in the amount of the appraisal gap. At the time of this writing, banks require you to have a minimum down payment of 20 percent of the appraised value. The bank will only loan you up to 80 percent of the appraised price. Hence, the borrowed balance will be lower since banks loan up to 80 percent of the appraised value, not the purchase price. The end result is a little more cash flow but a reduced **ROI**. Of all the properties I have evaluated for the sake of purchasing, none have appraised above the asking price, and at least 70 percent have appraised at a minimum of $7,000 below it.

As with anything related to housing, supply and demand determine whether the buyer or seller is in control. The seller has the controlling position when the supply is low and the demand is high, and the buyer is in control when the supply is high and demand is low. Expect larger appraisal gaps when the sellers are in control. Unfortunately, the scenario described occurs frequently enough to warrant a name. For this book, I will call it the Appraisal Problem.

How to Handle the Appraisal Problem

My approach to reduce the Appraisal Problem's impact is to use these five steps:

1. **Determine the appraised value before signing the purchase and sales agreement.**

   The process to estimate the value of the property is simple: Find three houses similar to the subject house located nearby and recently sold. These houses are comparable properties, so the appraised value will be similar to the prices these houses were sold for. Compare the asking price of the turnkey rental property with the value you obtain from the comparable property approach. If the value you obtained is significantly lower than the asking price, ask the turnkey provider to justify their price by providing their comparable properties.

2. **Negotiate the price based on the appraised value you obtained.**

   In the case of an appraisal gap, first, negotiate for lower or no closing costs equal to the amount of the appraisal gap. If the appraisal gap is greater than the closing costs, first negotiate for no closing costs and then negotiate for a reduced purchase price that equals the amount of the remaining difference.

3. **Negotiate for no appraisal gap before signing the purchase and sales agreement.**

   Read the purchase and sales agreement and make sure the contract has the appraisal contingency. Ensure that you are not contractually obligated to purchase the property if an appraisal gap exists. Negotiate to include the appraisal contingency and to remove the appraisal gap or reduce it to a value at which the financial performance of the property will still meet your criteria.

4. **Look to purchase properties when the market is more favorable to buyers.**

   Waiting for the market to be more favorable for buyers may not be an option because of how long this can take. Instead, be prepared to tell the turnkey provider no when it comes to properties with an appraisal gap. Also, be prepared to spend a lot of time negotiating with them until you receive a property that fits your criteria.

5. **Try to profit from the Appraisal Problem.**

   Profiting from the Appraisal Problem is not an obvious path and requires some care. Turnkey providers usually work in specific neighborhoods and tend to sell lots of properties near the property you are purchasing.

   Many of their clients will pay the asking price even if the property appraises well below that. What this will do is set comparable properties with values much higher than they really are, resulting in some forced appreciation. The forced appreciation from the Appraisal Problem will cause your property to increase in value at appreciation rates much higher than would be the case otherwise.

   My plan to profit from the Appraisal Problem is simple. Use the county auditor's website to identify how many properties the turnkey provider owns and has sold near the property you are looking to purchase. Again, many of these properties will be sold at the asking price, which is very likely to be above the appraised value for these properties. These numbers, along with the appraisal terms in the contract, should provide enough information to estimate a range for the forced appreciation. After you obtain this range, negotiate as described above for (2).

   What usually happens is, the appraisal will come back low, and the turnkey provider will not be willing to lower the price. They will sell the property to a different investor, and you will receive a new property to review. Sometimes it can take multiple properties before the property appraises at the asking price, but eventually, it happens.

Remember, the turnkey provider wants to sell you houses and protect their reputation. After the first or second property does not appraise, they will be more careful to send a property they believe will appraise at the asking price. Again, the properties sold afterward are likely to be at higher prices than their appraised values, which establishes comparable properties at higher prices. The end result: Your property will appreciate at a higher appreciation rate.

The Value of a Good Turnkey Provider

When you find a good turnkey provider, by extension, you get access to their knowledge, network, and business systems. Some benefits of arrangement include but are not limited to:

- A good turnkey provider will know their local markets very well and offer properties that are well-positioned to perform.
- Their property management teams will be top-notch, resulting in reduced expenses for you while you maintain your income.
- Their business will have systems to evaluate markets, look for below-market deals, renovate the property, find tenants, manage the rental, handle financials for owners, and provide customer service.

Usually, you want the company managing the property to be the same one that sold you the property. The main reason: You will be a long-term client with their company even after they sell you the property. That said, there are always exceptions to the rule. Several excellent companies out there outsource property management, which is why the criteria listed in this book do not eliminate turnkey providers who do not manage properties. So, how then would you determine whether to eliminate a company that outsources management? The questionnaire, listed below, for finding good turnkey partners includes many points to ask, all designed to evaluate the performance of property management. If the turnkey provider's answers are favorable, the management teams are likely performing.

Selecting a Turnkey Provider Using the Questionnaire

The first step in finding a turnkey partner is to make a list of providers working in the metropolitan areas that interest you. Perform an internet search and search real estate investment forums to help you craft that list. Regarding those investment forums, the turnkey provider's business is very much tuned toward something investors are very vocal about—namely, their money. This means that message boards dedicated to real estate investing, such as BiggerPockets (https://www.biggerpockets.com), provide an excellent source for reviews. If you find a turnkey provider with good reviews, chances are that provider is a good one.

Use the **Questionnaire for Finding Good Turnkey Partners** to fully vet a company. The questionnaire in the appendix is a more streamlined version for the sake of easy printing. The remainder of this section discusses that questionnaire, which is broken into two sections. The first section, During the Meeting, is a series of questions designed to gather information. The second section, After the Meeting, lists action items to help you verify and vet the turnkey provider. The objectives are to

- identify the likelihood of the Appraisal Problem,
- determine how much room there is to negotiate,
- determine whether the rental rates are near the market rate, and
- evaluate the quality of the renovation work.

During the Meeting:

Question 1. How many properties have you sold to investors?

The goal is to gauge the size of the turnkey company. A larger company is more likely to use good business processes and have a strong professional network established. It also means the business is not dependent on a single person.

Question 2. Can you provide referrals from your investor clients?

A turnkey provider who has sold lots of properties should be able to provide referrals.

Question 3. Do you own the properties you sell?

You do not want to deal with wholesalers or middlemen. By middlemen, I mean people or businesses who buy a turnkey property from a turnkey provider, increase the price, and then sell the property to an investor. I have spoken with middlemen; their whole goal is to add a charge that can be avoided by simply identifying the true turnkey provider. Wholesalers are investors who market for below-market property deals and then sell them to investors. This can be a fine option for a more active investor (or an investor who plans to renovate the property), but wholesalers are not likely to offer a turnkey property.

Question 4. Does your company own the management company that manages the properties you sell?

As I already mentioned, it is best if the turnkey seller is the company managing the property. This allows for a much smoother experience once you close on the property. Plus, the turnkey provider is locked into a long-term commitment and, therefore, is more likely to sell a true turnkey rental, i.e., a rental property where all management activities are fully taken care of.

Question 5. What is the average length of occupancy for a tenant?

Tenant turnover is usually the largest expense, and hence, it is important for the tenants to stay as long as possible. A good average occupancy for the type of single-family houses I target is above five years, although I feel that four years is acceptable.

Question 6. How much does the average tenant turnover cost?

For me, my properties average just below $2,500 for tenant turnover. This includes repairs and maintenance, cleaning, advertising, and the leasing fee—typically, the first month's rent from the new tenant. That said, I think I have been fortunate. I would budget more for turnover.

Question 7. How long does it take to clean, repair, and place a new tenant for tenant turnover?

As mentioned, tenant turnover is expensive. You want to complete the process as quickly as possible. A good management team will complete tenant turnover in two to three weeks on average. Note: The length of time will vary with market conditions.

Question 8. Do you use chargebacks?

A chargeback occurs when damage beyond normal wear and tear occurs and is the tenant's fault. For example, if the garbage disposal needs replacement because the tenant put an entire chicken down the sink, the repair costs would be charged to that tenant. My preference is to see property management willing to chargeback the tenant when the situation clearly merits it.

Question 9. What is the average collected scheduled rent?

Just because a tenant is contractually obligated to pay the rent does not mean they actually will. It is important to know how much of the scheduled rent is collected. A higher percentage gives you an idea of how well the property management team is screening potential tenants. Low collected rent is a serious red flag. It needs to be taken into consideration along with the vacancy rate, which is why you should ask how much of the scheduled rent is collected.

Question 10. What is your current vacancy rate?

This is another question meant to discern the management team's level of efficiency. Obviously, a lower vacancy is better, especially if the collected scheduled rents are high.

Question 11. Can you provide some example property brochures for properties you recently sold?

Make sure to request brochures for the different markets they operate in and the different price points they typically deal with. The brochures should include the asking price, the address, the square footage, the number of bedrooms and bathrooms, parking information, the current rental rate or the anticipated rental rate, property tax, an estimate for insurance, the management fee, the mortgage, and the HOA. The assumptions used to determine the mortgage will be listed and should include the loan-to-value ratio, interest rate, and the term. You then have some information compiled about the expected return. Unfortunately, some turnkey providers like to include all four returns lumped together (cash flow, appreciation, loan paydown, and depreciation). Make certain you know what they are including and absolutely compute the returns on your own.

Question 12. What percent of the properties you sell appraise at the asking price?

I mentioned early in this section how big of an issue the Appraisal Problem can be. Turnkey providers who abuse the appraisal process absolutely know they are doing it and will dance around this question. I usually receive an answer along the lines of, "Well, the appraisal process is very random and seems to come back all over the place." The reality is, the appraised value will be well below the asking price or sometimes at the asking price, which is systematic, not random.

Question 13. What will you offer me if the property does not appraise at the asking price?

Turnkey providers can offer a lot. In my case, they have covered my closing costs, reduced the price, and offered different properties to purchase. Make sure you do not overpay for a property. Remember, it is better to pass on properties until you find a winner.

Question 14. Do you offer any warranties on the renovations for the property?

Remember, the turnkey provider put the scope together for the renovations and, therefore, should be able to stand by their work. Again, ask to have the warranty for Year 3 instead of Year 1. They will not likely agree, but it is worth asking.

Question 15. Do you offer rental guarantees?

A rental guarantee refers to the assurance that you will receive the monthly rent regardless of whether the tenant has paid it. A good turnkey provider should have an excellent understanding of their management team, the rents collected in Year 1, and their eviction rates. If their management team is good, persuading the provider to concede on a rental guarantee for six months or the first year shouldn't be hard.

Question 16. How many evictions have you had to do in the last year?

Evictions are part of the business. A lower eviction rate means the management team is doing an excellent job of screening potential tenants. Keep in mind, though, that even the best management teams will have evictions.

Question 17. Can you tell me about the eviction process and include the average cost and average length of time to complete the eviction process?

To date, I have been fortunate—I have not had a single eviction. My management teams began the eviction process twice in the past, and both times, the tenants paid the owed rent. Regardless, evictions happen, and each state has different laws that affect the cost and time needed to complete the process. As mentioned earlier, I only buy rentals in landlord-friendly states.

Question 18. How much are the maintenance costs on average per month per property in years one, two, and three?

Turnkey providers may not know the exact number, but they should have a good idea of what to expect and therefore should be able to share an average percentage. Again, this information is useful for planning and identifying low-quality renovations. Be certain to compare multiple companies and remember, if it seems too good to be true, it likely is.

Question 19. Can you provide a detailed scope of work and a list of the materials used for your average renovation?

The scope of work refers to an itemized list of all the renovations completed by the turnkey provider on the property. The providers I use provide the scope and materials used during the renovation as part of the package they send to potential investors. A good turnkey provider will have systems in place for the renovation process that will include the materials. Again, look over the materials used and ask your inspector to review them and then tell you whether those materials are of low or average quality.

Question 20. What are your management fees?

The most recent trend slants toward lower management rates, but I advise caution here. Lower rates are not necessarily better. Typical rates are between 8 to 10 percent of the rent, with 10 percent being the standard. Some companies offer incentives that include a reduction in the rate, depending on how many houses you own. If the rate is below 8 percent, be certain you understand all their fees for maintenance, leasing, and bookkeeping.

After the Meeting:

- ☐ Confirm that the properties in the property brochures were recently sold. Markets change; so, recently sold properties will provide the most accurate information.

- ☐ Perform a quick desktop appraisal for each subject property in the brochures. Your appraisal does not need to be fancy. I typically use Zestimate on Zillow's website. To use this system, go to https://www.zillow.com, enter the property address, and the Zestimate should be displayed on the upper right corner of the page. Note: If the Zestimate and the asking price are vastly different, I pull comps and complete an actual appraisal using the comparable property approach discussed in the section **Estimate the Appraised Value**. I don't pull comps for all properties sent—only enough to gauge the effects of any potential Appraisal Problem.

- ☐ Use the county auditor's website to determine whether the sold price was less than, more than, or the same as the asking price shown on the property brochures. Comparing the sold price with the asking price is a good approach to determining how much negotiating room you will have. Not everyone is good at negotiating. Personally speaking, it is a weaknesses of mine; however, I find it much easier if I have an idea of what to expect.

- ☐ Determine how the rental rate compares to the market rental rate. You can find the market rental rate through https://www.RentOMeter.com or other sources such as https://www.zillow.com. In general, Rentometer provides pretty good rental rate information, and many property management companies will at least review Rentometer's results as part of their process to determine the market rent. These companies also take the additional step of pulling the rental rate from similar properties. The approach is almost identical to the comparable property appraisal method.
  - ◊ Are the rents listed in the property brochures realistic? Are the rents well above or well below market rates? You are looking for management teams that set the rents near the market rental rate.

- ☐ Review the scope of work provided in the property brochures to determine whether (1) the renovations are cheap and (2) the renovations meet the buying criteria. For reference, some questions based on renovation-specific buying criteria are below:
  - ◊ Was the roof replaced? If not, is the roof less than four years old?
  - ◊ Was the HVAC replaced? If not, is the HVAC less than two years old?
  - ◊ Was the hot water tank replaced? If not, is the hot water tank less than two years old?
  - ◊ Was the interior fully renovated?

Remember, if you are uncertain, follow up with the turnkey provider for more information.

- ☐ Compute the four profit returns (cash flow, appreciation, loan paydown, and depreciation) of a property to ensure there are example properties that satisfy your financial-specific purchase criteria (for example, a cash flow greater than $300). Remember, the numbers will reflect the market conditions; so, if the cash flow is low for what looks like a cash flow property, the market conditions may not be right for purchasing properties right now. You can always ask the turnkey company for older brochures to confirm.

- ☐ After comparing each turnkey provider, hire a company or reopen the search. Note: Even if you decide that the time may not be right to purchase, it is still worth asking the top one or two turnkey providers on your list to send property brochures.

Again, the questions in this checklist are intended to uncover the quality of turnkey providers. These are the same questions I use when screening potential turnkey partners. Utilizing the checklist should

- streamline the turnkey provider screening process for you,
- eliminate mistakes or prevent you from forgetting to gather the necessary information, and
- allow anyone with a sufficient understanding of the turnkey business to complete the screening process.

Now that we have discussed setting up your business plan, setting purchasing criteria, evaluating markets, and screening turnkey providers, we can move on to the most exciting part! Purchasing your first turnkey rental property. The discussion in Part 4 will help you with this process.

PART FOUR: PURCHASING A TURNKEY PROPERTY

CHAPTER 16

THE PREAPPROVAL PROCESS

> Where We Are At: Master Checklist Step 7
> - **Loan Preapproval Checklist**

Purchasing a property has multiple steps associated with it, which are all included below. If you have questions during the process, you can always reach out to your turnkey liaison. That said, let's discuss the first step to purchasing a property—the preapproval process.

Before diving in, it bears mentioning that the purchasing process for a turnkey rental property from a turnkey provider is very similar to that of purchasing a personal residence. Hence, your knowledge of the purchasing process, such as the preapproval step and closing process, will be transferable, though the purchasing process has some unique nuances that are turnkey-specific.

Beginning the Purchasing Process

First, inform your turnkey company that you are ready to purchase properties with them. The turnkey company will help guide you through the process and will start by requesting that you be preapproved by a lender.

Turnkey providers have a list of lenders, which they will send to you. Keep in mind, the lenders provided by the turnkey provider are familiar with that provider's business and, as such, will have an excellent idea of the risk involved. This will make it much easier for you to get preapproved. If you already have a lender and are pre-approved, let your turnkey provider know.

Preapproval Process and the Prequalification Process

There is a preapproval process and a prequalification process. The prequalification process is less rigorous. For the prequalification process, the lender reviews the financial information you provide and will then send you an estimated loan amount without pulling credit or verifying your financials.

For the preapproval, however, the lender will pull a credit report and verify the financial information you provide. Typically, the turnkey providers ask for a preapproval. If you are interested in shopping around for a lender, start with the prequalification process since the lender will not pull credit—which lowers your credit score—for this. Once you have settled on a lender, you can begin the preapproval process.

The Preapproval Process

The preapproval can take a little time. Use the **Loan Preapproval Checklist** to complete this process. The required documents might vary depending on your specific lender and loan type. You might be required to submit the same documents multiple times. Supply the information requested, and remember, from the lender's perspective, the loan is nothing more than an investment, and as such, they need to evaluate you and your plan for that purpose. For the lender, it is all about determining their risk by scrutinizing all aspects of your financial status.

The preapproval process begins with a mortgage application. The lender will want your social security number and will perform a credit check. The information the bank collects will be uploaded using the bank's browser-based portal. The lender will ask for

- bank account statements;
- a list of assets;
- a list of debts, including credit cards and other loans;
- a list of income sources;
- employment status; and
- past addresses.

The lender uses the results to determine how likely you are to repay the mortgage.

Banks use two metrics to help them calculate this: the debt-to-income ratio (DTI) and loan-to-value ratio (LTV). The DTI is the ratio of all your monthly debts divided by your monthly income. The equation for the DTI is given as:

$$DTI = \frac{Monthly\ Debts}{Monthly\ Income}.$$

The DTI ratio measures the strength of your personal finances. A lower DTI is viewed as a lower-risk candidate. The reason: Your monthly income is more likely to adequately service your monthly debts. To summarize the DTI:

- Lower DTI = Lower Risk
- Higher DTI = Higher Risk

The LTV is the ratio of the loan amount divided by the value of the property. The equation for this is given as:

$$LTV = \frac{Loan\ Amount}{Property\ Value}.$$

The LTV ratio measures the bank's financial risk with the property. A lower LTV represents less risk for the lender. The reason: In the event you are unable to pay the mortgage, the lender can foreclose and assume ownership of the property. The bank can sell the property to reduce their loss. A lower LTV means the loan balance is small compared to the value of the property. Hence, the bank is more likely to recover their investment. To summarize the LTV:

- Lower LTV = Lower Risk
- Higher LTV = Higher risk

If you are approved, the DTI and LTV ratios are used to determine the interest rate for the mortgage and mortgage type.

At the time of this writing, the lender is legally obligated to provide a loan estimate within three business days of receiving the mortgage application. The loan estimate will include

- whether you are approved,
- the terms of the mortgage,
- the mortgage type,
- the interest and principal payments, and
- an estimate of the closing costs.

Again, the preapproval process happens before you are under contract and is not completed by the underwriter. The underwriter has the final say about the mortgage and will verify the information once you are under contract to purchase a property.

The underwriter will request the same information previously collected for the preapproval process. They may also ask for additional information, which can vary based on who is requesting it. Since this additional information is highly variable and will change for each situation, it will not be discussed here.

A Final Note About the Preapproval Process

Lending regulations are complicated, with rules that change regularly. If a lender does not work out, do not give up. Instead, speak with another one. With lending, you need to be persistent and approach multiple lenders to accomplish your goals. The reason: Every lender is different; though their underwriting may be tied to the same regulations, their interpretation of the regulations can and will vary. This is not overly surprising, given that Fannie Mae's and Freddie Mac's lending regulations are thousands of pages long, and changes occur regularly.

For an investor, the pre-approval process can be one of the more frustrating steps to the turnkey rental business. For some, the nature of your employment might make it difficult to receive pre-approval for a personal loan. For example, having a job with a low base salary and a hefty stipend may cause issues. Unfortunately, the lending regulations are such that most lenders must use the taxable income for the pre-approval process, which corresponds to only the base salary and does not include the stipend. In this scenario, many lenders may not approve a loan. I mention this because the keyword is most. For those of you who fall into this category, shop around; eventually, you will find a lender who understands how your salary is paid and will be more likely to provide you with preapproval. Also, you can look for loan products outside of a conventional loan such as a nonconforming or commercial loan.

Once you are preapproved for a loan, the turnkey provider will begin to send property brochures. The systematic approach to evaluating property-specific information in these brochures is explored in the next chapter.

CHAPTER 17

HOW TO EVALUATE PROPERTIES

> Where We Are At: Master Checklist Step 8
> - **Property Evaluation Checklist**

Once you receive preapproval, begin evaluating the properties sent to you by the turnkey provider. Sometimes the evaluation process is short, which means a suitable property can be found after only a day or so. Other times, the process can take multiple weeks. Do not get discouraged if it takes a while, and absolutely hold to your purchasing criteria. Remember, a turnkey provider wants to sell you a house. If you pass on multiple houses and provide feedback as to why you are passing, the turnkey provider will try very hard to send or even reserve a house that meets your requirements. You absolutely do not want to be an investor that buys any property the turnkey provider sends because, going forward, the turnkey provider will be more likely to send their properties that have proven challenging to sell. The financial performance of these properties will likely be below the average of the turnkey provider's inventory.

The evaluation process begins when the turnkey provider starts sending their property brochures to you. The brochure could be a link to a website dedicated to the property or it could be an Excel file attached to an email. The properties sent for review will come from their existing inventory and newly arriving inventory. You can expect a large turnkey provider to have several new properties every week; hence, expect new property brochures weekly.

Your task as a turnkey rental investor is to filter through the prospective properties using the **Property Evaluation Checklist** until you find one that meets the purchasing criteria you established using the systems and processes introduced in parts 1 and 2. Your goal is to evaluate the properties quickly and efficiently because other investors will receive the property brochure too; thus, speed can be important.

The brochures sent by the various turnkey companies are similar and will include similar information such as

- a picture of the property,
- the property address,
- the number of bedrooms and bathrooms,
- the square footage of the property,
- whether the property has a tenant,
- the rental rate or target rental rate,
- the duration of the lease,
- the estimated property tax,
- the estimated insurance,
- the homeowner's association (HOA) fee if there is one,
- an estimated mortgage based on assumptions listed in the brochure for the interest rate, down payment, and loan term, and
- some financial estimates for performance.

The turnkey provider will sometimes include the scope of work for the renovations done to the property. Make sure to specifically request this from the provider. Again, use the **Property Evaluation Checklist** to evaluate the properties. The remaining sections in this chapter are devoted to the action items you'll find in this checklist.

Evaluating Curb Appeal

For the first step in evaluating a property, study the property photo included in the brochure. While this may not be a very technical process, it is important to make sure the property

- has good curb appeal, defined as a property that is pleasing to the eye;
- has a low-maintenance exterior finish such as brick;
- is surrounded by properties of similar value—use Google Maps (https://www.google.com/maps) to view the subject property and the surrounding neighborhood; and
- includes your target tenants (young professionals, families, retirees, etc.).

Remember, a potential tenant develops their first impression of a property exclusively based on how it looks. A property with good curb appeal is easier to sell and rent. In general, brick homes have fewer maintenance concerns than other exterior finishes. Again, you are looking for a neighborhood your target tenants will want to live in. Take note of whether the house is located in a cul-de-sac, if schools are located within walking distance, and if other such desirable amenities are included. If you have any hesitations about the property based on how it looks, pass those on to the provider; there are always more properties available.

Evaluating Property Specs

The second step to evaluating a property is to look at the location and the property's specs. Keep in mind the type of renters most likely to be interested in the subject neighborhood. If you are targeting families, look for properties with three and four bedrooms and two full bathrooms. The inclusion of a garage is another nice feature since people prefer inside parking, and the additional storage opportunities provided by a garage are also a perk.

Next, look at the square footage of the property; consider how much room the property offers in terms of your targeted family. The tenant's perception of whether a property is small or large will depend on the typical house in the neighborhood. If typical properties in the neighborhood are nine hundred to one thousand square feet, a house with 1,400 or more square feet will be perceived as more spacious and desirable. If houses in the area are only eight hundred square feet, houses with one thousand square feet would be considered decently sized. This holds true for other property features such as decks, garages, fencing, and the number of bedrooms and bathrooms. Again, make sure the subject property meets your buying criteria for the bedroom count and other property specs, and remember to evaluate the property based on how good of a fit it is for your portfolio.

Review the Scope of Work

The next step is to quickly review the scope of work, which, to review, is a detailed breakdown of the work and materials for the renovation of the property. Note: The purchase criteria for the business plan provided in the **Property Evaluation Checklist** is only designed for the purchase of houses with

- a brick exterior finish,
- a new or fairly new roof,
- a new or almost new HVAC,
- a new or almost new hot water tank, and
- a fully renovated interior.

I do not purchase rental properties with a septic system.

At this point, I want to define "almost new" as it applies to the renovation criteria. The average life expectancy for the different systems in a house can vary based on

- the quality of the system installed,
- the location of the house,
- how the different systems are maintained and serviced, and
- many other variables.

Typically, the average life expectancy of the different systems and building materials is given as a range in years. For establishing the purchase criteria, I recommend using the lower estimate for the life expectancy. Table 11 summarizes the lower-end life expectancies of some home systems and my purchase criteria.

Table 11. Life expectancy of some home systems and the corresponding buying criteria.

	Life expectancy (lower end)	Criteria used (no older than)
Hot water tank	8 years	2 years
Roof	25 years	4 years
HVAC	10 years	2 years

You will notice that the criteria I use for my business are quite lower than the lower end listed in the above table. For example, I require the hot water tank to be no more than two years old. I prefer to look for homes that meet the criteria listed to reduce maintenance expenses and improve the odds of not having any big maintenance expenses at the beginning of ownership.

Review the scope of work and confirm the subject property satisfies the renovation purchase criteria. Later, during your due diligence process, the inspector you hire is going to be your eyes on the property. So, absolutely ask this person about the expected life remaining in the different systems of any property you are considering buying. They can confirm that the information in the scope of work is accurate. If it is not, you should be able to terminate the purchase and sales agreement using the inspection contingency without losing your earnest deposit. Remember, your property inspector is a wealth of invaluable information, but you must ask questions, not expect them to volunteer everything you need to know.

Estimate the Appraised Value

The next step is to estimate the appraised value of the property. Certified appraisers use three methods to appraise real estate:

- The sales comparison method
- The replacement cost method
- The income method

Sales Comparison Method

The most common method for appraising a single-family turnkey property is the sales comparison method. This method relies on identifying at least three comparable properties. A comparable property is a property that

- has recently been sold,
- is located within a certain distance from the subject property, and
- is similar in age, size, and style.

The value of the subject property should be similar to the sold prices of recently sold, similar properties. Most properties are not going to be truly identical. For example, the subject property may have a finished basement, even though the only properties recently sold in that area that are similar in size have unfinished basements.

For cases like this, you (or a certified appraiser) will look for houses nearby that might differ in size but have finished and unfinished basements. By comparing these properties, you can estimate the value added by including a finished basement. The concession can then be applied to the subject property to determine an estimated value.

For turnkey investing, understanding how comparable properties are used to set the value for properties is relevant for

- the purchasing process,
- the negotiating process when buying, and
- estimating the appreciation rate of your property due to the Appraisal Problem.

The Replacement Cost Method

The replacement cost method yields an estimated value based on the costs to build the property taking into account the current cost of materials. This calculation is important to insurance providers and is certainly used to estimate premiums, but, to the best of my knowledge, the approach doesn't have much impact on the turnkey rental business.

Income Method

The last appraisal method is the income method, used to appraise the value of multifamily properties with more than four units. This method estimates the value of the property based on how much income the property produces. This method is not typically used for single-family properties.

Evaluate the Property Tax

If the property passes the eyeball test and the renovation criteria, the next step is to check the property taxes—something to look out for when evaluating the property's financial performance. This tax will affect the cash flow of a property. That is why, prior to calculating the cash flow, the ROI (based upon the cash flow), and the four returns, you need to determine the property tax for that home. This tax is determined by the county using the value of the property. When you buy the house, if the purchase price is significantly higher than the estimated value last used to determine the property tax, you can be certain the property tax will increase as soon as the property is reassessed.

A reassessment occurs when the county calculates the property tax based on the property value. In general, reassessment occurs every three years, but this can vary from county to county. I recommend going to the county auditor's website and estimating the property tax using the purchase price. Some county websites offer calculators for this purpose. You can also call the county auditor's office and ask.

Let's review a quick example to illustrate the importance of estimating the property tax. We'll assume the assessed value used to determine the property tax was $120,000 and that the assessment was done three years ago. Let's further assume that, at the time of the most recent assessment, the house was not up to date and had a lot of deferred maintenance. This property has since been fully renovated by the turnkey provider and is for sale at a price of $220,000.

The property tax listed in the brochure sent to you by the turnkey provider is likely to be the current tax rate based on the old, assessed value of $120,000. Let's assume the property tax listed in the brochure is $150 per month. When the property is reassessed at a value of $220,000, the property tax might increase to $250 per month (or more). If your calculation for the cash flow resulted in $320 per month based on the old taxes of $150 per month, the cash flow will decrease to $220 per month after the assessment.

Again, you should estimate the property tax. If estimating that takes up too much time (longer than ten minutes or so), make sure to discuss it with your turnkey provider. For example, you could let them know you will purchase the property once you finish evaluating the property tax and that you will have an answer for them quickly.

I recommend setting a timeframe with your turnkey provider, such as twenty minutes, which is reasonable since you can quickly call the county for an estimate. Your turnkey provider may let you reserve the property. It is important to provide feedback and be open and transparent with your providers. Remember, your goal is to establish a long-term relationship.

Estimate the Financial Performance

Now that you have the updated property taxes, it is time to compute the cash flow, the ROI based on the cash flow, and the other profit returns of the property such as the loan paydown, appreciation, and depreciation. Do not rely on the estimated returns listed in the brochure; always compute the four profit returns yourself.

I use an Excel spreadsheet for this purpose, set up with the appropriate formulas to do the calculations for me. That way, I can quickly enter the financial data needed and review the estimated returns. The purchase calculations I've plugged into my spreadsheet require a list of inputs, which are

- the purchase price,
- the appraised value,
- the estimated appreciation rate,
- your tax bracket,
- the loan-to-value ratio,
- the loan term,
- the loan interest rate,
- the closing costs,
- the monthly rental rates from years 1 and 2,
- the estimated property tax,
- the estimated property insurance,
- the HOA, and
- the property management fee.

From these inputs, the calculator estimates

- the invested funds (funds needed to buy the property),
- the cash flow for years 1 and 2,
- the cash-on-cash ROI,
- the ratio of the cash flow and gross rent,
- the loan paydown,
- the appreciation,
- the effective tax rate,
- the carryover losses,
- the total return, and
- the total ROI.

The spreadsheet for the purchase calculations, which includes the input and output information listed above, is shown below in Figure 10. The outputs are indicated with a box.

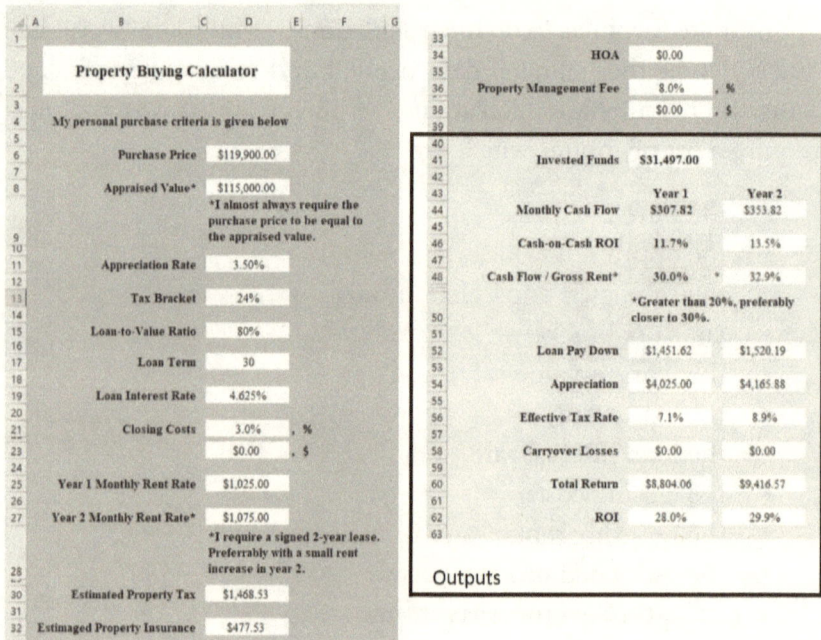

Figure 10. Turnkey Purchase Calculator.

The purchase calculator spreadsheet is available to you for free at:

https://scottastanfield.com

It takes me only a few minutes to enter the information, review the financial performance, and then decide if I want to purchase the property. You may be asking yourself at this point: What do the financial performance numbers mean? To answer that question, let's take a deeper dive into the cash flow, cash-on-cash ROI, and appreciation calculations.

Compute the Cash Flow

The cash flow is determined by subtracting the expenses from the rent as given below:

$$Cash\ Flow = Rent - Expenses.$$

For the expenses, I only sum the fixed expenses. which include the

- property management fee,
- mortgage payment,
- insurance, and
- property tax.

To illustrate, if the rental rate is $1,000 per month, and the sum of the property management fee, mortgage, insurance, and property tax is $700 per month, the cash flow then equals $300 per month:

$$\$1{,}000 - \$700 = \$300.$$

As long as the cash flow is around or greater than $300 per month, it will easily cover the typical maintenance and repair expenses. This is especially true if the property requires a brick finish, a new or fairly new roof, an HVAC, and a hot water tank.

Another approach to setting the cash flow requirement involves reviewing the typical budget for maintenance and repairs and vacancy. A typical budget allocates 10 percent of the gross rent for these expenses. Given this information, an investor could establish a cash flow requirement of at least 20 percent or more of the gross rent. My preference when using this approach is to strive for a cash flow closer to 30 percent of the gross rent. The property evaluation system in this book does not delve into a more detailed estimate of the costs of maintenance and repairs for one reason: Speed is of the essence. Remember, you will likely evaluate many properties. So, you need to manage your time wisely.

Compute the Cash-on-Cash ROI

The next step is to compute the cash-on-cash ROI using Eq. 3.1, shown below for your convenience:

$$ROI = \frac{Annual\ Return}{Invested\ Funds} \times 100.$$

The invested funds are determined by summing the down payment and the closing costs. The required down payment is usually 20 or 25 percent of the purchase price. You can offer a larger down payment if you prefer, but I tend toward a lower down payment to enhance leverage and reduce taxes.

The down payment in the formula is given as 20 percent multiplied by the purchase price or $40,000 for a $200,000 purchase price. I would budget another $6,500 for the closing costs (1 to 3 percent of the purchase price), which brings the invested funds to:

$$\$40,000 + \$6,500 = \$46,500.$$

The cash-on-cash ROI is given as:

$$\$300 \times 12 / \$46,500 = 7.7\%.$$

A cash-on-cash ROI between 7 and 10.3 percent will result in a cash flow of around $300 per month for the price point I like to target.

This value for the invested funds assumes the property appraises at the asking price. An appraisal gap would require more investment funds, which will increase the cash flow because the mortgage expense is lower. However, the cash-on-cash ROI will also be reduced. I almost always pass on properties that do not appraise at the asking price. A rare exception occurs when the property meets my purchase criteria, and I can negotiate a concession on the order of the appraisal gap. For example, if the appraisal gap is $5,000 and the turnkey provider pays for the closing costs, which are on the order of $5,000, then I will go forward with the purchase.

Estimate Appreciation

The next step is to estimate appreciation by accessing Zillow or any other online website, where you can estimate or get an estimate for appreciation. The rate provided is likely not going to be accurate, but it is still worth looking at it.

The main reason for estimating appreciation is to gain some idea of the total return of the property; this way, you can begin to develop a long-term plan. In general, my goal is to achieve a loan-to-value ratio well below 0.75 as quickly as possible because it allows for

- a cash-out refinance,
- a HELOC, or
- selling at a profit.

In general, the ability to adjust your portfolio because of a favorable loan-to-value ratio will allow you more options and flexibility with loan products and with determining your exit strategy.

When setting up your business based on cash flow, a better estimation for appreciation is not needed. For those who are buying for appreciation, however, you will want a better method to approximate appreciation. Review **Chapter 14 How to Evaluate a Market**, which walks you through the appreciation evaluation process. Remember, though, your methods must be done quickly so that you can complete the evaluation process in a timely manner.

Note: When selecting your appreciation market, it must be done with your portfolio and your personal finances in mind. Again, you want to have extra revenue that can offset the low cash flow produced by an appreciation property to mitigate your risks. Because of the inherent risk of appreciation properties, I would recommend more stringent criteria as outlined above.

Strategically Schedule Your Closing

The next step is to schedule the closing on or near the first business day of the month. Once you have identified a property that satisfies your criteria, call the turnkey provider to schedule the closing. While my preference is to close on the first business day of the month, I will allow for the first five business days.

The reason for this is very simple; if you are purchasing with a mortgage, you will make more money (up to one month's rent) by closing at the beginning of the month. The reason is as follows: The first mortgage payment will be due on the first day of the month, two months after the purchase date. If the purchase date is the LAST day of June, then ALL of June is counted as the first month, and July is counted as the second month. The first mortgage payment, then, will be due on August 1st.

To illustrate this strategy, let's assume the rent is $1,000 per month. If you own the property for only one day in June, the rent you will receive for June comes to $33.

$$\$1,000 \:/\: 30 \text{ days} = \$33/\text{day}$$

You will, however, receive the full rent of $1,000 for July since you owned the property for the entire month. Therefore, the total rent you will receive for June and July equals $1,033:

$$\$33 + \$1,000 = \$1,033.$$

This amount represents the total rent you will receive before you pay the first mortgage payment on August 1st.

Now, let's assume you set the closing date for June 1st. That way, you will have owned the property every day in June and July. The rent you will receive for June and July will then be $2,000:

$$\$1{,}000 + \$1{,}000 = \$2{,}000.$$

This is the total rent you would receive before you make the mortgage payment on August 1st, resulting in almost $1,000 more (one month's rent) that you will pocket by closing on the first of the month.

In general, I will not eliminate a good property if I cannot close within the first five business days, but I will pass on an average property because the turnkey providers I work with offer several new properties every week, allowing me to be more selective. You do not need to worry about this criterion if you are purchasing without a mortgage.

Remember,

- closing at the end of the month results in the bank making more money, and
- closing at the beginning of the month enables you to make more money.

This should come as no surprise: My preference is to make more money.

Determine Your Exit Plan

Thus far, I have mostly described the purchase side based on the purchase criteria, but with all investments, you should have an exit plan. As alluded to, the market cycle and total return are pertinent information when determining an exit plan. Given that the market is dynamic, it should come as no surprise that your long-term plan, and therefore, your exit strategy will constantly evolve.

To navigate the ever-changing nature of the rental market, whenever you purchase a property, evaluate the market cycle and quickly develop a long-term plan based on your set goals. Some of the questions you should ask yourself are:

- Do you want to own the property forever?
- Do you only want to own the property until the end of the expansion phase of the market cycle and then sell?
- Is the property you are buying a property likely to appreciate so that the profits from selling will finance the purchase of multiple properties? If so, perhaps only hold the property for ten years and then sell using a 1031 exchange so that you can avoid paying large maintenance bills.

Understand that your exit strategy is not set in stone and will change over time as the market changes. Also, note that it is okay to not have a definitive exit plan during the evaluation process. You can assemble your exit plan after completing the purchase as long as you stick to your purchase criteria, which will ensure that you are buying the property for the correct reasons.

Putting Everything Together: My Purchasing Criteria

We covered a lot of information in this chapter. At this point, I want to summarize my investment criteria, also listed in the **Property Evaluation Checklist**. These criteria, which are designed to maximize revenue and minimize expenses, are:

- I buy three- and four-bedroom houses with a minimum of two full bathrooms.
- I prefer houses with a brick exterior.
- At the time of writing, the typical purchase price I target is between $150,000 and $250,000.
- The roof cannot be older than four years.
- The HVAC and hot water tank cannot be older than two years.
- The interior needs to have been fully renovated.

- I do not purchase homes with a septic system.
- The monthly cash flow needs to be at least $300 per month after fixed expenses or, alternatively, greater than 20 percent of the gross rent (preferably closer to 30 percent of the gross rent).
- I only purchase properties that have a signed lease with a new tenant, and I prefer two-year leases.
- I set the closing date for the first five days of the month.

With the evaluation process complete, it is time to discuss the next step in the purchasing process: reviewing and signing the purchase and sales agreement. This will be the topic of the next chapter.

CHAPTER 18

PURCHASE AND SALES AGREEMENT

> Where We Are At: Master Checklist Step 9
> - **Purchase and Sales Agreement Checklist**

Once you have verbally committed to purchasing a property, your turnkey provider will send you a purchase and sales agreement. This agreement, which is a legally binding contract that lists all the terms and conditions between the seller and the buyer of the property, is a necessary part of all real estate deals.

Signing is usually done through an online portal such as DocuSign. Never sign anything without reading the document first. Remember, you can always have a lawyer review the document if needed. Use the **Purchase and Sales Agreement Checklist** when reviewing the documents involved.

Common components of the purchase and sales agreement include

- the buyer's and seller's full names and contact information,
- the property address and legal description of the property,

- the purchase price,
- a description of how the buyer will be paying for the property,
- a list of appliances and other items included in the sale,
- who, if anyone, is responsible for purchasing title insurance,
- any citations regarding property tax,
- the closing date,
- a list of contingencies that must be met for the transaction to take place,
- the terms of the earnest deposit,
- any options (contingencies) to terminate the contract, and
- a property disclosure.

Some common contingencies include

- the inspection contingency,
- the appraisal contingency,
- the financing contingency, and
- the title contingency.

The Inspection Contingency

The inspection contingency allows the buyer to terminate the contract if the inspection process identifies a problem with the property. The law around the inspection contingency can vary depending on the state. Always check with your turnkey provider if you have questions. Typically, the buyer will ask the seller to address any problems identified by the inspection or reduce the purchase price. If the problems are not addressed, the buyer can terminate the contract. Note: When buying properties from a true turnkey rental provider, most of the time, the seller will address the issues that come up in the inspection.

The Appraisal Contingency

The appraisal contingency allows the buyer to terminate the contract if the property does not appraise at the purchase price. As the buyer, you want to preserve the appraisal contingency and make sure no language involved can legally bind you to purchase when there is an appraisal gap. Make sure you understand what you are signing.

The Financing Contingency

The financing contingency gives the buyer some protection if they are unable to secure financing to complete the purchase. This is unlikely to occur since the turnkey provider will ask that you be preapproved by the lender. If you were preapproved and, later during the process, the lender decided not to finance the transaction, you could exercise the financing contingency to terminate the purchase and sales contract.

The Title Contingency

The title contingency gives protection to both the lender and the buyer. When a title inspection is completed, any issues, such as liens or gaps, should be uncovered. If such issues are found, they can either be fixed or the buyer can terminate the contract.

The Property Disclosure

The property disclosure is comprised of everything the seller has done to the property. This disclosure also lists everything wrong with the property that the seller is aware of. The seller is legally obligated to provide an accurate disclosure. Sometimes, the seller is not aware of any issues pertaining to the property, which is why an inspection is so important to ensure such issues are properly addressed.

Record Key Data

When reading through the purchase and sales agreement, make sure to document all the dates. Different items, such as the earnest money deposit, inspection, appraisal, etc., will each come with certain time frames to be scheduled within and a certain date to be completed by. When it comes to scheduling different aspects such as the inspection or appraisal, the times can vary based on who will be scheduling it. Reach out to your turnkey provider liaison with any questions in this regard.

Other Aspects to Watch Out For

When confirming the price, make sure to determine all other expenses such as the leasing fee, property tax, and closing costs. Remember, the purchase criteria require the property to be tenanted. Some turnkey companies will try to collect a leasing fee (usually one month's rent) in addition to the purchase price. Negotiate for no leasing fee. The leasing fee is paid by the owner, and you were not the owner when the tenant signed the lease.

Also, make sure the property tax is prorated instead of being passed onto you. For example, let's assume property tax equal to $1,500 is due at the end of June, and the closing date is June 1st. Further, assume the property tax represents the taxes owed for January through June. The turnkey provider may leave it to you to pay the full $1,500. Instead of agreeing to these terms, negotiate to prorate the property tax (please note that different states in the US may handle property tax at closing differently). For this example, the monthly rate would be $250 per month ($1,500/six months). I would negotiate to pay $250 for June since that is the only month in which you would be listed as the owner.

Also, confirm who is paying the closing costs, and then, lastly, confirm all the other expenses listed. Again, you can reference the **Purchase and Sales Agreement Checklist** when reviewing what to expect from such an agreement. In summary, as you read the purchase and sales agreement, you will want to

- confirm the purchase price,
- determine whether a leasing fee is included and have it

waved if the property is tenanted,
- make sure the property tax is prorated based on the settlement date,
- confirm who is paying the closing costs,
- confirm that the settlement date (closing date) will occur during the first five days of the month,
- confirm the amount of the earnest deposit,
- determine where to send the earnest deposit,
- check the delivery instructions and deadline for the earnest deposit,
- confirm that the contract includes a financing contingency without appraisal gap language,
- confirm the contract includes an inspection contingency, and
- record all dates for each contingency listed.

It is always good practice to record vital information and add it to your calendar to avoid missing anything important. Your turnkey provider will certainly remind you, but it is better to have no surprises. At this point, if all is in good order, sign the contract and be well on your way to closing on the property. Part Five is all about the post-signing management of the purchase.

PART FIVE:
AFTER YOU SIGN THE PURCHASE AND SALES AGREEMENT

CHAPTER 19

EARNEST DEPOSIT

Once you sign the purchase and sales agreement, you usually have twenty-five hours to send the earnest deposit. The earnest deposit, a deposit from the buyer equal to 1 to 3 percent of the purchase price, is held by the closing attorney or title company in an escrow account.

The earnest deposit offers some protection to the seller in the event that the buyer backs out of the contract. The buyer can terminate the purchase and sales agreement and receive the deposit back if the contract is terminated because of one of the contingencies listed in Chapter 18. Otherwise, the seller is entitled to keep the earnest deposit. During closing, the earnest deposit is applied to the purchase of the property as part of the down payment.

Recall from the previous section that the purchase and sales agreement with a turnkey provider will include

- the earnest deposit amount,
- the due date, and
- sending instructions.

Make sure to follow the details provided as instructed. Usually, the funds are wire-transferred or mailed overnight with a certified check. My preference is to wire transfer the funds because of the convenience. This does require a business checking account that allows you to initiate a wire transfer.

The purchase and sales agreement becomes a binding contract once it has been signed and the earnest money is received by the title company or closing attorney.

At this point, the steps you need to complete before closing are:

1. Acquire property insurance.
2. Begin the due diligence and inspection period.
    a. Title inspection
    b. Documentation inspection
    c. Physical inspection
3. Wait for the bank-scheduled appraiser to appraise the property.
4. Perform the wrap-up with the closing.

These steps will be discussed in detail in the following chapters. We will start with acquiring property insurance.

CHAPTER 20

PROPERTY INSURANCE

> Where We Are At: Master Checklist Step 10
> - **Insurance Broker Questionnaire**

It is crucial to ensure that property insurance is in place before closing. Otherwise, you could lose your entire investment if a fire or some other disaster occurs.

Your liaison through the turnkey provider will likely provide a quote for insurance. You can look into securing insurance independently, but I have not been able to find cheaper insurance than what the turnkey providers provide through their network. That said, you should still compare insurance policies for the coverage provided and premiums charged. When looking at the coverage, check whether the turnkey rental property requires special insurance. This insurance can be area-dependent and includes provisions based on the home's location such as whether it is in a flood plain, fire zone, hurricane-prone area, etc.

I recommend working with an insurance broker when checking insurance quotes independent of your turnkey provider's network. Use the **Insurance Broker Questionnaire** to find an insurance broker to help with your insurance needs. Below is a discussion on how to use the questionnaire.

When working with an insurance broker, begin by describing your business to them. It is important that the broker understands that multiple rental properties located in different states will be involved. A good broker can help you find the correct insurance at a good premium. Remember, understanding the ins and outs of insurance is not necessary. What is necessary, however, is to hire the right professional who can help your business. Below is a list of questions to help you find the right professional when seeking an insurance broker.

1. Are you an insurance broker or an insurance agent? My preference is to find a broker since these professionals are not tied to insurance products from a single company. Also, a broker works for their clients, whereas an agent works for an insurance company.

2. Are you independent or owned by an insurance company? Again, you are looking for an independently owned broker.

3. What is your experience? You want a broker with real estate experience who can handle insuring properties in different states.

4. Are you a national firm? We want a broker that understands the laws and regulations in the different states to ensure they have the right background to assist in a business with properties located in any state.

5. Do you reevaluate my coverage annually prior to renewing to find the lowest premiums? Insurance companies like to steadily increase the premiums (our cost) each year as part of their business plan to generate more revenue. We want

a broker that shops around for the lowest rates whenever a policy is set to renew.

6. Do you handle notifying the lenders if the insurance provider changes? This is important; we want a broker who does the leg work for us. Changing insurance providers can become a nightmare as it can take a lot of time on our end. If the insurance provider changes and the bank does not receive proof of insurance, the bank will purchase insurance on your behalf. You can bet that the premiums the bank receives will be higher. Remember, our business is a turnkey business designed to minimize the hours we need to work; hence, we want systems that leverage the time of the professionals we hire.

7. Do you have references from clients? Most insurance brokers that are equipped to handle our needs are going to have a large online presence. As such, there will be plenty of reviews available for us to read through, but you should still ask for references.

8. Can you provide a personalized policy for my business? The broker should be able to review your portfolio and make recommendations. Remember, we are not insurance experts. We need a qualified professional to help us understand the different insurance options available.

9. What does my policy include? My preference is to insure up to an additional 25 percent of the replacement cost of my properties. Your broker can provide excellent insight on many other options, but you will need to ask first. They may very well recommend something different. Please note: Coverage, deductibles, etc. may depend on the location.

10. How much will it cost?
11. Do I need an umbrella policy? Umbrella insurance is an extra layer of insurance that provides additional coverage for lawsuits, property damage, or other unexpected large expenses. I use umbrella insurance as part of my liability plan. Again, I am not an insurance expert, so ask your broker. They will be able to provide a much more articulate analysis of this insurance type. On a side note: The premiums for umbrella insurance can be considered a business expense, so speak with your CPA.

Once you have narrowed down the search to several candidates, you are going to want to receive quotes. You can likely get better rates by having the insurance broker bundle other insurance plans such as your personal residence, renters' insurance if you are a renter, life insurance, auto insurance, and an umbrella policy. Have the candidates provide an itemized quote—which is a breakdown of the price of each service offered.

To receive a quote, the insurance brokers will require some information. For rental properties, your brokers will likely ask

- for the property address,
- the name of the lender or a copy of the mortgage statement,
- the year the property was built,
- whether the property is currently tenant-occupied,
- whether the property has a fireplace,
- the age of the roof,
- the number of stories,
- the foundation type,
- the exterior finish,
- the primary heat source,
- the square footage of the house,
- the number of bathrooms,
- the number of bedrooms,

- whether the basement is finished—and if it is, the square footage of the finished basement,
- a list of any detached structures such as sheds, garages, and fences,
- whether the property has a swimming pool, and
- whether there are any pets.

My preference is to tabulate this information into an Excel sheet and send it to the broker. Insurance companies will then use this information to compute your premiums.

Once you have found an insurance broker and have received quotes for coverage, make sure that coverage is based on the actual replacement cost for your properties. The replacement cost is the estimated cost required to rebuild the property. Sometimes the coverage is only for a percentage of the replacement cost.

My preference is to pay a larger deductible so that the percentage of the replacement cost is around 125 percent. My objective with this criterion is to insure against disasters instead of minor damage. For my business plan, the insurance expense for a turnkey rental property was never great enough to justify including purchasing criteria to achieve lower premiums.

The ins and outs of insurance can be complicated, but remember, you do not have to be an expert on insurance practices. You do need to hire the right professional, which we covered in this chapter. The next step during the purchasing process, due diligence, will be explored next.

CHAPTER 21

DUE DILIGENCE AND THE INSPECTION PROCESS

> Where We Are At: Master Checklist Steps 10-12
> - **Due Diligence Checklist**
> - **Inspector Questionnaire**

Due diligence occurs once the property is under contract and before you take ownership. The purpose of due diligence is to mitigate your risk as the buyer by verifying the information provided by the seller, inspecting the physical property, and verifying that the title of the property is clean. The purchase and sales agreement will provide a deadline that must be met for you to exercise any of the contingencies. It is extremely important not to go past deadlines. As such, the due diligence process can be broken into three steps, namely,

1. the title inspection,
2. documentation inspection, and
3. physical inspection.

If you are planning to title the property in a land trust or an LLC, now is the time to have your attorney prepare the documents and inform the closing attorney or title company. The closing attorney or title company might be able to title the property in your name to satisfy the mortgage requirements and then transfer the title to your LLC or trust, which will save you time later. They may also be able to directly title the company into your LLC or trust.

The sections that follow describe the action items included in the **Due Diligence Checklist**.

Title Inspection

It should come as no surprise that the transfer of ownership of any property is well documented by a government agency, in this case, the county auditor and county recorder. This documentation contains a wealth of important information such as ownership changes (title transfers), loans, liens, and any other pertinent issues recorded throughout the history of the property.

When a lender issues a loan for a property, the property is used as collateral, which requires a publicly available record. This record is attached to the title of the property. The title inspection protects the lender in the event that another lender is already using the property as collateral for a mortgage.

A title inspection is also a good way to determine whether a lien exists on the property. A lien, another type of documentation attached to the title of a property, can occur when the property owner does not pay a bill such as property tax or an invoice from a contractor. The contractor can then record a lien. What the lien does is notify the closing attorney or title company that the owner of the property owes money. These liens are typically transferable to whoever owns the property.

The purpose of the title inspection is to identify problems with the property's title. The title company or closing attorney will complete a process called the chain of title, which is simply a complete history of everything recorded with the title of the property. The title contingency allows you as the buyer to terminate the purchase and sales agreement if the title has problems such as a lien.

Title Insurance

The purpose of title insurance is to protect you from mistakes made to the chain of title. For example, if the chain of title does not reveal any problems and then, after closing, it is determined that a lien is attached, the title insurance will cover your financial losses due to this mistake.

My recommendation is to always buy title insurance. It is worth a slightly smaller ROI to mitigate risk. For you, the title inspection is actually simple. Buy title insurance so that if there is a problem, the title company or closing attorney will notify you of it. It does not have to be any more complicated than this.

Documentation Inspection

Once the seller performs a documentation inspection, which refers to the process of confirming that the information provided by the seller is accurate, you will receive verifying documentation. The typical documents collected by you from the seller include

- the seller disclosure,
- a copy of the current lease,
- copies of recent utility bills,
- verification of security deposits,
- documents for the HOA,
- verification of the scope of work, and
- a copy of the seller's tax returns.

Be certain to review the seller disclosure carefully. While the disclosure is not a substitute for the property inspection, it could provide valuable information as to whether the property is worth buying before spending money on an inspection.

Further, verify the HOA fee by reviewing the HOA documents. Additionally, some neighborhoods with HOAs may have specific rules for the percentage of renters allowed in the neighborhood. It is important that you review the HOA documents to determine the risks with the property.

Typically, for a turnkey property, you won't collect a copy of the seller's tax returns. You do want to verify the property has a tenant by receiving a copy of the lease. The lease will also verify the rental rate that the turnkey provider disclosed. If the property is rented, you will want to verify the security deposit.

The Physical Inspection

It is the licensed property inspector's job to provide a physical inspection of the property. I have seen other investors wave the inspection. Absolutely never do this, especially since you are not likely to walk any of your properties. Even so, avoid inspecting the property yourself unless you are qualified to do so. Remember, the inspection process is intended to lower your risk.

The turnkey provider will likely provide a list of inspectors, and while the list provided is probably okay to use, my preference is to hire my own. More information on how to hire a good inspector can be found using the **Inspector Questionnaire** in the appendix.

Once the inspection report is ready for review, you will receive a copy. Sometimes, the liaison is missed in the process and does not receive the report. Check the recipients of your email message (to which the report copy was attached) to make sure the liaison was included; if not, forward the copy to them as well.

I find it very helpful to speak directly to my inspector after they finish the inspection and the property is still fresh in their memory. Make sure to confirm with your inspector the age of the roof, hot water tank, and HVAC system. You should ask their opinion of the quality of the materials used in the renovations. Have the inspector confirm (1) that permits were pulled for the work, and (2) the work completed was to the standards of the local building code. If the scope of work does not match what the inspector finds during the inspection, be certain to notify the turnkey provider. It is also a good idea to ask them to verify the items listed in the property disclosure. Remember, you can exercise the inspection contingency to terminate the contract without penalty if needed.

The inspection report will always include something, even for fully renovated properties or newly built properties. The liaison you use will have their team of contractors or in-house renovation team address everything identified in the inspection report. The turnkey providers that I use immediately address everything without me having to ask. Review the before and after photos of the repairs for the property taken by the turnkey provider to ensure everything was properly handled. If you are uncertain about any aspect of these repairs, request that the inspector revisit the property.

The Appraisal Process

The appraisal process happens once the property is under contract. During due diligence, a certified appraiser will estimate the value of the property using the methods described in the section **Estimate the Appraised Value**.

Even if you purchase the property with cash, you should still have the property appraised since the appraisal process protects you. If you are purchasing the property with a mortgage, the lender will schedule the appraisal for you. Once the report is complete, it will be emailed to you. Make sure that the liaison is included in the email; if they are not, immediately forward the report to them.

If the property does not appraise, meaning the appraised value falls below the asking price, the bank will notify you. The turnkey provider will also send an addendum for you to sign to waive the appraisal contingency. Do not sign the addendum or at least do not do so immediately. Prior to signing, be sure to:

1. Calculate the performance of the property based on the appraisal gap.
2. Negotiate with the turnkey provider.

If the appraisal gap is on the order of the closing costs, try to negotiate for the turnkey provider to cover the closing costs. If the appraisal gap is greater than the closing costs, negotiate for the turnkey provider to cover the closing cost and reduce the purchase price by the difference. I prefer to negotiate the closing costs first instead of trying to lower the purchase price because the purchase price will be used as a comparable property when determining the value of the houses that sell after the property I am purchasing.

If the turnkey provider is unwilling to negotiate, terminate the purchase and sales agreement and have them send you more property brochures so you can look for another property. Remember, maintain your posture by not giving in as this will equate to a stronger performing portfolio down the road.

The due diligence process is an extremely important factor in reducing the risk associated with your investment. Most of the time you spend after signing the purchase and sales agreement will involve completing the due diligence process. Once this is done, you can move on to closing on the property, a topic we will cover in the next chapter.

CHAPTER 22

THE CLOSING PROCESS

During the due diligence process, the lender will email you requests to verify your financial documents. Once the bank is ready (meaning the financing is secured) and the other processes are complete, the bank will notify the closing attorney or title company as to who will talk to you about finalizing the date for closing.

The goal of the title company will be to close near the closing date provided in the purchase and sales agreement, but sometimes this date can slide. Pay attention to the purchase and sales agreement because missing the target closing date can terminate the contract. At any rate, do not give in if the proposed closing date is early and falls at the end of the month. Banks know that they make more money when the closing is scheduled at the end of the month. When this happens, simply inform everyone you are unavailable to sign until the first business day of the month.

The turnkey liaison will reach out to schedule the closing. Once the date is set, the bank will schedule a traveling notary to meet you at a time and location of your choice to sign the closing documents. The notary will collect a copy of your driver's license and lead you through the signing process, which will take between forty-five minutes and one hour.

Prior to closing, the bank must send you a closing disclosure, which contains pertinent information about the loan such as:

- The loan details
- Estimated total monthly payment
- Closing costs
- The amount of cash needed to close
- Contract details

Prior to the meeting, be certain to verify the information in the disclosure and to wire the funds needed (you will find this figure listed under the "amount of cash needed to close" section within the disclosure). When wiring these funds, follow the wiring instructions provided by the closing attorney or title company carefully.

Also, depending on the type of loan and the state in which your property is located, your spouse may need to sign as well. Be sure to check on this matter with the title company in advance. Once completed, the notary will mail the documents overnight, and you will receive a copy of everything covered at the meeting. The bank will review the paperwork and verify the signed documents. If all is in good order, the purchase is then finalized, and the bank will fund the purchase. At this point, you own the property, and it is time to celebrate the purchase.

CHAPTER 23

WHAT TO EXPECT GOING FORWARD

> Where We Are At: Master Checklist Steps 14-15
> - **Post-Purchase Checklist**

After closing, the turnkey provider will let you know that everything is set. You will likely receive a welcome email with instructions for setting up a new account with their portal system. Every turnkey provider I have worked with has used a portal system to communicate with their investor clients. For guidance on your next steps, follow the action items listed in the **Post-Purchase Checklist**.

The portal can be linked to your business checking account, which you can use to deposit payments or submit funds to cover expenses. As for repair expenses, if they fall under a specified threshold such as $300, they will automatically be taken care of without your approval. For repairs above this threshold, you will need to approve the work order.

Typically, the bank uploads monthly financial statements and then sends an automated email to let you know when they are available for viewing. A copy of the lease and other documents will be uploaded to your portal as well.

Some companies assign a customer service liaison, but most rely exclusively on the portal to communicate day-to-day items, only calling or emailing if something major should occur such as tenant turnover.

As mentioned, executing the business processes from this point on should only take you a few hours per month. Your time will be mostly spent monitoring the financial performance of your business and deciding on how and when to purchase more properties.

CHAPTER 24

REPLACING OR FINDING PROPERTY MANAGEMENT

> Where We Are At: Master Checklist:
> - **Property Management Questionnaire**

Under ideal conditions, your initial screening for a turnkey provider will result in an excellent business partner with a top-notch property management team. Unfortunately, there is always the risk that the property management team will turn out to be not as good as you thought.

My current turnkey rental business employs five different property management companies, which are all excellent. During the first year of business, shortly after purchasing a turnkey property with a new turnkey provider, I discovered that the property management team that provider used at the time did not perform to my standards. A poorly performing management team may be

- disorganized,
- slow to fill vacancies,
- unresponsive,

- slow to schedule maintenance, and
- remiss in addressing tenant concerns in a timely manner.

At that time, I had not yet refined the business processes provided in this book, which, looking back, would have eliminated the company from contention. At any rate, I replaced the underperforming team with a different property management company that I am still working with today.

If you see signs (such as those listed above) that the property management team is not performing, do not hesitate to replace them. Property management is the single most important decider on whether the property is profitable or not, at least in the short term. To reinforce how important property management is, you can purchase the perfect investment property, with the best location, at the absolute best time in the market cycle and still lose money if your property management team does not perform. The good news is, replacing the team is an easy fix. Review the **Property Management Questionnaire** to help you select a good team. The remainder of this chapter discusses that questionnaire in detail.

To begin the process, make a list of at least three property management companies. You can perform an online search and check real estate investment forums for information. As for the latter option, investors will be quick to leave reviews regarding their property management. This means that message boards dedicated to real estate investing, such as BiggerPockets (https://www.biggerpockets.com), are an excellent source of this type of information. If you find a property management company with good reviews, chances are, that company will be excellent. You can always submit a post asking for reviews if you do not find any. Bad experiences tend to be posted far more often than good ones.

Once you have a list of companies, use the **Property Management Questionnaire** to fully vet each company. The questionnaire is organized into five sections dedicated to the different areas of property management that matter to a rental business.

These sections are

- general questions,
- questions about communication between the management company and their clients,
- questions about the statistical performance of the management company,
- questions about marketing the property, and
- questions about the company's fee structure.

The action items in the questionnaire and my brief description are given below.

General Questions:

1. How long has your company been in business?
   - Look for an experienced company as opposed to a new one with little to no experience in the industry.

2. How many employees does your company have?
   - It is important to find a larger company that is not dependent on one person.

3. Have you done business under other company names? If so, what are the names of those companies, and why did you rebrand?
   - Many companies rebrand at some point by changing names. Once you know the past company names, you can look for old reviews. Some companies will seek to rename because their prior name no longer describes their business. For example, a company named Atlanta Property Management might consider changing its name to National Property Management if its business grows beyond the Atlanta area.

4. What types of properties will your company not manage?
   - For example, some companies may not manage lower-end properties. Knowing the property types that a management company accepts is useful for future plans and provides some insight into their experience level.

5. How many properties does your company manage?
   - This question will help you gauge the size of the company, especially when evaluating the performance of their operation using the questions below in the Statistical Performance Questions section.

Communication Questions:

1. Does your company use an online system that I can access to receive copies of my monthly financial statements, the lease, and the property management agreement?
   - You absolutely need a company that utilizes such systems; this really simplifies the operation of the turnkey rental business.

2. How will your company communicate with me, and how often will I hear from your team?

3. How and when are maintenance and vacancy issues communicated to me?

4. Who will be my main point of contact? How long has this person been with the company?

Statistical Performance Questions:

1. What is the occupancy rate for the properties that have been under your management for the last three months?

- The occupancy rate should be above 90 percent if the property management team is performing well.

2. What is the average length of stay for a tenant?
    - This length will vary depending on the asset class (apartments, single-family homes, student housing, etc.). In general, the average length of stay for single-family homes should exceed four years.

3. What percentage of the rent is collected?
    - A management team should collect at least 90 percent of the scheduled rent.

4. Is your company able to complete a full rehab if needed? If so, what is the average time and cost for such a rehab?
    - Although each situation is different, the property management team should be capable of renovating properties. You will want to compare their costs with other candidates.

5. What is the average length of time for a tenant turnover?
    - This is a measure of how long it takes the property management team to rent the property. The average length of time should be less than four weeks and ideally be around two weeks if only minor repairs are needed.

6. What is the average cost of your tenant turnovers?
    - Tenant turnover is one of the larger expenses of rental properties. A lower average cost means the management team is performing at a high level.

7. What is the average percentage of the gross rents used toward maintenance?

- A smaller value (below 3 percent) is a good indication that the property management team is performing at a high level.

8. How many evictions has your company had in the past year, and how were they handled?
    - Evictions happen to even the best property management teams. The teams that are performing at a high level will have fewer evictions than those performing at less optimal levels.

9. What is the average length of time for an eviction?

Marketing Questions:

1. What is your company's marketing strategy for finding tenants?
    - Look for companies with a well-defined system that uses many different marketing strategies and websites. Some strategy examples include yard signs, social media listings, and listings in at least three to four dedicated rental websites such as https://www.Zillow.com, https://www.Apartments.com, and https://www.Trulia.com.

2. Does your company handle the marketing in-house or is it outsourced?

3. What are the processes and screening criteria your company uses to screen potential tenants?
    - Seek out a property management team that has clear, well-defined screening systems with screening criteria that will find quality tenants.

Fee Structure Questions:

1. What is your monthly management fee?
   - The traditional fee is 10 percent of the monthly rent, but the trend over the last few years has been to charge lower. I have seen rates as low as 8 percent. I have also seen companies charge a flat rate as low as $100 per month regardless of the rental rate.

2. What is your tenant placement fee?
   - The typical fee is one month's rent.

3. What is your maintenance up-charge fee?
   - The maintenance up-charge fee is usually equal to a percentage of the quote received for the work. The management team will tack on a fee in addition to the contractor rate. Typical rates are 10 to 15 percent.

4. Are there any other fees that I have not asked about? If so, what are they, and what are the associated costs?

To conclude, solid property management is crucial to the success of your turnkey rental business. Again, use the questionnaire presented above to help screen potential management teams. Now that we've discussed so many processes at length, we'll explore some long-term strategies that will help your turnkey rental business succeed in Part Six.

PART SIX:
EXIT AND LONG-TERM STRATEGIES

CHAPTER 25

LONG-TERM RENTAL PERFORMANCE

Your goal as a turnkey rental investor is to identify properties that perform and that you can own for many years. As mentioned, there are advantages to owning property for a long time.

I've talked to many who have voiced a misconception about the performance of rentals and who struggle to understand how buying a property can scale up into many properties. Those who do not understand or doubt the process simply lack a sufficient grasp of the details. Let's clarify the process with the following example.

Example 25.4 Financial Performance and Scaling for Cash Flow and Appreciation Properties

Making long-term plans for your investment property first requires understanding how your properties are likely to perform through the years as your portfolio matures. Long-term success in this business often comes down to making projections using the correct financial model. I have bundled the model I use into this example. For this exercise, we seek to

- assemble and evaluate a financial model to predict the performance of an average cash flow and an average appreciation property for a twenty-year horizon,
- determine when the financial returns from the portfolio are sufficient to purchase more properties,
- determine how many properties can be purchased using only the monetary returns from the portfolio generated after twenty years of service,
- determine the financial performance of the portfolio of properties on a year-by-year basis, and
- identify specifically the advantages of owning each property for a long time.

For the full mathematical treatment, see **Example 25.4 Projected Financial Performance and Scaling for Cash Flow and Appreciation Properties** in **Appendix D: Mathematics for the Examples**.

Assumptions

Any time you make long-term projections—in any business—certain assumptions must be made. The assumptions for this example were mostly arrived at using historical national averages. Your portfolio might perform better or worse than national averages, but the idea behind projecting the future of your portfolio will allow you to scale or adjust your business plans to meet your goals. The assumptions for this example are:

- The annual appreciation rate for cash flow properties was 2 percent.
- The annual appreciation rate for appreciation properties was 5 percent.
- The maintenance expense was 5 percent of the gross rent.

- The vacancy expense was 4 percent of the gross rent.
- The rental rate was increased each year based on the historical national average.
- Property tax and property insurance increased at a constant 1 percent every year.
- A 24 percent tax bracket was used for tax purposes.
- The mortgage terms were constant, with an interest rate of 4.625 percent, a thirty-year fixed term, and a loan-to-value ratio of 80 percent.
- Appreciation was included to determine the purchase price of new purchases.

As with the results from any model, the assumptions made can have a profound effect on the accuracy of the results. In this example, the appreciation is assumed to be constant and represents an average rate. Recall that most of the appreciation occurs toward the end of the expansion phase and during the hyper supply phase and that there is very little if any appreciation during recovery. A decrease in property value also occurs during the recession phase. Hence, appreciation is not evenly distributed each year, and therefore, the results in this example cannot capture this reality.

Furthermore, expenses such as property tax and insurance, which were modeled as increasing at an annual constant rate, will change as the property value fluctuates. So, a constant yearly increase would not depict reality. This especially holds true for property tax, which will only increase when the property is reassessed by the county auditor.

A similar argument holds for the financials used in the calculations for this model for the properties. Remember, this model uses the average values for the different dependent variables, and while they are modeled as constant, i.e., as having a constant growth rate, they do not actually follow this rule. For example, modeling the rent as increasing by a constant amount each year would not capture reality.

Also, the portfolio was not burdened with overhead expenses for asset protection and tax preparation, which would include setup costs to draft an LLC or trust, pay registered agent fees, pay state renewal fees, pay umbrella insurance, and pay the CPA.

To summarize, the results obtained will change depending on the assumptions; as such, the results shown below will vary with the results obtained in practice. That said, the general trends presented are valid. Understanding the model is important when you plan to use the results to guide decisions.

Scaling Results for Cash Flow Properties

The results for an investor who elects to only invest in cash flow properties are shown below in Table 12.

Table 12. Scaling results for cash flow properties. The portfolio results are shown for the indicated year.

Year	Number of Properties	Cash Flow	Loan Paydown	Appreciation	Total
1	1	$2,281	$1,514	$2,398	$6,193
7	2	$5,573	$3,368	$5,509	$14,350
11	3	$8,991	$5,410	$8,945	$23,346
14	4	$12,776	$7,614	$12,656	$33,046
16	5	$19,811	$9,869	$16,460	$46,139
18	6	$24,466	$12,294	$20,550	$57,310
20	7, 8	$32,598	$17,148	$28,506	$78,252

The profits from a single cash flow property purchased in Year 1 are shown to be sufficient to buy more properties in years 7, 11, 14, 16, 18, and 20.

So, what do all these numbers mean? Let's break down each column in Table 10 to get a better understanding.

The Year and Number of Properties Columns

The Year column represents the year when the accumulated profits from the portfolio were sufficient to purchase a new cash flow property. The Number of Properties column represents the number of properties in the portfolio. In Year 1, the portfolio includes one property. In Year 7, the accumulated profits are sufficient to purchase a second property. Additional new purchases occur in years 7, 11, 14, 16, 18, and 20 (two are purchased in year twenty).

The Cash Flow, Loan Paydown, and Appreciation Columns

The Cash Flow, Loan Paydown, and Appreciation columns represent the profit of the portfolio for the year indicated in the Year column. For example, in Year 11, the annual cash flow produced by the three properties in the portfolio is $8,991. Similarly, those three properties produced $5,410 and $8,945 in loan paydown and appreciation, respectively.

The Total Column

The Total column equals the total profit returned by the portfolio for the year indicated. The total is the sum of the cash flow, loan paydown, and appreciation.

Total = cash flow + loan pay down + appreciation

For example, in Year 20, the portfolio includes eight cash flow rental properties. The annual profit from the portfolio produced during Year 20 was $78,252:

$32,598 in cash flow
+
$17,148 in loan paydown
+
$28,506 in appreciation
= $78,252 Total Return.

Let's put this into perspective. In this example, you would have purchased the first property with a down payment and closing costs totaling $27,577. Your initial purchase would have produced a return during the first year of ownership of $6,193. That means, the ROI will equal 22.5 percent:

$$\$6,193 / \$27,577 = 22.5\%$$

Without contributing more than the initial $27,577, the portfolio will grow to eight properties, and the annual return in Year 20 will be $78,252.

Next, it is worth reviewing the total profit generated by each property over twenty years, which is shown below in Table 13.

Table 13. Breakdown for the returns from each cash flow property in the portfolio after 20 years. Note: Properties 7 and 8 were purchased in Year 20, and the results shown are after one year of service.

Property	Cash flow	Loan Paydown	Appreciation	Total
1	$63,178	$38,841	$61,828	$163,848
2	$45,249	$27,087	$44,001	$116,337
3	$33,668	$19,994	$32,648	$86,310
4	$24,390	$14,333	$23,523	$62,246
5	$17,610	$10,511	$17,131	$45,252
6	$10,708	$6,534	$10,482	$27,723
7	$3,389	$2,249	$3,563	$9,201
8	$3,389	$2,249	$3,563	$9,201
Total	$201,581	$121,798	$196,739	$520,118

The property column refers to the different properties in the portfolio. The cash flow, loan paydown, appreciation, and total columns reflect the profit returns from the corresponding property for the entire time of ownership.

For example, Property 1 produced $63,178 in cash flow after twenty years of service, which is, again, actual cash in your pocket. The property also produced $38,841 in loan paydown and $61,821 in appreciation for a total return of $163,848:

$$\$63{,}178 + \$38{,}841 + \$61{,}821 = \$163{,}848.$$

The ROI is 594 percent:

$$\$163{,}848/\$27{,}577 = 594\%.$$

This corresponds to an average annual ROI of 29.7 percent:

$$594\%/20 \text{ years} = 29.7\%.$$

The other properties in the portfolio generated lower returns than Property 1 but similar ROIs because the properties have not been owned as long. For example, Property 2 was purchased in Year 7, which means you would have only owned the property for thirteen years.

Summing the cash flow, loan paydown, and appreciation for all properties in the portfolio results in a total return of $520,118. Remember, the only out-of-pocket funds is the initial investment of $27,577 (the down payment and closing costs for the initial property). The ROI for the portfolio is 1,886 percent:

$$\$520{,}118/\$27{,}577 = 1{,}886\%.$$

Clearly, this is a very powerful result and should help guide you through the scaling, shown in my example, to purchase additional properties (the subject of parts six and seven of this book).

Scaling Results for Appreciation Properties

The results for an investor who elects to only invest in appreciation properties are shown below in Table 14.

Table 14. Scaling results for appreciation properties. Results shown are the portfolio results for the year indicated.

Year	Number of Properties	Cash Flow	Loan Paydown	Appreciation	Total
1	1	-$676	$3,156	$12,500	$14,9780
7	2	$594	$8,603	$35,178	$44,374
11	3	$2,576	$15,517	$70,878	$88,971
14	4	$5,066	$23,821	$98,997	$127,883
16	5	$3,727	$32,720	$136,430	$172,877
18	6	-$4,449	$43,194	$180,496	$219,241
20	7	-$17,251	$55,471	$232,164	$270,383

By capitalizing on mostly appreciation and loan paydown, the profits from a single appreciation property purchased in Year 1 are shown to be sufficient to buy more properties in years 7, 11, 14, 16, 18, and 20.

As shown, at the end of Year 20, the portfolio includes seven rental properties. For Year 20, the profits from the portfolio of seven properties are:

- a loss of $17,251 in cash flow,
- a gain of $55,471 in loan paydown,
- a gain of $232,164 in appreciation, and
- a total return of $270,383.

These results were achieved after an initial out-of-pocket investment of $57,500. Note: The total return of $270,383 from the portfolio of appreciation properties in Year 20 is greater than the total return of $78,252 from the cash flow properties.

The ROI is 470 percent:

$$\$270,383 / \$57,500 = 470\%.$$

This corresponds to an average annual ROI of 23.5 percent:

$$470\% / 20 \text{ years} = 23.5\%.$$

The total returns of each appreciation property and the entire portfolio is shown below in Table 15.

Table 15. Breakdown for the returns from each appreciation property in the portfolio after twenty years. Note: Property 7 was purchased in Year 20, and the results shown are after one year of service.

Property	Cash flow	Loan Paydown	Appreciation	Total
1	$30,597	$106,895	$446,491	$583,983
2	$16,785	$82,607	$344,716	$444,108
3	$8,080	$64,607	$268,906	$341,593
4	$1,720	$48,438	$201,508	$251,666
5	-$3,153	$36,528	$150,772	$184,147
6	-$6,197	$23,398	$94,836	$112,037
7	-$4,218	$8,373	$33,166	$37,321
Total	$43,614	$370,846	$1,540,395	$1,954,855

The initial funds used to purchase the first property are shown to compound to a value of $1,954,855 after 20 years.

In Table 15, Property 1 produced $30,559 in cash flow after twenty years of service. Again, this result shows that, over time, the revenue growth will eventually result in positive cash flow. Property 1 also produced $106,895 in loan paydown and $446,491 in appreciation for a total return of $583,744 after twenty years of service.

Summing the cash flow, loan paydown, and appreciation for all the properties in the portfolio results in a total return of $1,954,616. This total resulted from an initial out-of-pocket investment of $57,500 (the down payment and closing costs for the initial property). The corresponding ROI is 3,399 percent:

$$\$1,954,616 / \$57,500 = 3,399\%.$$

The greater return from the portfolio of appreciation properties comes at the cost of higher risk and thus, as mentioned, is only a suitable investment for high-income earners. The total carryover losses for the appreciation portfolio are $276,886 over those twenty years of service. Remember, an investor can begin by purchasing cash flow properties and then slowly adding appreciation properties to their portfolios.

A Note About Maintenance and Repairs

Based on the results from this analysis, my preference is to hold properties instead of trying to avoid major expenses by selling; this is because the revenue growth should cover the expenses, and the savings gained by selling early will likely be negated by the expenses for selling. Remember, though, each property is different; often, they will have specifics that will deviate from the national average. As such, each property should be evaluated independently. It may be better in some cases to sell rather than pay for major repairs.

Secondly, the total repair expense after twenty years of service for the first property purchased is $28,017 and $32,997 for the cash flow and appreciation properties, respectively. These values are likely too low and can be adjusted accordingly.

When adjusting the repair expense, consider this important question: Will these funds actually be sufficient to replace the roof, replace the hot water tank, replace the HVAC system, and cover the repairs that occur over the life of the property? The answer depends on many factors, some of which you cannot control. However, the purchase criteria and who you hire to handle the property management are two options you can control. Remember, good property management will find quality tenants and monitor the property on a routine basis.

If you think the model is not accurate, by all means, adjust the numbers accordingly. In the end, the results from the modified model should still conclude that the cash flow (profit) increases at a faster rate than the maintenance cost if reasonable values, that reflect historical national averages, are used. Again, the goal of the purchasing criteria used in the turnkey rental business plan is to increase the probability that this will happen.

A Summary of the Key Findings

Let's summarize the key findings and the answers to the initial questions made at the beginning of this example.

- How many properties can be purchased using only the monetary returns from a portfolio of cash flow properties after twenty years of service?
    ◊ Seven properties can be added after the first purchase for a total of eight properties.

- How many properties can be purchased using only the monetary returns from a portfolio of appreciation properties after twenty years of service?
    ◊ Six properties can be added after the first purchase for a total of seven properties.

- When are the financial returns from the portfolio of cash flow properties sufficient to purchase more properties?
    ◊ The initial purchase of the first cash flow property results in a portfolio of eight properties, with new purchases in years 7, 11, 14, 16, 18, and 20 (two were bought in year twenty).

- When are the financial returns from the portfolio of appreciation properties sufficient to purchase more properties?
    ◊ The initial purchase of the first appreciation property results in a portfolio of seven properties with new purchases in years 7, 11, 14, 16, 18, and 20.

- The revenue for the portfolio of cash flow or the portfolio

of appreciation properties is predicted to increase at a greater rate than the expenses.
- ◊ If the expenses are outpacing the cash flow for properties purchased using the criteria in this book, your property management team is likely not performing well.

- The appreciation properties in the first year of service produce a monthly loss in cash flow, but after enough years of service, they will produce a monthly cash flow.

- How do the results from this example compare to the actual performance of my portfolio?
  - ◊ The performance of my portfolio before the COVID-19 pandemic outperformed the results from the example because my maintenance and vacancy expenses were lower than the models.
  - ◊ The performance of my portfolio after the COVID-19 pandemic greatly outperformed the results from this example because of the high appreciation rates.
  - ◊ Note: My portfolio of turnkey rental properties is only seven years old, which partially contributes to the deviation.

To conclude, holding rental properties for a long time can result in a very impressive **ROI**. The key is to reinvest the earnings from the four returns and let your portfolio mature over time. As your portfolio matures, the equity increases as the loan paydown occurs. This equity is not a realized monetary return unless you can access it. How to access your equity, which was touched upon earlier, is explained in greater detail in the next two chapters.

CHAPTER 26

LENDING PRODUCTS

To scale up the number of properties in our business, as indicated in the previous section, we need to know how and when to gain access to the equity of our properties. Multiple lending products can be used to liberate this equity, including but not limited to

- selling,
- refinancing,
- obtaining a home equity loan, and
- acquiring a home equity line of credit (**HELOC**).

A really important component of operating a turnkey rental business (and, really, any real estate business) is looking for and identifying sources of financing. While I have indicated several financing options with conventional lenders, you can find many other potential sources with private or secondary market lenders. In this chapter, we will discuss refinancing and the other lending products listed. Selling will not be discussed here since it has a dedicated chapter in this book.

Refinancing

Refinancing is a loan product that can utilize the equity of a property or capitalize on lower interest rates. When you refinance, the bank pays off the existing loan with a new loan. If the money received from the new loan is greater than the funds needed to pay off the existing one, you can choose to receive the difference in cash or reduce the borrowed balance. As for the latter, receiving cash from refinancing is known as a cash-out refinance.

Let's look at a quick example of how refinancing can work for rental properties. First, we'll assume that the appraised value of a property is $200,000, and the current mortgage balance is $50,000. We will assume that the initial mortgage balance was $100,000, and the interest rate was 4 percent. The equity of the property is $150,000:

$$\$200,000 - \$50,000 = \$150,000.$$

There are two refinancing options to explore, namely,

1. a cash-out refinance, and
2. a refinance.

Cash-Out Refinance

The objective of the cash-out refinance is to pull cash from the equity that can be used to purchase another property. At the time of this writing, Freddie Mac loan regulations required a loan-to-value ratio of at least 75 percent for a cash-out refinance. So, let's assume the bank can do a cash-out refinance for a loan-to-value ratio of 75 percent. For a property that appraises at $200,000, this means the bank can give you a loan of up to $150,000:

$$75\% \times \$200,000 = \$150,000.$$

For the cash-out refinance, this would result in a new loan with a balance of $150,000, replacing the old loan with the $50,000 balance. Since the old loan only requires $50,000 to pay it off in full, the investor would receive the remaining funds at closing. In this example, the investor would receive up to $100,000:

$$\$150,000 - \$50,000 = \$100,000.$$

The actual value you would receive will be a little less because of the closing costs. Your monthly mortgage payment would increase from $477 to $716 (use Eq. A.1). The $100,000 received could be put to work by purchasing properties.

At the time of this writing, that $100,000 would be enough money to purchase two more properties at $200,000 each, which would, in turn, produce around $300 per month after fixed expenses. The increase in cash flow then equals $361:

$$-\$716 + \$477 + 2 \times \$300 = \$361,$$

which represents an increase in your monthly profits of $361 at the cost of increasing the debt of your portfolio. Remember, too, the additional properties will provide additional loan paydown and appreciation. Assuming the three properties are worth $200,000 each, the annual appreciation rate of 3 percent would result in an increase in equity after the first year of $18,000:

$$3\% \times 3 \text{ properties} \times \$200,000 = \$18,000.$$

The greater return from appreciation results from the monetary value of the assets in the portfolio increasing with the additional purchase.

The cash received at closing from the cash-out refinance is not taxed (the taxes are deferred) because the property was not sold. The advantage here might not be obvious at first, but think about how amazing it would be to receive a check for $100,000 and not have to pay taxes.

Moreover, the money received can be spent on anything you choose, although the smart choice would be, most likely, to roll the money into another investment. That said, your business may be mature enough at that point for the cash flow to cover your personal expenses even after the cash-out refinance. If so, you may simply prefer to finance some sort of large purchase with the cash such as a boat.

Refinance

The objective of refinancing is to lower the mortgage payment to increase cash flow by reducing the borrowed balance. When the market interest rate is lower than your current interest rate is the best time to refinance. Speak with your CPA about refinancing as some of the expenses involved can be treated as business expenses.

Looking back at our example, we can see how refinancing would result in receiving a new loan with a $50,000 balance (plus closing costs). The funds available from refinancing, again $100,000, are used to pay off the balance of the original mortgage in full and lower the borrowed balance of the new loan. The mortgage payment would go from $477 to $239, producing an increase in cash flow of $238:

$$\$477 - \$239 = \$238.$$

The loan paydown for the new mortgage would be lower, and you would not receive additional leverage for appreciation. The appreciation for one year at an appreciation rate of 3 percent would result in an equity gain of $6,000:

$$3\% \times \$200,000 = \$6,000.$$

The overall result for the portfolio would be similar debt, lower expenses, and an increase in profit.

At first glance, you might wonder why someone wouldn't want to do a cash-out refinance. There are many good reasons, including

1. the end of the market cycle is approaching, making it preferable not to take on more debt and instead focus on lowering expenses to increase profits,
2. you have exhausted the number of conventional mortgages and cannot purchase more properties with a conventional loan,

3. the rates of the loan products available to you are too high for a cash-out refinance to make sense,
4. you want to lower the equity as a liability strategy, and
5. the investor might want to deleverage (similar to item (1)).

The correct choice is all about the status of your portfolio, where the market is at and where it is heading, your current business plan and goals, and your risk tolerance.

In regard to (4), if you wish to lower the equity as a liability strategy, the probability of a lawsuit is lower when there is less money (or less equity) held in your business. This strategy does require the use of a limited liability company to legally segregate your business assets from your personal assets. Unfortunately, I am not legally allowed to offer advice on this subject since I am not a lawyer. In addition, laws and asset protection vary from state to state. I recommend seeking professional advice from an attorney and using the limited information provided here to begin the conversation.

Home Equity Loan

A home equity loan, also referred to as a second mortgage, is an additional mortgage for the property in which the loan amount is based on the equity. In general, it is much harder to get a home equity loan for a rental property than for a personal residence. Start by talking with the lender for the primary mortgage as their risk from a home equity loan is lower than that for a bank that is not the primary mortgage lender. Expect the rate to be higher than the current market mortgage rate. The term is also not likely to be a thirty-year term; expect a shorter term such as fifteen or twenty years.

Let's illustrate the pros and cons of receiving money through a home equity loan with a quick example. Let's assume the mortgage balance for the primary mortgage is $50,000, and the appraised value for the property is $200,000. Let's also assume you have found a lender that will give you a home equity loan in which the combined loan-to-value ratio of the primary and secondary mortgage needs to be 60 percent or less. A 60-percent loan-to-value ratio results in a leveraged balance of $120,000:

$$60\% \times \$200,000 = \$120,000.$$

The maximum borrowed balance for the second mortgage is given as the difference between the allowable leveraged balance and the balance of the primary mortgage, or $70,000:

$$\$120,000 - \$50,000 = \$70,000.$$

Some of these funds will go toward the closing expenses. Let's assume the remaining balance after the closing costs is $65,000. At closing, the title company or closing attorney will wire the funds ($65,000) to your account.

Since you have not sold a property, no income taxes will be charged to these funds. Be certain to discuss with your CPA the tax ramifications because some or all the expenses involved in acquiring the home equity loan might be eligible to be treated as business expenses.

For the home equity loan, let's assume the term is fifteen years and the interest rate is 6 percent, making the monthly payment $590.70 (use Eq. A.1). Remember, the first mortgage is still in place, so the total debt service will be the first and second mortgage payments, which will reduce your cash flow for the property.

One advantage of a home equity loan is that the primary mortgage is not paid off. Remember, a mature loan produces more loan paydown than a new loan if the mortgage terms are the same. In terms of net cash flow, purchasing a second property using the funds from the home equity loan will likely result in cash flow lower than the monthly payment for the home equity loan.

The leveraged return from appreciation will be greater since there are two properties instead of one. Remember, though, leverage works both ways. For example, the appreciation rate can be negative, such as during a recession. If the appreciation rate is -3 percent, the loss from two properties appraised at $200,000 each is -$12,000:

$$-3\% \times \$200{,}000 \times 2 = -\$12{,}000.$$

The loss from one property would be -$6,000. For these reasons, a home equity loan should not be used unless you understand the risks. Most likely, a home equity loan is suitable during the beginning or middle of the expansion phase when the appreciation rate is likely positive and will remain so for multiple years.

Home Equity Line of Credit (HELOC)

A home equity line of credit (HELOC) refers to a loan product that works similarly to a credit card in that your available balance is directly determined by the equity of your property. In general, HELOCs are difficult to obtain for a rental property, but the advantages of using this loan product instead of refinancing or selling are substantial; hence, obtaining a HELOC can be worth the effort.

The funds available from a HELOC are available during a five- or ten-year window known as the draw period. During this period, you do not have to make payments unless you spend the funds from the HELOC. The payment during the draw period is an interest-only payment. The interest rate is usually a variable rate tied to an index.

Recall, when you refinance cash out of the property, assuming the interest rate is the same, the mortgage payment will increase. Again, this higher debt service results in less cash flow. If the funds from the refinance are not immediately put to work with a new purchase, the total profits will be lower while you are looking to utilize the capital from the refinance. However, with a HELOC, the expenses for the property remain the same until you spend the HELOC. Again, no payments are due until you spend some of those funds.

After the draw period described above, a repayment period commences that lasts for twenty or twenty-five years. During the repayment period, you will be unable to spend the HELOC funds. The payments during this period include both the interest and principal of the funds.

The advantages for HELOCs include:

- Lower closing costs
    - ◊ The closing costs of a HELOC will be lower than the costs to refinance and are typically $500 or less. This results in more buying power.
- An easy closing process
    - ◊ HELOCs require fewer documents, and the closing process can be completed relatively quickly.
- No monthly debt service until you use it
- A low, interest-only payment during the draw period
    - ◊ A lower debt service, which provides more cash for investing
- A higher borrowed balance (a loan-to-value ratio greater than 75 percent)
    - ◊ Greater leverage by enabling a large, borrowed balance
- You don't need to replace the original mortgage
    - ◊ Maintains a higher ROI from the loan paydown

Since a HELOC does not replace the original mortgage, the loan paydown remains unchanged. Recall that the loan paydown for a mortgage is greater for a mature mortgage. For a mature mortgage, the loan paydown will be much higher than that of a new mortgage if the interest rates are similar. If you refinance, the returns from cash flow and the loan paydown could be significantly reduced.

HELOC Example

Let's look at a quick example using a HELOC. The balance for the HELOC will typically be determined using the loan-to-value ratio. For this example, we'll assume the property appraises at $200,000 and has a mortgage balance of $50,000. The lending institution may compute the HELOC balance using a loan-to-value ratio of 50 percent, which results in the maximum total borrowed funds of $100,000:

$$50\% \times \$200,000 = \$100,000.$$

The HELOC balance will be the maximum total borrowed funds minus the balance owed for the primary mortgage or $50,000:

$$\$100,000 - \$50,000 = \$50,000.$$

The monthly interest-only payment for a 5 percent interest rate during the draw period is $208.33:

$$(5\% / 12 \text{ months}) \times \$50,000 = \$208.33.$$

Note: A full payment of $208 occurs only if you spend the full $50,000. Your monthly principal and interest payment during the repayment period is $330 per month for a 5 percent interest rate and a twenty-five-year repayment period.

The interest rate for a HELOC is not fixed and will vary with the index. To illustrate the risk, let's assume you were projecting an interest rate of 5 percent during the repayment period (which involves a $330 monthly payment), but instead, the interest rate climbed to 10 percent. The monthly payment would then be $483. The lender will provide information regarding how much the rate can increase, so be certain to evaluate the worst-case scenario.

Is a HELOC Right for You?

So, which loan product is the best choice for your needs? To help you answer this question, you should build a financial model for each scenario: HELOC, refinancing, home equity loan, and selling the property. Once you have a model in place for each, you can determine which one makes the most sense and aligns best with your goals. The market cycle, interest rates, and your personal goals are all important factors when deciding the best option. In most cases, the option that provides the best return is the one you will want to select.

The HELOC option might result in the best return on your money, but other factors bear consideration such as whether you want to hold the property into the foreseeable future. In general, you will want to look for a HELOC if the current market interest rate is significantly higher than that of your existing loan. If the rate is significantly lower than that of the current loan, refinancing is a viable option.

In general, HELOCs are an excellent option to obtain at any time during the market cycle since there are no monthly payments unless you choose to use the funds. Remember, interest rates will likely increase during the hyper supply and recession phases, which will increase your HELOC payment. In this regard, the funds can be held as a reserve for major expenses, at least for the five or ten years of the draw period. As with all major business decisions, speak with your CPA as some expenses associated with a HELOC can be treated as business expenses.

The terms for HELOCs will vary a fair amount between lending institutions, so you should shop around. Smaller banks or credit unions are more likely to offer HELOCs. When the real estate market is strong, the loan-to-value ratios offered increase. The highest loan-to-value ratio I have seen offered for rentals was 80 percent. This particular lending institution was willing to allow up to four HELOCs and did not require being the primary lender. Really good terms such as this are usually only available when the real estate market is really strong.

When evaluating the HELOC option, be sure to use the maximum payment during the draw and repayment period as it is a good practice to build plans using worse-case scenarios. Think back to Example 13.3. Specifically, recall that the results from this example showed that the cash flow increased at a greater rate than the expenses. The additional cash flow should easily handle the debt service requirements during the repayment period.

With how inflation impacts the purchasing power of money, a HELOC represents one of the best short positions available since the principal payments do not start until after the draw period ends. Just remember, the interest rate is variable. So, extreme caution must be exercised when using a HELOC.

To summarize:

- The funds available from a HELOC can make an excellent reserve fund.
- HELOCs can offer more leverage than other lending products.
- Try to utilize a HELOC when you do not want to replace the mortgage.

The lending products discussed in this chapter are one of two methods used to access equity. The second approach, selling the property, is discussed in the next chapter.

CHAPTER 27

SELLING PROPERTIES

While I usually do not sell properties as an exit strategy, there are plenty of good reasons to sell, and I have certainly benefited from doing so. For example, investors who opt to invest in appreciation properties will likely utilize selling strategies more than those who invest exclusively in cash flow properties. The reason is simple: Refinancing equity out of an appreciation property will result in negative cash flow; however, selling can result in the ability to purchase multiple cash flow properties without the need to pay capital gain tax. If you plan to sell a property, make sure to speak with your CPA about how to minimize your capital gain tax. Your CPA will most likely recommend selling using a 1031 tax exchange. Also, make sure you discuss selling with your turnkey provider or property management team prior to beginning the process. Most will suggest that you wait until the property is vacant, but remember, it is your property; you need to do what is best for you, even if it means selling while the property is occupied.

Most people's initial thoughts about selling real estate are to simply list their property with a real estate agent. While this is certainly a viable approach, it is not always the most advantageous.

Many options are out there, and like anything else, each has merit. Selecting the correct option will depend on market conditions, which play a role in the profitability of each option. For example, lots of expenses come with selling properties, some of which can be greatly reduced by selecting the appropriate time and strategy. The different selling options include but are not limited to

- selling with a real estate agent,
- selling directly to an investor,
- selling directly to your tenant,
- selling to your tenant with a lease option, and
- selling to an investor with seller's financing.

Regardless of which option you choose to sell your property, the results will very much depend on whether the market is a buyer's market or a seller's. I do my best to sell only during a seller's market. First, though, it is important to understand the difference between a seller's and buyer's market. The latter market type means there are too many sellers and not enough buyers. In this type of market, a seller will likely have to concede to the buyer's request during closing, which will certainly result in lower profits. The opposite is true in a seller's market, when there are too many buyers and not enough sellers.

The rest of this section is dedicated to evaluating the pros and cons of each selling option by comparing their gross profits and other nonmonetary benefits and disadvantages. The financial models utilized are basic and can be expanded to model variations based on the listed options and other scenarios. I've condensed the results into some generalized rules on how to select the most profitable option that fits your specific requirements. In the examples provided, it is clear that the different selling options will require some estimates for the appraised value of the property, the mortgage balance, and the rental rate. The estimates for these parameters are tabulated below in Table 16.

Table 16. House parameters.

House Parameters	
Appraised Value	$180,000
Mortgage Balance	$95,500
Rental Rate per Month	$1,500
The housing parameters shown are used below to illustrate the different selling options discussed.	

Selling Option #1: Selling with a Real Estate Agent

My experiences selling properties with real estate agents have been mixed; the result is, of course, dependent on the agent. An exceptionally talented agent can bring a lot of value that can be difficult to find elsewhere. Since having a talented agent is crucial, proper screening is a must. The questionnaire titled **Real Estate Agent Questionnaire** can assist with your search.

It is important to understand how a seller's market affects real estate agents. In this type of market, successful agents have listings, i.e., they are representing sellers. The agent's job is actually very easy if they represent a seller in a seller's market. In contrast, agents who represent buyers end up spending a lot of money driving around and working a lot of hours with very little monetary gain. For this reason, agents compete fiercely with other agents for sellers during a seller's market.

Remember, everything in real estate is negotiable. If you are the seller in a seller's market, you hold all the power at the negotiation table—not just with the buyer but with the real estate agents as well. This means that you can negotiate for lower real estate commissions but can likely only successfully negotiate for lower rates during a seller's market.

The typical real estate commission rate equals 3 percent. That means 3 percent of the sale price goes to the buyer's agent and another 3 percent goes to the seller's agent, for a total commission of 6 percent. In a strong seller's market, you can easily negotiate a 2 percent commission for the selling agent. I would not recommend trying to negotiate the buyer's agent commission to below 3 percent, however. Remember, the buyer's agent has already worked hard for little monetary gain. If you lower their rate, they may simply show their clients other homes.

Reducing your commission from 6 to 5 percent will save $1,000 for every $100,000 the house sells for. Note: Your agent (the seller's agent, in other words) is going to try to convince you that (1) you should pay 6 percent, and (2) you should pay them 3 percent of that 6 and the buyer's agent something less than 3 percent. Remember, this is in their best interest, not yours.

As to other expenses, in a strong seller's market, it is much easier to sell the property for more than the listed price without paying closing costs or repairs. In this type of market, the home is more likely to sell for more than the appraisal value of $180,000. The opposite occurs in a buyer's market in which the home is more likely to sell for less than the appraised value. One expense I recommend regardless of whether it is a buyer's or seller's market is to have a professional cleaning done. During a seller's market, I don't recommend staging (decorating with furniture, pictures, etc.). During a buyer's market, however, staging becomes more important. If staging is necessary, the real estate agent will handle renting the necessary materials.

A comparison of the expenses in a buyer's and seller's market is shown below in Table 17.

Table 17. Estimated expense summary when selling with a realtor.

Expenses	Buyer's Market	Seller's Market
Appraisal Fee	$0	$0
Closing Costs	$5,400	$0
Real Estate Commissions	$10,800 @ 6%	$9,000 @ 5%
Renovation/Repairs	$5,000	$0
Cleaning	$300	$300
Staging	$500	$0
Utilities and Holding Costs	$800	$400
Total	$22,800	$9,700
The expenses when selling should be lower for a seller's market, including the agent commissions.		

As shown in Table 17, the estimated expenses for the seller are lower during a seller's market, possibly as low as $9,700. During a buyer's market, you might have to pay as much as $22,800 (possibly more). Remember, this is just an example to show how selling with a real estate agent can vary between a seller's and buyer's market. The main concepts to keep in mind are: Make sure to get some estimated values for your property if you are selling and remember to negotiate for favorable terms if it is a seller's market.

To summarize, you will find the most value using an agent when:

- It's a strong seller's market because your seller-related expenses are lower.
- When you anticipate complications that are likely to require

the services of an agent's strong network of professionals.
- You want to sell the property quickly.
- You want to minimize your time during the selling process.

Selling Option #2: Selling Directly to an Investor

For new turnkey rental investors, you will quickly learn that active real estate investors will go to great lengths to contact you, hoping to persuade you to sell your properties to them. I receive ten or more letters and postcards every week and upwards of twenty text messages and phone calls daily. This constant pestering can be a serious annoyance, though it can be greatly reduced, depending on how you title your properties. The reason is straightforward: If the name of the owner on the title is 123 Main Street Trust or 123 Main Street LLC instead of your name, it is much harder for active investors to determine who to call. This can also be used to your advantage in other ways as will be described in this section.

To sell to an investor, you need to understand their business plan. For starters, investors are going to advertise themselves as someone who

- can close quickly by purchasing all in cash,
- allows you to avoid agent commissions,
- will buy without any need for you to make repairs to the property, and
- will not ask you to clean the property.

Their goal is to send thousands of letters and text messages and make just as many phone calls trying to find a motivated seller—someone who must sell the property quickly to avoid losing it to foreclosure. The active investor (the good ones, anyway) understands that a truly motivated seller will likely accept a below-market price offer.

Our goal is to turn the tables and utilize the free marketing (free for us) to shop around for an inexperienced active investor. This is much easier than you would expect; real estate gurus preach a lot about active business plans such as wholesaling and flipping, both of which require constant marketing to find motivated sellers. I should make it clear that these business plans can, when executed properly, be very lucrative; however, they do require a lot of time.

At any rate, we are looking for inexperienced, active investors who have been told no or mostly no for their entire active, short real estate careers. The reason: They will be very excited to speak to you. Remember, you only need one investor who is willing to overpay for a property.

The benefits of selling your property this way can best be illustrated by estimating profits based on the expenses shown in Table 18.

Table 18. Expense summary when selling to an investor.

Expenses	Buyer's Market	Seller's Market
Appraisal Fee	$0	$0
Closing Costs	$0	$0
Real Estate Commissions	$0	$0
Renovation	$0	$0
Cleaning	$0	$0
Staging	$0	$0
Utilities and Holding Costs	$0	$0
Total Expenses	**$0**	**$0**

Note: When you sell the property to an investor, they typically purchase the property as is and are willing to cover closing costs in a buyer's or seller's market. Therefore, your selling expenses are $0.

As shown, the expenses can equal nearly $0 in such a scenario. Even inexperienced active investors will almost certainly not purchase at the appraised value, but I have heard about situations in which they considered offers $10,000 and $15,000 below the appraised value.

For this example, let's assume the sales price you and the active investor settle upon isn't the appraisal value of $180,000 that we are using for our assumptions but is instead $165,000 cash, with the tenant in place and your mortgage balance at $95,000. Thus, your gross profit is calculated as $70,000:

$$\$165,000 - \$95,000 = \$70,000.$$

I would not likely sell to an investor during a strong seller's market because you are more likely to get a better offer by going with Selling Option #1. The above approach will work best when the market only slightly favors sellers or when you want to sell quickly and want to sell as is.

Is It Worth It?

For full disclosure, my preference is to not deal with active investors. The process requires the turnkey investor to spend a lot of time talking with many active investors, most of whom won't work out for various reasons. Almost all of them will want to walk the property, which requires notifying your property management team so that they can then notify the tenant. In general, I do not find the potential increase in profits worth the effort; however, I wanted to at least mention this approach for those who might be interested in it.

Selling Option #3: Selling Directly to your Tenant

The benefits of selling your property directly to the tenant are significant and include

- no real estate agent commissions,
- no cleaning and maintenance expenses, and

- no holding costs from utilities and your mortgage.

This option is easily my favorite, but it does not happen often. The best approach is to have your property management team include a credit score as part of the screening criteria. Ideally, you want to set the minimum credit score so that your future tenant can qualify for financing. Note: Just because you select favorable screening criteria to find a potential buyer does not mean you will locate one.

Prior to the end of the lease, have your management team include the option to purchase the property when they begin the renewal process. For example, many property management companies begin sending notices to the tenant about renewing three months in advance (some even sooner). You will want to offer three options on the notice, namely, to

1. renew for one year at $1,500 per month,
2. renew for two years at $1,400 per month in Year 1 and $1,450 per month in Year 2, or
3. purchase the property for $180,000.

You can improve your odds by providing some help to your tenant such as letting them close on the first business day of the month; that way, they can enjoy two full months without a mortgage payment. I also recommend setting the price using an appraiser so that the tenant won't feel like you are taking advantage of them. In addition, the tenant will order an inspection.

The sell-specific expenses are listed below in Table 19.

Table 19. Expense summary when selling to your tenant.

Expenses	Buyer's Market	Seller's Market
Appraisal Fee	$500	$500
Closing Costs	$0*	$0*
Real Estate Commissions	$0	$0
Renovation	$0*	$0
Cleaning	$0	$0
Staging	$0	$0
Utilities and Holding Costs	$0	$0
Total	$500	$500

When selling to a tenant, I recommend paying any closing costs with the title company or closing attorney. The expense should be minor. Also, renovations are usually minimal and will depend on what the inspection report includes. My preference is to pay for an appraisal to set the price.

I have purposely included other common expenses in the table to illustrate why this method is my favorite. The gross profits received from the sale is $80,000:

$180,000 - $95,000 - $500 = $80,000.

The pros are obvious; you can eliminate a lot of the expenses listed in Table 19 that are usually accrued when selling. On the other hand, the process does take considerable time and offers no guarantees that your tenant will choose to purchase the property. This method works well for any market you choose to sell in.

Selling Option #4: Selling Using a Lease Option

A lease option refers simply to a standard rental lease with a purchase option clause built into the agreement. The option clause provides the tenant with the choice to purchase the property at the end of the lease; if the tenant chooses this option, the property owner is obligated to sell to them.

The benefits for a landlord are

- additional income, and
- lower expenses when selling the property.

The tenant benefits by

- having the option to purchase after living in the property and
- locking in the sales price.

The flexibility of the option comes at a financial cost to the tenant. Typically, the two costs are

1. a rent credit, which is an increase in the monthly rental rate, and
2. a lease option rate, which is a one-time payment due at closing.

The rent credit is collected each month; if the tenant does not purchase the property at the end of the lease, the property owner keeps the credit. However, if the tenant exercises their purchase option, typically, the rent credit is applied to the tenant's down payment. The monthly rent credit may have tax implications, so please consult with your CPA.

Be advised that some lenders do not like lease options and will not allow the rent credit to be applied as part of the down payment. If you are entering into a lease option, make sure to help the tenant understand that they may need to shop around for a lender.

The lease option rate is a one-time payment the tenant pays to you, the property owner, at closing and is usually between 1 to 3 percent of the sales price. There are many nuances with lease options, so seek professional help if you decide to implement lease options as an exit strategy.

Lease option contracts typically include the sales price, the duration of the lease, the rent credit, and the lease option rate. The sales price is usually the current market value, which presents some risks to you (the landlord) if, at the end of the lease, the value of the property is greater than the agreed-upon sales price. You can use several approaches to minimize your risk in this situation; for example, you can

- determine where the market is regarding the market cycle—remember, the appreciation rate is greatest at the end of the expansion phase;
- estimate the current appreciation rate and the anticipated appreciation rate; or
- set the lease option rate at or slightly above the projected appreciation rate.

Selling a property with a lease option is tricky and not relevant to most investors since the strategy requires a special lease (a lease option). Also, your turnkey provider may not be comfortable with this arrangement. At any rate, it can be a very lucrative approach.

The expenses for selling with a lease option are shown below in Table 20.

Table 20. Expenses for the lease option sale.

Expenses	Buyer's Market	Seller's Market
Appraisal Fee	$0	$0
Closing Costs	$0*	$0*
Real Estate Commissions	$0	$0
Renovation	$0*	$0*
Cleaning	$0	$0
Staging	$0	$0
Utilities and Holding Costs	$0	$0
Total	**$0**	**$0**

When you sell the property to your tenant with a lease option, you may have repair costs and closing costs, especially in a buyer's market.

As shown, the expenses are low in general. Remember, though, in a strong buyer's market, you will likely have to cover some portion of the closing cost. I do not include the closing cost because the potential buyer (tenant) is already attached to the property and does not want to move; thus, you will have a better chance at negotiating successfully.

The lease option parameters, which include the rent credit, the lease option rate, and the lease term, are shown below in Table 21.

Table 21. Lease option parameters.

Lease Option Parameters	
Lease Option Term, Years	1
Lease Option Rate @ 3%	$5,400
Rent Credit @ 10%	$1,800

At the end of the lease (after one year), if the tenant chooses not to exercise their option to purchase, the landlord will keep the rent credit of $1,800. If the tenant chooses to exercise their option to purchase, the landlord will make $90,400:

$$\$180,000 - \$95,000 + \$5,400 = \$90,400.$$

The additional $5,400 in the above estimate is the lease option credit. Remember, this is a simplistic model intended to illustrate the pros and cons of the strategy.

I have seen situations in which landlords abused their lease options. They intentionally screen for tenants who will unlikely ever be able to purchase the property, hoping to collect additional rent from them that way. Please do not do this as it is, in my opinion, unethical. Remember, you can make good money from a turnkey rental business without having to resort to dirty tactics.

Selling Option #5: Selling Using Seller Financing

Seller financing occurs when the landlord becomes the lender for the buyer. This type of financing may not be relevant as an exit strategy for most investors because usually, to be eligible, you must own the property clear and free (no mortgage).

The benefits to the seller include but are not limited to

- monthly income you can collect without worrying about collecting rent, paying for repairs, paying insurance premiums, and paying for property taxes;
- a lower annual tax liability since you collect your profits over the course of several years; and
- access to a mortgage rate above the market rate if you wish to finance the mortgage.

The benefits to the buyer include but are not limited to

1. a faster, cheaper closing process,
2. more flexibility with the underwriting criteria and mortgage terms than working with a bank, and
3. any seller-financed loans will not appear on the buyer's credit report.

Concerning benefit (2), the buyer might be able to secure financing with a lower down payment than what an institutional lender will allow. It is challenging for buyers to find seller financing; hence, you should be able to find many interested buyers and potentially get a higher sales price than would otherwise be possible.

The risks to seller financing mostly apply to the buyer. A savvy seller will require a higher interest rate than the market rate to lower their risks. Understand that you can, if needed, repossess the property through foreclosure should the buyer stop making payments. If this happens, you own the property clear and free and are, at that point, experienced with operating the property as a rental and can make that transition. Hence, your risk is fairly low.

If interested in using seller financing, seek professional help setting up the lending documents. Regarding the financials, the monthly mortgage payment is calculated the same way you would the payment for any other mortgage using Eq. A.1.

Assuming the property parameters shown in Table 22, you might be able to sell the property for $185,000 even in a buyer's market. Again, adjust the values accordingly.

Table 22. Expenses for the seller using seller financing

Expense Items	Cost
Closing Costs	$0
Legal Expenses	> $0
Real Estate Commissions	$0
Renovation	$0
Cleaning	$0
Staging	$0
Utilities and Holding Costs	$0
Total	$0

Note: When you sell the property using seller financing, you will probably have legal costs.

For a quick idea of the potential profits, let's assume the following:

- A sales price of $185,000
- The market interest rate for a mortgage is 4.5 percent.
- The loan terms you have negotiated are a 6.5 percent interest rate, a twenty-year term, and an 85 percent loan-to-value.

Based on these terms, the mortgage payment would be $1,172 per month (use Eq. A.1). If the buyer chooses to repay the loan over the twenty-year term, the total money you will receive is $281,379. If they choose to refinance, you will be paid out in full by the new lender. Note: You can include a penalty for early payoff. Remember, everything is negotiable.

Summary of the Different Selling Options

A brief summary of the selling options follows below.

Option #1: Selling with a Real Estate Agent

The best times to do so are when

- you want or need to sell quickly,
- you want to minimize your time during the selling process,
- you anticipate complications during the selling process, and
- it is a seller's market.

Option #2: Selling Directly to an Investor

Consider this option if:

- The selling expense is close to $0 for you.
- You need to sell the property in as-is condition.
- You are certain this is the best choice for your current situation (not recommended).

Option #3: Selling Directly to your Tenant

The benefits include:

- Your expenses are minimized (no commissions, cleaning or maintenance fees, or holding costs).
- It is a good method in a buyer's or seller's market.
- A solid profit—but bear in mind, it does not happen often.

Option #4: Selling Using a Lease Option

The benefits include:

- Additional income for the landlord.

- Lower expenses when selling.
- A solid profit, but first, be sure to check with your turnkey provider as to whether this is a viable option.

Option #5: Selling Using Seller Financing

This option allows you to:

- Collect a monthly income without the expenses of repairs, insurance, property taxes, and property management.
- Lower your annual tax liability by collecting your profits over the course of years.
- Grants you access to above-market interest rates for the mortgage.

To conclude, selling represents one of two methods you can use to access the equity in your properties. The other method involves utilizing one of the different lending products available such as a refinance or a HELOC. Again, access to your equity is crucial to increasing the size of your portfolio and represents one of several long-term strategies. In Part Seven, we will focus on some other long-term strategies to grow your turnkey rental business.

PART SEVEN:
LONG-TERM STRATEGIES

CHAPTER 28

MAXIMIZING CASH FLOW

Many investors take an interest in owning a turnkey rental business because the cash flow can provide the kind of supplemental income that could lead to financial freedom or early retirement. Remember, if you're interested in retirement as a goal, you must determine how much net income you will earn, not base this goal on your net worth. Financial freedom or early retirement becomes possible once the cash flow in your business is greater than your personal expenses.

As such, there may come a time when you will want to change your strategy toward paying down debt rapidly. Note: Paying down debt will also result in an increase in cash flow. Increasing cash flow and reducing debt might be an attractive option if you are ready to focus on other activities or simply want peace of mind. You may also want to use this strategy if the market is approaching a recession. This section discusses methods that will allow you to pay off mortgages at an accelerated rate.

Snowball Effect

First, we'll go over one method to deleverage rapidly: the snowball effect. This approach is commonly used to help people pay off credit card debt. Concerning credit cards, the idea is simple: Make the minimum payment for each credit card and then pay extra toward the credit card with the lowest balance. Once the credit card with the lowest balance is paid off, the extra cash can be put toward the next credit card with the lowest balance.

The same concept can be applied to your portfolio of properties. In general, the properties in your portfolio will have different mortgage balances and different cash flows. To use the snowball effect, select one property and make an extra payment each month toward it so that the extra payment is the cash flow from your portfolio. When this mortgage is paid in full, the cash flow will increase since the expenses have decreased. The additional revenue makes paying the next property go faster.

There are several criteria to choose from when determining which property to pay off first, including

- the lowest mortgage balance,
- the highest interest rate, and
- the ROI.

When selecting a property using the ROI, compute the annualized ROI for each property based on the interest saved. Select the property with the highest ROI. An example of how to determine this was provided in **Chapter 6 Return on Investment**.

The concept of using the snowball effect to pay off mortgages rapidly is simple and powerful. For example, let's assume your portfolio of turnkey rental properties contains ten properties with financials similar to those tabulated below in Table 23.

Table 23. *Example of Portfolio Financials.*

Property Pro Forma	
Purchase Price	$119,900
Annual Rent	$12,300
Annual Mortgage	$5,918
Annual Cash flow	$3,452
Annual Escrow Funds	$1,813
The financials shown are used to illustrate the power of the snowball effect.	

To make the example easier, let's assume the properties are all new purchases and the mortgage balances are $95,920 for a thirty-year fixed mortgage. Further, ignore loan paydown for simplicity.

Each property produces an annual cash flow of $3,452, which is $34,520 for the portfolio of ten properties:

10 properties x $3,452 = $34,520.

Since the loan paydown is ignored, $34,520 extra is applied to the mortgage balance. This results in paying off the mortgage in two years and nine months:

$95,920 / $34,520 = 2 years, 9 months.

Since the mortgage payment on one property is now officially $0, the annual profit of the portfolio would increase by the mortgage payment, which is $5,918 (annual payment). During the following year, the extra payment would increase to $40,438:

$34,520 + $5,918 = $40,438.

Again, ignoring loan paydown, the next mortgage would be paid off in about two years and five months:

$95,920 / $40,438 = 2$ years, 5 months.

As the equation shows, this payoff happened four months quicker than it did for the first mortgage. Those are powerful results. The snowball effect is paying off the debt approximately 27.5 years faster than would happen by making minimum payments.

Arbitrage Strategies

Arbitrage refers to an investment strategy that allows you to invest borrowed funds in an investment vehicle with a return greater than the cost of borrowing the funds. For example, if the funds were borrowed at an interest rate of 5 percent and invested in a financial vehicle that produced a gross return of 12 percent, the result is a net return of 7 percent:

$$12\% - 5\% = 7\%.$$

The funds for an arbitrage strategy could come from many sources, including credit cards, a lender, or even the escrowed property tax and insurance. Each of these sources carries various levels of risk. The best approach to illustrate how arbitrate works is by providing some examples. The objectives for the examples that follow are to

- illustrate how arbitrage works for different scenarios and
- illustrate how the extra funds generated from arbitrage strategies can decrease the time required to deleverage the portfolio debt.

Escrow Arbitrage

For this example, let's look at how the escrowed property tax and property insurance can be used in an arbitrage strategy. Understand that any strategy using such escrow funds presents significant risk. It is imperative that you only implement an arbitrage strategy using these funds if you

- have a complete understanding of the risks,
- have an excellent investment plan for these funds, and
- have an excellent plan to mitigate the risks if the plan does not perform.

Remember that the mortgage payment has four components, namely,

- the principal,
- the interest,
- the property tax, and
- the property insurance.

Regarding the property tax and property insurance, the lender puts these funds into an escrow account monthly. Typically, property tax and property insurance are paid every twelve or six months, which provides a twelve- to six-month window in which these funds can be invested.

To use this approach, first, contact your lenders and eliminate the escrow accounts for the properties in your portfolio. Let's assume your portfolio includes ten properties with financials like those summarized below in Table 24.

Table 24. Example of Portfolio Financials.

Property Pro Forma	
Purchase Price	$119,900
Annual Rent	$12,300
Annual Mortgage	$5,918
Annual Cash flow	$3,452
Annual Escrow Funds	$1,813

By eliminating the escrow account, the funds available for an arbitrage strategy are $18,130:

$$\$1,813 \times 10 \text{ properties} = \$18,130.$$

These funds will then be deposited into your business account.

By eliminating the escrow accounts, the property tax and insurance will no longer be paid automatically by your lender, making those payments your responsibility. Additionally, the strategy requires the identification of a low-risk investment in which you can place the funds.

Let's further assume that the investment vehicle you select produces a 3 percent annualized return. A 3 percent annualized return results in a monetary return of $701:

$$3\% \times \$18,130 = \$701.$$

While an extra $701 may seem like a small sum, it does represent a little over two months' cash flow for a typical cash flow property. It is a little more complicated than this example since the invested funds are moving in and out of your account on a six- or twelve-month schedule, depending on when the property tax and insurance payments are due. Also, the balance builds incrementally every month, so the invested principal is not constant. Regardless, the funds can still be put to work in an investment to produce a return.

Credit Card Arbitrage Strategy

A credit card can also be used in an arbitrage strategy. Before getting into the example, I want to quickly discuss the perception of credit card debt. In general, most people label credit card debt as bad debt. I do not disagree with this generalized statement; however, the details matter when classifying debt as bad or good.

For example, would you be willing to borrow $5,000 from a credit card if those funds produced a profit of $10,000 and you deemed the risks acceptable? In this scenario, I would say the debt was good debt with the caveat that the investment carried significant risk because of the presumably high credit card interest rate. That said, the investor's experience may have significantly reduced the risks for the investment, making it a well-calculated risk worth taking. Similarly, borrowing $5,000 to purchase some sort of high-end television is bad debt because the debt is tied to a depreciating asset.

At any rate, to illustrate how a credit card can be used in an arbitrage strategy, let's assume you acquire a credit card that has a 0 percent interest rate for an eighteen-month promotional period. The approach is simple: Pay your monthly expenses in your personal budget using the 0 percent interest rate credit card. By using the credit card, it frees up the funds you would have used to pay your expenses so that they can be applied to an investment.

Let's say you are able to charge $4,000 per month to the credit card, which would provide an additional $4,000 per month to be applied in a snowball effect strategy, described in the section **Snowball Effect**. These charges might include daycare, groceries, gasoline, etc.

Further, assume the mortgage balance for the property to be paid off is $50,000, and the cash flow of your ten-property portfolio is $2,877 per month. For these assumptions, an extra monthly payment of $6,877 can be made:

$$\$4,000 + \$2,877 = \$6,877.$$

Thus, the mortgage will be paid in full in seven months:

$$\$50,000 / \$6,877 = 7 \text{ months}.$$

Remember that the promotional interest rate for the credit card does not expire until after eighteen months. The next step is to save the cash flow from the properties to pay the credit card balance in full before paying any interest. The cash flow will increase to $3,468 per month since the mortgage was paid off.

The credit card balance at the end of seven months is $28,000:

$$4,000 \times 7 \text{ months} = \$28,000.$$

This balance can be paid in full in eight months:

$$\$28,000 / \$3,468 = 8 \text{ months}.$$

Both the mortgage and the credit card will be paid off in fifteen months. Without the additional funds from the frontloaded strategy, the property would have been paid off in eighteen months:

$$\$50,000 / \$2,877 = 18 \text{ months}.$$

Utilizing a credit card and the snowball effect results in a profit by reducing the mortgage interest and collecting additional cash flow. In this example, the additional cash flow is collected for three months. Again, the strategy carries significant risk, so exercise care if you decide to use it.

In Summary

Maximizing cash flow using the snowball effect can be a powerful strategy for those wanting to rapidly deleverage without selling any properties. My preference is to maintain a leveraged position and let time increase my revenue, but of course, your preference may be different.

The arbitrage strategies discussed in this chapter represent a lot of risk, which should be evaluated before you move forward. Again, these strategies are long-term options; it is up to you to decide what is right for your business plan. Now, let's focus on how to scale your portfolio.

CHAPTER 29

HOW TO SCALE YOUR TURNKEY BUSINESS

> Where We Are At: Master Checklist Step 16
> - **Monthly Business Management Checklist**

Monthly management of your turnkey rental business is vital to the success of your business. Use the **Monthly Business Management Checklist** to complete this step. This checklist is broken into two parts:

- Financial Tracking
- Business Scaling

The action items listed under financial tracking, discussed earlier in **Chapter 5 Financial Bookkeeping**, are, as mentioned, all about monitoring the financial health of your business. Our discussion will now focus on implementing the action items for business scaling.

Implementing business scaling actions can be thought of as building structures with building blocks. Many different structures can be built using such blocks, which include

1. a cash-out refinance,
2. a refinance,
3. a home equity loan,
4. a home equity line of credit,
5. selling with a realtor,
6. selling to an investor,
7. selling to your tenant,
8. selling using a lease option,
9. selling using seller financing,
10. applying the snowball effect, and
11. utilizing an arbitrage strategy.

Your objective is to build and modify your current portfolio using these blocks. While the example to be discussed shortly in this chapter illustrates how to manually perform the action items, I use calculations in an Excel spreadsheet to streamline the process. This tool, along with several others, is available on my website:

https://scottastanfield.com/

More "blocks" are certainly available than I have included here, so do not limit yourself. For the purposes of this book, the eleven listed blocks are plenty. Additionally, **Example 25.4 Projected Financial Performance and Scaling for Cash Flow and Appreciation Properties** shows how powerful scaling can be. Notably, a single cash flow property could, over a twenty-year timeframe, result in a portfolio of eight properties. Similarly, an appreciation property over a similar timeframe could result in a portfolio of seven properties. This example illustrates why scaling is good but does not demonstrate how to scale, which we will now discuss.

The general approach to scaling is to evaluate each block with the intent of defining the risks and then determine how each block will change the portfolio's

- revenue,
- expenses,

- assets,
- debt, and
- effective tax rate.

Understand that market conditions will establish how each block will change your portfolio's financial information. For example, the mortgage interest rate will fluctuate with the market as will many other dependent variables. Again, the objective is to define each block based on the current market conditions and then assemble the blocks to accomplish your goals.

Example 29.5 Executing the Business Scaling Action Items

The mathematical development for this section is given in **Example 29.5 Executing the Business Scaling** in **Appendix D: Mathematics for the Examples**. The discussion below is designed to summarize the key results while demonstrating the business scaling action items in the **Monthly Business Management Checklist**.

Let's assume your portfolio includes three properties, located at 123 Main Street, 456 Cemetery Road, and 789 High Street. You have owned these properties for multiple years. You purchased all three out-of-pocket. By that, I mean you used funds accumulated from another income source such as a job. The funds used to purchase the properties, therefore, did not come from profits made from your portfolio.

Today happens to be the date you scheduled to execute your Monthly Business Management Checklist. At this point, you are ready to execute the business scaling action items. To do this, you must first look at the different properties within your portfolio, determine your portfolio's financial state, and check the different loan products available to you. Your main goal is to determine how your current portfolio can best be used to provide the funds needed to purchase more properties and scale your business without using out-of-pocket funds. The steps for this effort, which are also listed in the checklist, are described below.

Step 1. Determine the cash funds in your business account.

The cash balance, which is the accumulated cash flow produced by your portfolio, is $48,201 (the math is provided in the appendix). The funds shown here were acquired over multiple years of owning the three properties in your portfolio.

Step 2. Determine how much cash is in your personal account for investing.

For this example, the cash funds from your personal account that you wish to contribute to investing are $0.

Step 3. Estimate the equity for the properties in your portfolio.

The equity in your portfolio for each property is

- $63,872 for 123 Main Street,
- $52,350 for 456 Cemetery Road, and
- $40,629 for 789 High Street.

These values were obtained by subtracting the current mortgage balance from the appraised value. I use Zestimate for a quick estimate of the appraised value, then determine the current mortgage balance from my monthly mortgage statements.

Step 4. Estimate the loan-to-value ratio for each property in the portfolio.

The loan-to-value ratio for each property is

- 0.55 for 123 Main Street,
- 0.63 for 456 Cemetery Road, and
- 0.72 for 789 High Street.

These values were determined by dividing the current mortgage balance by the appraised value.

Step 5. Estimate the funds from the different loan products and selling options for each property with a loan-to-value ratio of less than 0.75.

For simplicity, I opted to forgo evaluating selling options and arbitrage strategies. The four loan products to be evaluated include refinance, cash-out refinance, a home equity loan (HEL), and a home equity line of credit (HELOC). Note: The loan-to-value ratio is below 0.75 for all three properties in your portfolio. The results for each property are shown below in Table 25.

Table 25. Funds available by property by loan product.

	Refi	Cash-Out Refi	HEL	HELOC
123 Main	$0	$23,750	$27,207	$34,713
456 Cemetery	$0	$12,228	$16,527	$23,191
789 High	$0	$507	$4,806	$11,470
Total	$0	$36,485	$48,540	$69,374

The cash received from the HEL is greater than the funds received from the cash-out refinance because the closing costs are significantly lower.

Step 6. Estimate your total investment funds.

The total funds available is the sum of the funds in steps 1, 2, and 5. The sum of Steps 1, 2, and 5 for a refinance is $48,201:

$$\$48{,}201 + \$0 + \$0 = \$48{,}201.$$

The sum of steps 1, 2, and 5 for a cash-out refinance is $84,686:

$48,201 + \$0 + \$36,485 = \$84,686.$

The sum of steps 1, 2, and 5 for a home equity loan is $96,741:

$48,201 + \$0 + \$48,540 = \$96,741.$

Lastly, the sum of steps 1, 2, and 5 for a HELOC is $117,576:

$48,201 + \$0 + \$69,374 = \$117,576.$

Step 7. Determine how many properties you can purchase with the total funds reported in Step 6.

Contact your turnkey provider to determine the price of a new purchase if you are not sure. For this example, it is assumed that you can purchase a new cash flow property for $170,000. For a loan-to-value ratio of 0.8 and for closing costs at 3 percent of the purchase price, the funds required to buy the property are $39,100:

$(1 - 0.2) \times \$170,000 + 3\% \times \$170,000 = \$39,100.$

The number of properties you can purchase is determined by dividing the total funds available from Step 6 by the required investment funds ($39,100). For the refinance, the number of properties is one:

$\$48,201 / \$39,100 = 1.$

For the cash-out refinance, the number of properties is two:

$\$84,686 / \$39,100 = 2.$

For the HEL, the number of properties is two:

$\$96,741 / \$39,100 = 2.$

Lastly, for the HELOC, the number of properties is three:

$\$117,576 / \$39,100 = 3.$

The number of properties you can purchase through each loan product and the remaining cash available is summarized below in Table 26.

Table 26. Number of properties and remaining cash.

	# Properties	Cash Remaining
Refinance	1	$9,101
Cash-Out Refinance	2	$6,486
HEL	2	$18,541*
HELOC	3	$276*

*Fewer funds could be obtained from the HEL to purchase two properties. The remaining cash for the HELOC would be undrawn funds.

Step 8. Determine the total ROI and the financial impact of each loan product.

When I complete Step 8 for my business, I first establish a baseline by determining the ROI and financial state of my current portfolio. My preference is to compute the ROI based on out-of-pocket funds. The total invested funds are $87,898. The baseline is shown below in Table 27.

Table 27. Baseline state of a portfolio comprised of three properties.

Profit Returns		Financial State	
Cash Flow	$8,760	Revenue	$42,638
Loan Paydown	$6,369	Expenses	$38,731
Appreciation	$8,598	Assets (Prop. | Cash)	$485,798 | $48,201
Total	$23,727	Debt	$266,656
ROI	**27.0%**	Effective Tax Rate	8.8%

As shown, the profit returns from your portfolio are projected to be

- $8,760 per year in cash flow,
- $6,369 per year in loan paydown, and
- $8,598 for the coming year in projected appreciation.

The total return, which is the sum of the cash flow, loan paydown, and appreciation, equals $23,727:

$$\$8,760 + \$6,369 + \$8,598 = \$23,727.$$

The ROI is 27 percent and is given as the total return divided by the invested funds:

$$\$23,727 / \$87,898 = 27\%.$$

Remember, the financial state of the portfolio entails a list of essential financial information that, once estimated, completely defines the financial state of the portfolio. When building or changing your business plan, the overview of your financial state will help you determine which direction to take the plan. As discussed in Chapter 12 and shown in Table 24, the key financial projections needed to define the financial state of your current portfolio include:

- Revenue = $42,638
- Expenses = $38,731
- Assets = $485,798 with $48,201 in cash
- Debt = $266,656

I like to also include the effective tax rate, which, for the baseline, is 8.8 percent:

- Effective Tax Rate = 8.8%.

The performance of the existing portfolio (the baseline) is the first building block. The financials shown are a projection of the performance of your portfolio for the next physical year; hence, they represent the annual return. The return from depreciation (not shown in the table) reduced your tax rate of 24 percent to an effective tax rate of 8.8 percent.

With the financial state of the baseline fully defined, it is time to define the financial state for all the different options (building blocks) available to you. You can

1. refinance without purchasing a new property,
2. refinance and purchase one new property,
3. cash-out refinance without purchasing a new property,
4. cash-out refinance with purchasing up to two new properties,
5. obtain a home equity loan without purchasing a new property,
6. obtain a home equity loan with purchasing up to two new properties,
7. obtain a home equity line of credit without purchasing new properties, and
8. obtain a home equity line of credit with purchasing up to three new properties.

To review, these eight options are the different building blocks we seek to define for this example in Step 8. We could also include the different selling options and arbitrage strategies. The selling options would likely be worth considering in a seller's market. At any rate, there are a lot of moving pieces (eight, currently), which is why I use Excel to evaluate my options.

What I typically do for Step 8 is define the blocks and then move to the next step in the business scaling action items list. For this example, I am going to diverge from that path to describe the different blocks in more detail. Afterward, I will continue with the execution of the business scaling action items.

Option 1: Refinancing without Purchasing Any New Properties

Building Block 2. The second block computed (the first was the baseline) is for the purpose of refinancing the portfolio without the need to purchase any new properties. The annualized financial state for this option is shown below in Table 28.

Table 28. Financial state of your portfolio after refinancing without purchasing new properties.

Profit Returns		Financial State	
Cash Flow	$11,943	Revenue	$42,638
Loan Paydown	$5,489	Expenses	$36,428
Appreciation	$8,598	Assets (Prop. | Cash)	$438,472 | $48,201
Total	$26,029	Debt	$280,518
ROI	**29.6%**	Effective Tax Rate	9.1%

As shown in the table, Option 1: Refinancing without Purchasing Any New Properties modifies the financial state of your baseline by

- increasing your cash flow from $8,760 to $11,943,
- decreasing your loan paydown from $6,369 to $5,489,
- not changing your appreciation,
- decreasing your expenses from $38,731 to $36,428,
- decreasing your assets from $485,798 to $438,472 without changing your cash assets,
- increasing your debt from $266,656 to $288,518,
- increasing your ROI from 27 to 29.6 percent, and
- increasing your effective tax rate from 8.8 to 9.1 percent.

Overall, Option 1 capitalizes on the lower interest rates to reposition your portfolio, a trend that will repeat for each option. You will want to review all the changes to the financial state of your portfolio and decide if those changes fit your needs. All eight blocks, evaluated in Step 8, will present different changes to your baseline financial state. Your objective is to evaluate the changes, evaluate the risks, and pick the option you think is best for your goals.

Option 1 could be advantageous if you want to increase your cash flow and decrease your expenses or if you are in a market that is at the end of the expansion phase, making it a reasonable precaution if you are concerned about a recession, especially since the assets still include $48,201 in cash.

Option 2: Refinancing and Purchasing One New Property

Building Block 3. The financial breakdown for Option 2: Refinancing and Purchasing One New Property is shown below in Table 29.

Table 29. State of the portfolio after refinancing and purchasing one new property.

Profit Returns		Financial State	
Cash Flow	$15,284	Revenue	$59,438
Loan Paydown	$8,099	Expenses	$52,408
Appreciation	$11,997	Assets (Prop. | Cash)	$608,472 | $9,101
Total	$35,380	Debt	$416,518
ROI	**40.3%**	Effective Tax Rate	7.7%

As shown in the table, Option 2 modifies the financial state of your baseline by

- increasing your cash flow from $8,760 to $15,284,
- increasing your loan paydown from $6,369 to $8,099,
- increasing your appreciation from $8,598 to $11,997,
- increasing your expenses from $38,731 to $52,408,
- increasing your assets from $485,798 to $608,472 and decreasing your cash assets from $48,201 to $9,101,
- increasing your debt from $266,656 to $416,518,
- increasing your ROI from 27 to 40.3 percent, and
- decreasing your effective tax rate from 8.8 to 7.7 percent.

As shown, Option 2 would again capitalize on the lower interest rate while providing all the benefits discussed for Option 1, refinancing without purchasing any new properties. By purchasing a new property, your cash reserves are substantially lower while your expenses are much higher. The end result is a much higher ROI of 40.3 percent, with a hefty increase in your total return of $35,380.

Option 2: Refinancing and Purchasing One New Property could be suitable for the end of the expansion phase, especially if the leases for your existing properties have recently been renewed. Remember, expenses will increase with this option; so, it is important to lower your risk by waiting for the leases to renew or until you have enough funds to handle tenant turnover.

The property purchased was a cash flow property with a purchase price of $170,000. The financial state of the specific property you purchase will alter the financial state shown in Table 29. It could be advantageous to purchase higher price point properties (appreciation properties) to reduce your effective tax rate.

When I am considering purchasing a new property, I try to reduce my tax rate to an effective rate of 0 percent while maintaining my current level of carryover losses (preferably $0 in losses). It is tricky at best to accomplish in practice, but you should be aware of this approach.

Option 3: Cash-Out Refinance without Buying a New Property

Building Block 4. The financial state for Option 3: Cash-Out Refinance without Buying a New Property is shown in Table 30.

Table 30. State of the portfolio after a cash-out refinance without purchasing a new property.

Profit Returns		Financial State	
Cash Flow	$10,234	Revenue	$42,638
Loan Paydown	$6,187	Expenses	$37,438
Appreciation	$8,598	Assets (Prop. | Cash)	$438,472 | $83,721
Total	$25,019	Debt	$316,219
ROI	**28.5%**	Effective Tax Rate	8.1%

As shown in the table, Option 3: Cash-Out Refinance without Buying a New Property modifies the financial state of your baseline by

- increasing your cash flow from $8,760 to $10,234,
- slightly decreasing your loan paydown from $6,369 to $6,187,
- not changing your appreciation,
- decreasing your expenses from $38,731 to $37,438,
- decreasing your assets from $485,798 to $438,472 but increasing your cash assets from $48,201 to $83,721,
- increasing your debt from $266,656 to $316,219,
- increasing your ROI from 27 to 28.5 percent, and
- decreasing your effective tax rate from 8.8 to 8.1 percent.

This might be a good option if you want to increase cash assets while waiting for a good investment opportunity, increase your cash reserves in anticipation of an upcoming recession, or lock in lower interest rates.

Option 4: Cash-Out Refinance and Purchase Two New Properties

Building Block 5. The financial state for Option 4: Cash-Out Refinance and Purchase Two New Properties is shown in Table 31.

Table 31. State of the portfolio after a cash-out refinance with purchasing two new properties.

Profit Returns		Financial State	
Cash Flow	$16,916	Revenue	$76,238
Loan Paydown	$11,407	Expenses	$69,399
Appreciation	$15,398	Assets (Props. | Cash)	$778,472 | $5,521
Total	$43,720	Debt	$588,219
ROI	**49.7%**	Effective Tax Rate	6.2%

As shown in the table, Option 4 modifies the financial state of your baseline by

- increasing your cash flow from $8,760 to $16,916,
- increasing your loan paydown from $6,369 to $11,407,
- increasing your appreciation from $8,598 to $15,398,
- increasing your expenses from $38,731 to $69,399,
- increasing your assets from $485,798 to $778,472 but decreasing your cash assets from $47,236 to $5,521,
- increasing your debt from $266,656 to $588,219,
- increasing your ROI from 27 to 49.7 percent, and
- decreasing your effective tax rate from 8.8 to 6.2 percent.

Option 4 is an aggressive choice best utilized during the early or middle of the expansion phase, though it really comes down to your personal risk tolerance and goals. As shown, this option greatly increased your cash flow from $8,760 to $16,916, but take note, your cash flow is lower on a per-property basis.

Something else I want to point out here is that the interest rate—one of the more important variables—is lower when the market is good such as during the expansion phase. It will likely be higher when the market is struggling. For this reason, repositioning your portfolio requires projecting where the market is headed. You need to stay one step ahead of the market. Again, having newly renewed, two-year leases with proven tenants will lower your risks if you decide to use Option 4.

If concerned about your ability to gauge the market accurately, you can always choose a more conservative option. Remember, too, the ROI for more conservative options, such as refinancing, is still excellent. Additionally, the remaining action items in this chapter's checklist are designed to help you correctly identify the market. The refinancing options that have been presented thus far are summarized below in Table 32.

Table 32. Summary of the refinance options.

	Base	Opt. 1	Opt. 2	Opt. 3	Opt. 4
Cash Flow ($)	8,760	11,943	15,284	10,234	16,916
Loan Paydown ($)	6,369	5,489	8,099	6,187	11,407
Appreciation ($)	8,598	8,598	11,997	8,598	15,398
Expenses ($)	38,731	36,428	52,408	37,438	69,399
Assets ($)	485,798	438,472	608,472	438,472	778,472
Cash Assets ($)	48,201	48,201	9,101	83,721	5,521
Debt	266,656	280,518	416,518	316,219	588,219
ROI (%)	27.0	29.6	40.3	28.5	49.7
Effective Tax Rate (%)	8.8	9.1	7.7	8.1	6.2

Option 5: Home Equity Loan Without Purchasing New Properties

Building Block 6. The portfolio financials based on the option of obtaining a home equity loan without purchasing new properties are shown below in Table 33.

Table 33. State of the portfolio after a home equity loan without purchasing new properties.

Profit Returns		Financial State	
Cash Flow	$6,797	Revenue	$42,638
Loan Paydown	$7,286	Expenses	$39,777
Appreciation	$8,598	Assets (Props. | Cash)	$438,472 | $95,013
Total	$22,680	Debt	$328,854
ROI	**25.8%**	Effective Tax Rate	5.0%

As shown in the table, Option 5: Home Equity Loan Without Purchasing New Properties modifies the financial state of your baseline by

- decreasing your cash flow from $8,760 to $6,797,
- increasing your loan paydown from $6,369 to $7,286,
- not changing your appreciation,
- slightly increasing your expenses from $38,731 to $39,777,
- decreasing your assets from $485,798 to $438,472 but increasing your cash assets from $48,201 to $95,013,
- increasing your debt from $266,656 to $328,854,
- decreasing your ROI from 27 to 25.8 percent, and
- decreasing your effective tax rate from 8.8 to 5.0 percent.

The real advantage of Option 5 is the increase in your cash assets, which reaches $95,013 in the example. You might choose this option if you want the funds available while you wait for a good investment or if your first mortgages are mature. In the case of the latter (the mature state of those first mortgages), your return from the loan paydown will be substantial, and resetting with a new loan may not be in your best interest. Lastly, the typical closing costs for a home equity loan are lower than a cash-out refinance, which provides you with more cash.

Option 6: Home Equity Loan and Purchasing Two New Properties

Building Block 7. The financial breakdown for Option 6: Home Equity Loan with Two New Property Purchases is shown below in Table 34.

Table 34. State of the portfolio after a home equity loan with two new properties.

Profit Returns		Financial State	
Cash Flow	$13,337	Revenue	$76,238
Loan Paydown	$12,521	Expenses	$71,764
Appreciation	$15,398	Assets (Props. | Cash)	$778,472 | $17,576
Total	$41,355	Debt	$600,854
ROI	**47.0%**	Effective Tax Rate	4.3%

As shown in the table, Option 6 modifies the financial state of your baseline by

- increasing your cash flow from $8,760 to $13,337,
- increasing your loan paydown from $6,369 to $12,521,
- increasing your appreciation from $8,598 to $15,398,
- increasing your expenses from $38,731 to $71,764,

- increasing your assets from $485,798 to $778,472 but decreasing your cash assets from $48,201 to $17,576,
- increasing your debt from $266,656 to $600,854,
- increasing your ROI from 27 to 47 percent, and
- decreasing your effective tax rate from 8.8 to 4.3 percent.

Option 6 is another very aggressive option that can rapidly expand your portfolio. While this option results in two new purchases, your cash assets are still respectively high at $17,576. The enhanced cash flow from Option 6 and your cash assets will quickly award you sufficient funds to purchase a third property for your portfolio.

This option is best employed during the early or middle expansion phase because of its higher risk. Again, your risk is lowered if the leases for the initial properties in your portfolio have been recently renewed, preferably with two-year leases. Due to the potential difficulty in finding a lender for a home equity loan, the enhanced performance of Option 6 may not be worth the effort when the results from a cash-out refinance offer similar results.

Option 7: Home Equity Line of Credit Without Purchasing New Properties

Building Block 8. The portfolio breakdown for Option 7: Home Equity Line of Credit Without Purchasing New Properties is shown below in Table 35.

Table 35. State of the portfolio after a home equity line of credit without purchasing new properties.

Profit Returns		Financial State	
Cash Flow	$8,760	Revenue	$42,638
Loan Paydown	$6,369	Expenses	$38,731
Appreciation	$8,598	Assets (Props. | Cash)	$438,472 | $116,611
Total	$23,727	Debt	$266,656
ROI	**27.0%**	Effective Tax Rate	8.7%

As shown in the table, Option 7 modifies the financial state of your baseline by

- not changing your cash flow,
- not changing your loan paydown,
- not changing your appreciation,
- not changing your expenses,
- decreasing your assets from $485,798 to $438,472 but increasing your cash assets from $48,201 to $116,611,
- not changing your debt,
- not changing your ROI, and
- slightly decreasing your effective tax rate from 8.8 to 8.7 percent.

As shown, the financial state is exactly the same as the baseline except your cash assets are greatly enhanced. The HELOC balance is listed as part of your cash assets even though it is actually a line of credit. If a draw occurs from the HELOC, your debt and expenses will increase. Option 7 is excellent if you are waiting to find a good investment or to reposition before a recession as your expenses will not change until you draw funds.

A word of caution is warranted: The interest rate for HELOCs is variable. If the market weakens, there is a good chance the interest rate will increase, which will, in turn, increase the monthly payment to service the HELOC debt. Fortunately, you will not have a monthly payment unless you spend some of the HELOC, just as would be the case for credit card payments.

Option 8: HELOC with Three New Purchases

Building Block 9. The last building block option we will cover is Option 8: HELOC with Three New Purchases. The financials for this option are shown below in Table 36.

Table 36. State of the portfolio after a home equity line of credit with purchasing three new properties.

Profit Returns		Financial State	
Cash Flow	$16,855	Revenue	$93,038
Loan Paydown	$14,199	Expenses	$88,598
Appreciation	$18,798	Assets (Props. | Cash)	$948,472 | $276
Total	$49,978	Debt	$751,900
ROI	**56.7%**	Effective Tax Rate	3.7%

As shown in the table, Option 8 modifies the financial state of your baseline by

- increasing your cash flow from $8,760 to $16,855,
- increasing your loan paydown from $6,369 to $14,199,
- increasing your appreciation from $8,598 to $18,798,
- increasing your expenses from $38,731 to $88,598,
- increasing your assets from $485,798 to $948,472 but decreasing your cash assets from $48,201 to $276,
- increasing your debt from $266,656 to $751,900,

- increasing your ROI from 27 to 56.7 percent, and
- decreasing your effective tax rate from 8.8 to 3.7 percent.

Option 8, yet another very aggressive option, will result in doubling the size of your portfolio at the cost of reducing your cash assets to essentially $0. Moreover, some of the funds used to purchase the three new properties are tied to a variable interest rate loan.

After the draw period, the debt service will increase substantially. As mentioned in **Example 25.4 Projected Financial Performance and Scaling for Cash Flow and Appreciation Properties**, the revenue gained from a rental property has historically grown at a faster rate than its expenses. This additional revenue will likely service the larger debt of the full principal and interest payment during the repayment period. If the market turns before the advantages of this option bear fruit, you may find yourself in a bad position. For this reason, Option 8 is best utilized early in the expansion phase and is best suited if you have a strong financial situation that can help hedge your risk.

A summary of all these home equity options (options 1 through 8) is shown below in Table 37.

Table 37. Summary of the refinance options.

	Base	Opt. 5	Opt. 6	Opt. 7	Opt. 8
Cash Flow ($)	8,760	6,797	13,337	8,760	16,855
Loan Paydown ($)	6,369	7,286	12,521	6,369	14,199
Appreciation ($)	8,598	8,598	15,398	8,598	18,798
Expenses ($)	38,731	39,777	71,764	37,731	88,598
Assets ($)	485,798	438,472	778,472	438,472	948,472

	Base	Opt. 5	Opt. 6	Opt. 7	Opt. 8
Cash Assets ($)	48,201	95,013	17,576	116,611	276
Debt	266,656	328,854	600,854	266,656	751,900
ROI (%)	27.0	25.8	47.0	27.0	56.7
Effective Tax Rate (%)	8.8	5.0	4.3	8.7	3.7

Table 38, shown below, should help you make a side-by-side comparison of all eight options.

Table 38. Percent change in the financials for the baseline case for the eight options evaluated.

	Opt. 1	Opt. 2	Opt. 3	Opt. 4	Opt. 5	Opt. 6	Opt. 7	Opt. 8
Cash Flow	36.3	74.5	16.8	93.1	-22.4	52.2	0	92.4
Loan Paydown	-13.8	27.2	-2.9	79.1	14.4	96.6	0	123
Appreciation	0	39.5	0	79.1	0	79.1	0	119
Expenses	-5.9	35.4	-3.3	79.2	2.7	85.3	0	129
Assets	-9.7	25.3	-9.7	60.2	-9.7	60.2	-9.7	95.2
Cash Assets	0	-81.1	73.7	-88.5	97.1	-63.5	141.9	-99.4
Debt	5.2	56.2	18.6	120.6	23.3	125.3	0	182
ROI	9.6	49.3	5.6	84.1	-4.4	74.1	0	110
Effective Tax Rate	3.4	-12.5	-8	-29.5	-43.2	-51.1	-1.1	-58

The numbers shown correspond to the percent change in the baseline based on each option. For example, Option 8 increases

- the cash flow by 92.4 percent from the baseline,
- the loan paydown by 123 percent,
- the appreciation by 119 percent,
- the expenses by 129 percent,
- the assets by 95.2 percent,
- the cash assets by -99.4 percent,
- the debt by 182 percent,
- the ROI by 110 percent, and
- the effective tax rate by -58 percent.

By summarizing the results into one table, it becomes much easier to compare the eight options. If your goal was to maximize your cash assets, you might select Option 7, which corresponds to the option with the largest increase in your cash assets. At this point, we'll return to the steps in the business scaling checklist.

Step 9. Determine how many years have passed since the beginning of the last real estate recession.

The purpose of this step is to identify which phase the market is in with respect to the real estate market cycle. The last real estate recession began in 2007 and bottomed out in 2009. For the purpose of this example, let's assume you were evaluating scaling options during the summer of 2021. The number of years from the beginning of the last real estate recession to 2021 is fourteen:

$$2021 - 2007 = 14 \text{ years.}$$

Remember, the average period for the real estate market cycle is 18.6 years, and the shortest and longest periods were seventeen and twenty-one years, respectively. At fourteen years in, the current market cycle likely has three to five years until it ends. Remember, though, the last phases of the market cycle are not the best times to expand your portfolio, at least not without exercising caution.

Step 10. Determine whether it's a buyer's market or a seller's market.

For this step, evaluate market-generated data and determine whether it is a seller's or a buyer's market. For a strong seller's market, I would consider the different selling options discussed earlier in **Chapter 27 Selling Properties**. The selling option might be advantageous if you have a lot of carryover losses as these losses can be used to offset capital gain tax, although using a 1031 tax exchange is likely still the better option.

Step 11. Estimate the likely phase for the real estate market.

Your calculations in steps 9 and 10 will provide a lot of insight into determining the phase of the market cycle. Additionally, you should consider what is going on in regard to market-generated data, which you can then compare to the discussion about the different phases defined back in **Chapter 10 The Real Estate Market Cycle**.

For example, between 2016 to 2019, the market was in the expansion phase. In the summer of 2021, demand for housing was high, appreciation rates were high, and the number of new builds was starting to ramp up but were still low compared to the available inventory. In 2021, the market was likely in the last quarter of the expansion phase. Remember, the average period for the real estate market cycle is 18.6 years, and, by 2021, the cycle had lasted for fourteen years. Again, this points toward it being the last quarter of the expansion phase.

Step 12. Build a plan based on market-generated data and then take action. The plan from the checklist (in other words, taking my plan and tailoring it to design a plan that fits your goals and resources) is summarized below.

- Recession Phase: Buy property only after the bottom of the market. Look for cash flow or appreciation properties

tenanted with two-year leases, depending on your personal goals.
- Recovery Phase: Buy cash flow or appreciation properties with two-year leases.
- Expansion Phase:
  - ◊ Early in the expansion phase—buy appreciation or cash flow properties.
  - ◊ Middle of the expansion phase—buy cash flow properties with two-year leases.
  - ◊ Last quarter of the expansion phase—Consider waiting to buy. Only buy cash flow properties with two-year leases that are producing $300 per month or greater than 20 percent (preferably closer to 30 percent) of the gross rent. Use the current cash flow as a bellwether indicator for the market. Instead, focus on financing options that increase cash flow, reduce debt, and/or increase reserve fund.
- Hyper Supply Phase—wait to buy properties. Instead, focus on financing options and strategies that increase cash flow, reduce debt, and increase the reserve fund.

Notice that the process outlined includes no step about listening to outside noise. When I am evaluating my options, I do not listen to real estate agents telling me that the market could not possibly go down. Nor do I listen to turnkey providers insisting that I should purchase properties that were cash flow-negative because of the anticipated appreciation.

Instead, the process is very much about evaluating the options based on market-generated data. During the evaluation, if I do not find rental properties that fit my purchase criteria, I do not make a purchase. If you don't find any properties that fit yours, consider it a clear signal that buying may not be a good idea and won't help you accomplish your goals and objectives.

There will be many who feel that sitting out of the market because it seems to be in the last quarter of the expansion phase or hyper supply phase is foolish since there is no exact method to determine when the next real estate recession will occur. For those with this mindset, adjust the criteria provided here to suit your risk tolerance, but understand, buying at the height of the market before a recession could cost you many years and money to recover. Moreover, the returns from the turnkey rental business are already excellent. Most times, it is worth being content with a good return instead of squeezing for more at a substantial risk.

My personal preference has always been to err on the side of caution when investing. For those who do buy at the wrong time and then find themselves deeply underwater, take comfort in knowing that the value will most likely increase to above what you purchased it for, as long as you selected a good property in a desirable location. Hopefully, you will receive monthly cash flow while you wait.

I do think a strong portfolio of single-family rentals that are cash flow properties represents a lower-risk investment in real estate. This is one of the perks of rental investing—even when the market goes into a recession, and the value of your portfolio drops down as much as 30 percent, depending on the type of real estate, it will still produce monthly income. The single-family houses advocated in this book should still perform during a recession. I am not against other asset classes; I just prefer the lower risk associated with this methodology.

In summary, we discussed how to execute the action items for the business scaling section in the **Monthly Business Management Checklist**. The objectives were to

- illustrate how a portfolio scales up using real financial numbers based on the actual numbers for some of the properties in my portfolio,
- achieve scaling mostly by utilizing different financial instruments to access the equity in your properties such as

refinancing or selling, and
- learn to evaluate options—which is all about looking at how the different options modify your financial state (cash flow, expenses, debt, and assets) and then selecting the option that best achieves your goals.

Now that you better understand how to scale, let's discuss other long-term plans such as succession, i.e., passing the business to an heir(s) or selling the business.

CHAPTER 30

SUCCESSION PLANS

A succession plan refers simply to how you plan to exit your business when ready to retire. This chapter presents two approaches:

- Passing the business to heirs
- Selling the business off one property at a time

These strategies are in addition to the strategies discussed earlier in **Chapter 27 Selling Properties**. The discussion that follows is intended as an introduction to succession plans and, as such, should also assist you in having a more informed discussion with your estate attorney on the matter.

Passing To Heirs

For many, determining a succession plan dedicated to passing the turnkey rental business to their heirs is important, while others might be more interested in selling their business. Turnkey rental businesses are set up to operate independently of the owner, making it an ideal choice to leave to a successor with relative ease.

A business can be transferred to an heir or another person by

1. selling them the business,
2. bequeathing the business as a gift and drawing income from the new owner,
3. selling with seller financing as previously discussed, or
4. selling part of the business and retaining some of the assets for income.

Options 1, 3, and 4 are selling options and were already discussed in **Chapter 27 Selling Properties**. As for bequeathing the business as a gift, each year, you gift a portion of the business to your heir. For tax purposes, there are annual limits for gifts; thus, depending on the size of your business, you might be able to slowly transfer the business without paying too much transfer tax. This option centers around how gifts are coded for tax purposes, so be certain to build the plan with your CPA and estate attorney.

Establishing a succession plan, beyond this quick introduction, is outside the scope of this book. However, as mentioned, the brief description provided can help start your conversion for developing a succession plan with the appropriate professional.

Selling the Business Off One Property at a Time

This exit strategy, which some investors utilize to slowly exit their business without paying capital gain taxes, is simple. After the property has served as a rental, notify the property management team that you will not renew the lease. Then, move into the property and, after living in it for two years and one day, sell it.

The property is then treated as a personal residence for tax purposes because you, the seller, lived there for two of the last five years. At the time of this writing, no capital gain taxes are applied to profits below $250,000 (for filing single) and $500,000 (for married, filing jointly) if the property is a personal residence. The plan after selling is to move into another recently vacated rental property and repeat the process.

Developing a succession plan for your business comes down to establishing objectives, seeking professional help, and building a plan that you will modify over time. The treatment here is purposely short but should point you in the right direction to get started. Now that we've concluded our discussion on long-term strategies, let's move on to **Part Eight**, which is all about taxes and retirement accounts.

PART EIGHT:
TAXES AND RETIREMENT ACCOUNTS

CHAPTER 31

REAL ESTATE TAXES

All investment vehicles have distinct advantages and disadvantages. For example, one advantage of long stock positions is the liquidity of the shares; however, real estate is usually treated as an illiquid investment since buying and selling property typically takes months. Hence, properties are not easily converted to cash. While the illiquidity of property, in itself, can be considered a disadvantage, it also comes with some pros such as slowing down the number of emotional transactions from market participants during challenging times.

One advantage of real estate is the ability to purchase property with borrowed funds. This book has spent a fair amount of time discussing loans, leverage, and leveraged returns. In my opinion, leveraged returns, which represent the enhanced ROI caused by purchasing with borrowed funds, is one of the two biggest advantages of rental properties. The other—and perhaps the biggest advantage—is the tax benefits, which include

- depreciation,
- not having to pay social security and Medicare taxes from the rental income if the income is taxed as passive income,

and
- the 1031 tax exchange.

The Tax Benefits of Rental Property Investing

The objectives of this section are to

1. identify, define, and list the benefits of the different tax advantages listed above,
2. provide the framework to compute the tax savings for each tax saving benefit, and
3. discuss how to include the tax benefits in the evaluation process for purchasing and refinancing properties.

I've built in this framework to demonstrate the importance and magnitude of the tax benefits for the taxation of rental properties. Once your framework is in place for tax benefits, you can adopt tax-specific criteria into your business plan. That being said, the framework and examples established here are for typical rental properties. These examples illustrate the concepts only; results can and will vary depending on each specific situation.

Generally speaking, real estate taxation can be broken into two categories: annual taxes and one-time tax events. Annual taxes are the taxes paid every year for the taxable gains of the turnkey rental business while one-time tax events result from selling properties. The tax code and laws are constantly changing, so make sure to discuss them with your CPA.

Annual Taxes

You are required to file an annual tax return for your turnkey real estate business. The specific requirements will depend on your business structure, which simply refers to how the properties are titled and how the business is structured. For example, the properties could be titled in your personal name, a limited liability company (LLC), a trust, or some sort of combination. The business owner has the option to tax their LLC as

- an s-corporation (s-corp),
- a c-corporation (c-corp), or
- a sole proprietor.

Various advantages and disadvantages come with those three structures, a discussion of which is beyond the scope of this text. The structure that you decide is best for your business now may alter as the financial performance of the business changes. It is best to talk with your CPA every year or even every quarter so that you do not miss out on any tax-related opportunities and can amend your long-term plan as appropriate.

Annual Tax Example

Let's look at a simple example, which is meant to

1. illustrate how to compute the tax savings for a typical property,
2. illustrate how much money is saved,
3. provide a working definition for the different tax benefits, and
4. use the model to scale the benefit to a portfolio of properties.

To begin, let's assume the property's financial performance at the end of the year is as shown below in Table 39. The annual gross revenue (annual rent collected) was $12,300. The allowable business expenses include.

- property tax of -$1,469,
- property insurance of -$478,
- mortgage interest of -$4,404,
- property management of -$984, and
- depreciation of -$3,488.

Table 39. Example property financials.

Property Pro Forma	
Purchase Price	$119,900
Revenue from Rent	$12,300
Property Tax	-$1,469
Property Insurance	-$478
Mortgage Interest	-$4,404
Property Management	-$984
Depreciation	-$3,488

Other expenses for the property would likely include

- repairs and maintenance,
- leasing fees,
- office supplies, and
- professional services.

Many other expenses could qualify as business expenses, so be sure to discuss the matter with your CPA. For simplicity, the list above includes all the fixed expenses for the property and are the only expenses under consideration for this example.

Your taxable income, the income reported to the Internal Revenue Service (IRS), is calculated as the difference between the gross revenue and the allowable business expenses. Looking at Table 39, your total allowable expenses are $10,823:

$1,469 + $478 + $4,404 + $984 + $3,488 = $10,823.

For this example, your taxable income is $1,477:

$12,300 - $10,823 = $1,477.$

The income taxes owed are given as your tax bracket times the taxable income. If your tax bracket is 24 percent, the income tax or tax liability comes to $354:

$24\% \times \$1,477 = \$354.$

The property made a profit of $4,965 for the year; you'll notice that the profits exceed the taxable income of $1,477. This is because the expenses shown are much higher than the actual cash expenses paid by your business. Your business did not actually pay $3,488 for depreciation. Instead, depreciation lowered your taxable income, which lowered your tax liability and resulted in an effective tax rate lower than your tax bracket.

The effective tax rate is given as the income tax paid divided by the actual earnings. For this example, your effective tax rate is approximately 7.1 percent:

$\$354 / \$4,965 = 7.1\%.$

That is, the depreciation expense reduced the tax bracket from 24 to 7.1 percent, illustrating how powerful depreciation is in real estate investing and why I've listed it in this book as an amazing benefit.

Depreciation

Depreciation is a non-capital expense that represents the anticipated cost of the property wearing out over time. The previous example illustrated the power of depreciation by reducing the tax rate. In Chapter 7, we discussed the concept behind depreciation and how it contributes to a return on your investment. Here, we are going to build on that concept by taking a deeper dive into the actual effects that depreciation can have on your taxes.

Recall that the IRS allows for depreciation to be claimed every year for 27.5 years. Since depreciation is considered an expense, it can then be used to offset taxes. You can calculate the return from the depreciation expense by

(1) determining your original cost basis and depreciation basis,
(2) dividing your depreciation basis by 27.5 years, and then
(3) multiplying by your tax bracket.

The original cost basis refers to the purchase price when you first purchased the property. To determine the depreciation basis, separate the original cost basis into the price of the land and the price of the building. There are several methods to separate the original cost basis into the building and land value, for example:

1. Asking your CPA to separate the original cost basis (adjusted purchase price) into the land and building values by multiplying the basis by 0.8. Your CPA does this by assuming the building value is 80 percent of the basis, which is not always accurate but does hold for most properties.
2. Using the tax assessment from the county auditor's website. Review the auditor's website because sometimes the building value is closer to 90 percent of the purchase price.
3. Having the property appraised (not recommended).

For this example, the purchase price (original cost basis) was $119,900. So, the cost of just the building comes to $95,920:

$$\$119,900 \times 0.8 = \$95,920.$$

The cost of the building then becomes your depreciation basis. To determine how much of the depreciation basis can be used for tax purposes each year, you then move on to Step 2 and divide by 27.5, which gives $3,488:

$$\frac{\$95,920}{27.5} = \$3,488.$$

As shown above and in Table 39, $3,488 is the amount of depreciation you can claim in Year 1. To determine your return from depreciation, you then want to multiply your claimable depreciation amount by your tax bracket. For this example, I used the 24-percent tax bracket. The result is $838:

$$\$3,488 \times 0.24 = \$838$$

This is your return from depreciation and reduces your overall tax bill by $838. The estimate for the depreciation return

(1) assumes that the property was owned for the entire tax year,
(2) does not take into consideration whether the depreciation expense reduces the taxable income into a lower tax bracket, and
(3) assumes that the entire depreciation expense is eligible to reduce your taxable income.

Regardless of these limitations to the estimated return, using the method above to estimate the depreciation return should allow you to quickly evaluate the tax impact when evaluating a new property.

When consulting with your CPA, be sure they use the entire purchase price as the building value if you have a condo and you do not own the land. CPAs will typically default to 80 percent without looking at the details, which could result in lower depreciation. For example, if the purchase price was $200,000, the difference in the depreciation deduction between 0.8 and 0.9 is $727 per year:

$$(0.9 - 0.8) \times \$200,000 / 27.5 = \$727 \text{ per year.}$$

For a condo of the same price, this would result in lowering your depreciation by double or $1,455 per year. The bottom line: Make sure to discuss these issues with your CPA and always ask questions.

As mentioned, the above example for the depreciation expense holds for all years of service except for the first and last years. During the first and last year of service, the depreciation is prorated, which is defined as a distribution of a quantity (in this example, depreciation) over a shorter time period.

For example, $1,000 per month prorated over two weeks is $500.

The prorated values shown below in Table 40 for depreciation were provided by the IRs (at the time of this writing).

Table 40. Depreciation Rates for Property Service Dates.

Service Date of the Property	Percentage of Cost Basis
January	3.485%
February	3.182%
March	2.879%
April	2.576%
May	2.273%
June	1.970%
July	1.667%
August	1.364%
September	1.061%
October	0.758%
November	0.455%
December	0.152%

The full-year depreciation rate is 3.6364 percent:

$$1 / 27.5 = 3.6364\%.$$

If you purchase a property in March, the service date is in March, and the first-year depreciation rate would be 2.879 percent. The corresponding depreciation expense in Year 1 would be $2,762:

$$2.879\% \times \$119,000 \times 0.8 = \$2,762.$$

To determine the depreciation expense for the twenty-seventh year of service, simply take the sum of all the depreciation claimed in previous years and subtract that figure from the depreciation basis. Again, for the example provided, the depreciation basis is $95,920, and the total depreciation claimed at the end of twenty-seven years of service would be $94,449.54. Hence, the depreciation expense for the last year of service is $2,470:

$$\$95,920 - \$94,450 = \$2,470.$$

One last note on depreciation: It may seem complicated, but do not let it intimidate you. Instead, find an experienced CPA who can handle your taxes and provide tax-related advice for your business. Remember to efficiently implement the Master Checklist outlined in Chapter 2. You do not need to be a tax professional, a lawyer, or any other such professional. You need only know how to interview and hire the right qualified professionals. The questionnaires included in the section **Appendix B: Questionnaires** are intended to streamline this process, thereby increasing your likelihood of hiring top talent.

Expenses for Real Estate Professionals vs. Non-Real Estate Professionals

There can be some limitations to how expenses are treated based on your classification as a real estate professional or a non-real estate professional for rental taxation.

For the first option, classifying yourself as a real estate professional, expect your rental income to be taxed as active income (ordinary income). Real estate professionals can, as of the time of this writing, offset their total taxable income with a loss reported by their turnkey rental business. They must also pay self-employment tax based on their earnings.

The profits of a turnkey rental business for non-real estate professionals, on the other hand, are taxed as passive income. For taxpayers who fall into this category, no self-employment tax must be paid on your rental income; however, there are restrictions on how a reported loss (passive loss) from your turnkey rental business can be applied to your ordinary taxable income. The reported passive loss from your turnkey rental business may be eligible to offset your ordinary taxable income, but you will run into caps based on how much money you made for that year. For high earners, you will not be eligible to lower your taxable income based on your reported loss from your turnkey rental business. Instead, the loss becomes a carryover loss, which can be used to offset taxable gains in later years.

To illustrate carryover losses, let's return to the Annual Tax Example from earlier in this chapter. The taxable income was given as:

Property Revenue - Allowable Business Expenses.

Let's assume the allowable business expenses totaled $13,000. The property revenue was $12,300, which yields a taxable income of -$700:

$12,300 - $13,000 = -$700.

If you are classified as a real estate professional, you could offset your taxable income by the reported loss of $700. If unable to offset your taxable income by that loss, then the $700 becomes a carryover loss, which can be applied in later years to offset your taxes.

Determining whether you are eligible to be treated as a real estate professional for tax purposes is beyond the scope of this book. The reason: I have been given different answers on the subject from different CPAs. This is almost certainly because my specific situation has changed over the years. Please speak with your CPA, as their answer and advice will be dependent on your specific situation.

Adjusting the Cost Basis

As mentioned briefly in previous sections in this chapter, the original cost basis for the rental property can be adjusted for various reasons. For example, the basis might include the purchase price, the closing costs, and renovation expenses made to the property. The basis might also be the estimated value when the property was put into service, which could vary significantly from the purchase price if the time between purchasing and putting the property into service is extensive (years). Adjusting the basis of rental properties is beyond the scope of this text; however, I wanted to mention this so that individuals who might qualify for an adjustment are aware of it.

How to Include the Depreciation Return in Your Business Plan

At this point, you should have a sufficient foundation regarding how depreciation works and how it can affect your portfolio; now, let's discuss ways your depreciation return can be incorporated into your overall business plan. We will discuss the topic presented in this section based on how it affects two different groups:

- For Real Estate Professionals
- For Non-Real Estate Professionals

For Real Estate Professionals

For investors classified as real estate professionals who choose to invest in high price point rentals with large depreciation expenses and low cash flow, the negative taxable income from the portfolio can substantially lower your taxable ordinary income. The return from depreciation, which is the reduction of the tax expense, increases with the tax bracket.

If interested in this approach, it is important to remember that the cash flow covers day-to-day business expenses such as maintenance and repairs and tenant turnover. The negative cash flow predicted in **Example 25.4 Projected Financial Performance and Scaling for Cash Flow and Appreciation Properties** applies to a fully leveraged position. Lowering the leverage (with a higher down payment) will result in positive cash flow and a position with lower risk. Remember, however, the strategy of building a portfolio of appreciation properties is best suited to high-income individuals, especially if they will be treated as real estate professionals for tax purposes.

For Non-Real Estate Professionals

For non-real estate professionals, it is not advantageous to accrue carryover losses. While such losses can be used in later years to offset taxes, the value of the carryover losses, i.e., your buying power, will be reduced by inflation, which is why I prefer to not deal with these losses. For passive investors (those taxed as non-real estate professionals), my preferred strategy is to select cash flow properties that result in a tax liability as close to $0 as possible for your situation.

In practice, achieving a tax liability of $0 without carryover loss is very hard if not impossible because of variable operational expenses such as maintenance and tenant turnover. A more realistic goal is to select properties or lending options that modify your portfolio so that your effective tax rate is below 5 percent.

Based on the historical performance of rentals, we know that the revenue they provide tends to grow at a faster rate than expenses. Hence, the carryover losses accumulated during the early years of your business will likely offset your income tax during later years. Your goal is to try to minimize the number of years your carryover losses will sit unused.

Tax Example for Real Estate Professional

To summarize the discussion thus far and further reinforce the power of rental taxation, I've included this example: Assume you are classified as a real estate professional for tax purposes and own a turnkey rental business with a portfolio of many properties. Further, assume your profit at the end of the year was $50,000, and the reported taxable income at that time showed a loss of $60,000. Lastly, assume your ordinary taxable income from a job equals $100,000. Your gross income for the year was $150,000:

REAL ESTATE TAXES

$$100,000 + 50,000 = 150,000.$$

Your taxable income, therefore, is $40,000:

$$100,000 - 60,000 = 40,000.$$

Since tax amounts are separated into earning brackets, the amount you pay is separated as well. The income tax you will owe using the most recent single-filer tax brackets is as follows:

1. The first $10,275 you earned is taxed at 10 percent.
2. Any amount greater than $10,275 and up to $41,775 is taxed at 12 percent.
3. Any amount from $41,776 to $89,075 is taxed at 22 percent.
4. Any amount from $89,076 to $170,050 is taxed at 24 percent.

So, the taxes you pay on your taxable income of $40,000 will be $4,594:

$$\text{Taxes Paid} = 0.10 \times (\$10,275) + 0.12 \times (\$40,000 - \$10,276)$$
$$= \$4,594$$

The income taxes you would owe, assuming you do not own a turnkey rental business, equals $17,835:

$$\text{Taxes Paid} = 0.10 \times (\$10,275) + 0.12 \times (\$41,775 - \$10,276) + 0.22 \times (\$89,075 - \$41,776) + 0.24 \times (\$100,000 - 89,075) = \$17,835$$

To summarize, your tax expense would be $4,594. Without the portfolio, you would have paid $17,835 in taxes. The addition of the portfolio saved you $13,241 in taxes:

$$\$17,835 - \$4,594 = \$13,241.$$

This results in a $50,000 increase of your gross annual revenue. While this example reflects an extreme case, it still clearly illustrates the power of depreciation expense and rental taxation, especially as it relates to a large portfolio of properties. In my opinion, this is a pretty impressive result.

1031 Tax Exchange

As we saw in the last section, depreciation is a very powerful tax-saving expense. Unfortunately, after 27.5 years, you can no longer claim depreciation for that property. The good news: You can use another excellent tax-saving vehicle called the 1031 tax exchange, which will

- reset depreciation and
- delay paying capital gains and depreciation recapture when a property is sold.

What is the 1031 Tax Exchange?

This type of exchange occurs when you sell a property and then use the funds from that sale to purchase another property. Specific rules must be followed exactly when you use this procedure to avoid paying taxes on the capital gains.

a. The property you purchase must be under contract three months after you sell, and closing must occur one year after you sell.
b. The property or properties you purchase must have a combined appraised value that is at least the same as the property you sold.
c. The money earned by selling the property cannot ever be placed into your personal or business account.

If concerned about the time constraints presented in regulation (A) above, don't fret. The time requirements for a 1031 exchange are normally not an issue since a good turnkey provider typically sends multiple properties per week that meet your buying criteria if your criteria are similar to what is recommended in this book.

For regulation (C), if the money were to be transferred to your personal or business accounts, taxes are then owed. To properly keep track of these funds, the closing attorney or title company will open an escrow account in which to deposit those funds, which will then be used on the purchase side without you ever personally receiving them.

I am sure there are other rules involved, but those mentioned in the above list are sufficient to get you started. These and other regulations can always change, so be sure to check with the appropriate professionals.

How to Perform a 1031 Tax Exchange

The rules may seem like a real hurdle, but they are not as hard as they look. To perform a 1031 tax exchange, simply

1. give notice to your property management team that you are going to sell the property using a 1031 tax exchange and will not be renewing the lease,
2. wait for the property to be vacant if possible, and
3. notify the turnkey provider that you want to purchase properties using a 1031 exchange.

Regarding step (3), the turnkey provider will understand your request and will notify the title company or closing attorney. If you are selling with a real estate agent, inform that agent that the property will be used in a 1031 exchange. Make certain the title company or closing attorney understands this fact as well.

With that said, why would someone go through all this hassle? As always, let's illustrate with an example that shows regulation (B) in action. Let's say, you purchase a property for $119,900, and then, ten years later, its worth grows to $200,000. Let's assume that the mortgage balance is $77,000. The equity and gross proceeds from selling your property then comes to $123,000:

$$\$200{,}000 - \$77{,}000 = \$123{,}000.$$

Let's also assume that you have identified three properties worth $200,000 each for a total value of $600,000. This total value is much greater than the $200,000 value of the sold property; so, this meets criteria (B), mentioned above for the 1031 exchange.

Assuming a loan-to-value ratio of 80 percent results in a down payment of $40,000 per property:

$$80\% \times \$200,000 = \$40,000 \text{ per property.}$$

Therefore, the total down payment needed is $120,000:

$$\$40,000 \times 3 = \$120,000 \text{ in total for all 3 properties.}$$

Since the total needed to buy these three properties ($120,000) is less than the gross proceeds from selling ($123,000), sufficient funds will be left over to finance the purchase of the three properties.

The capital gain, without including any of the typical expenses when selling, comes to $80,100:

$$\$200,000 - \$119,900 = \$80,100.$$

Your expenses will reduce your capital gain, which will, in turn, lower your capital gain tax. For simplicity, I am ignoring any expenses involved. Let's assume the depreciation expense you claimed upon ownership of the property totals $34,880. For this example, without using a 1031 tax exchange, you would pay a capital gain tax on a capital gain of $80,100 and a depreciation recapture tax on the $34,880 depreciation expense. Thus, the total tax you would pay would equal $24,740.

By having to pay $24,740 in taxes, you would lower your gross profit to $98,260:

$$\$123,000 - \$24,740 = \$98,260$$

Since $98,260 is less than the $120,000 needed to purchase three more properties, you would only be able to purchase two more properties. By using a 1031 exchange, you can use the entire sum received at closing to trade one property for three properties without having to pay $24,740 in taxes.

Depreciation Reset

Say that the years remaining in which to depreciate the sold house was 17.5 years; if that is the case, you can reset the timeline using the 1031 tax exchange. Your new purchases would then have 27.5 years of depreciation. Moreover, the return from the depreciation for the sold property would be $831:

$$24\% \times 80\% \times \$119,900 / 27.5 = \$831.$$

The property, having appreciated to $200,000, would have a depreciation return of $1,386:

$$24\% \times 80\% \times \$200,000 / 27.5 = \$1,386.$$

The only way to realize the higher depreciation return would be to reset depreciation by exchanging the property. For this example, three properties were purchased, which resulted in a depreciation return of $4,158:

$$3 \times \$1,386 = \$4,158.$$

This is a substantial increase.

You can use a 1031 tax exchange to forgo paying capital gains and reset depreciation for as long as you want. I have heard about inherited properties that have delayed capital gains and depreciation recapture taxes for multiple generations using the 1031 tax exchange.

Capital Gain Tax

Capital gain taxes become due whenever you make a profit from selling a property. Your profit is taxed as a long-term capital gain or as ordinary income. Long-term capital gain tax refers to taxes paid from the profits made from selling a property you owned for longer than one year. Any profits from selling a property you have owned for less than one year are taxed as ordinary income, which will be at a higher rate than the long-term capital gain rate. In general, most if not all capital gain tax situations for a turnkey rental business will come in the form of long-term capital gain tax.

Lastly, personal residences have different, more favorable tax rules. A property is treated as a personal residence for tax purposes if you have resided in the property for two out of the last five years.

As of this writing, no taxes are owed when filing single if the profits from selling a personal residence are less than $250,000. For married couples filing jointly, no capital gain tax is applied to the sale of a personal residence for profits under $500,000.

How to Calculate Capital Gain Tax

The method used to calculate capital gain tax is a bit convoluted, but it is worth illustrating, which we will do by computing the capital gain tax for the property sold in the previous section. To summarize,

- the sold price was $200,000,
- the loan balance was $77,000, and
- the gross profit was $123,000.

The values used for the different expenses in the following example are shown below in Table 41.

Table 41. Tax-related expenses for capital gain taxes.

Cost Basis	**$119,900**
Depreciation	$34,880
Agent Commissions	$12,000
Closing Costs	$5,000
Repairs and Cleaning	$4,000
Carryover Losses	$5,000

The original cost basis simply refers to the price you paid to buy the property adjusted by your closing costs and renovation costs at the time of purchase. For selling purposes, the original cost basis can be adjusted for many different expenses outside of the selling expenses listed in the table. For a typical turnkey rental property, the adjusted cost basis is given as:

Adjusted Cost Basis
= Original Cost Basis - Depreciation
+ Suspended Losses + Agent Commissions
+ Closing Costs + Repairs

For the subject property, your adjusted cost basis of $111,200 is determined as follows:

$$\$119{,}900 - \$34{,}880 + \$5{,}000 + \$12{,}000 + \$5{,}000 + \$4{,}000$$
$$= \$111{,}020$$

The capital gain of $88,980 is given as the sale price minus the adjusted cost basis:

$$\$200{,}000 - \$111{,}020 = \$88{,}980.$$

Hence, a higher adjusted cost basis is beneficial for tax purposes. The next step is to calculate depreciation recapture—the gain realized from the sale due to selling a depreciable capital property. The depreciation tax rate (at the time of this writing) is 25 percent. To determine the depreciation recapture of $8,720, the following calculation is used:

Depreciation Recaptures
= Recapture Rate x Depreciation
= 0.25 x $34,880 = $8,720

The capital gain tax of $10,820 is determined as:

Capital Gain Tax
= (Capital Gain - Depreciation)
x Long Term Tax Rate
= ($88,980 - $34,880) x 0.2 = $10,820

The long-term tax rate is either 0, 15, or 20 percent and is dependent on your income and whether you are filing separately or married.

The total taxes owed equal $19,540:

$$Taxes = Capital\ Gain\ Tax + Depreciation\ Recapture$$
$$= \$10,820 + \$8,720 = \$19,540$$

This example is important to note for the following reasons:

1. The carryover losses that accumulated through the years are not lost. As shown, your carryover losses offset capital gain tax by increasing your cost basis.
2. In prior examples, we did not include how expenses could reduce the cost basis. This example included expenses, which lowered the original tax payment of $24,740 to $19,540.
3. Using a 1031 tax exchange is an option that can offset taxes and save you even more money. In this example, it saved $19,540.

I have heard stories in which investors have chosen not to claim depreciation and then sold their property, yet still had to deal with depreciation recapture. The reason: When adjusting the basis for the different selling expenses, the IRS states that the depreciation recapture is the **allowed OR allowable** depreciation.

The bottom line: Take depreciation each year, and, if you want to sell the property, try doing so using a 1031 tax exchange. If you want money from the property, look into refinancing and HELOC options. Also remember, the same argument about inflation and shorting the dollar holds here. Namely, the spending power of the money you receive from your depreciation return will be greater than the depreciation recapture if the value of the dollar goes down. Note: This ignores the different tax brackets involved.

To summarize our discussion of rental property taxes, the tax benefits for rental investing have a significant impact on the money you make from your portfolio. Though I kept the examples in this chapter simple, I hope to have at least conveyed the complexity of rental taxes. This level of complexity is exactly why you should prioritize partnering with a good CPA as part of your business plan.

CHAPTER 32

RETIREMENT ACCOUNTS

Retirement accounts can provide many tax advantages such as allowing your investments to grow tax-free. Several different types of retirement accounts will be explored in this section, including self-directed IRA and 401k plans. The purpose of this chapter is to provide a brief and limited review of these two retirement accounts since they could have some impact on your turnkey rental business.

Self-Directed IRA

You can use a self-directed IRA (traditional IRA) to build your turnkey rental portfolio. When using this IRA type, taxes are deferred to a later date. Specifically, you pay tax when you receive a distribution (when you receive funds from that retirement account). The funds in the account grow tax-free. At the time of this writing, receiving distributions before you are 59.5 years old results in a tax penalty. The traditional IRA also has an annual contribution limit that changes often.

In general, all retirement accounts come with government-mandated regulations, which include the types of investments you are allowed to invest in. Your ability to build and manage a turnkey rental business is greatly limited by such retirement account regulations. Make sure you understand the current rules and regulations because they change often (usually on a year-to-year basis), and many times, not to your benefit.

Disadvantages of Rental Investing in a Self-Directed IRA

Building a turnkey rental portfolio based on a self-directed IRA comes with many disadvantages, including but not limited to:

- Limited and/or unfavorable loan products.
- The tax benefits from real estate are nullified.
- All expenses must be paid from the IRA.
- The buying and selling process are complicated.

Unfavorable Loan Products

Qualifying for a loan to purchase rental properties with a traditional IRA is challenging. If you can find a lender, the loan products available through this method will have very unfavorable terms such as loan-to-value requirements of 50 percent, interest rates significantly greater than the market rates, and loan terms much shorter than thirty years.

Recall that the return from appreciation is a leveraged return in which the "lever" is approximately the ratio of the purchase price and the down payment. For a 50-percent loan-to-value ratio, you would need a down payment of 50 percent of the purchase price. In this scenario, the lever is two:

$$1 / 50\% = 2.$$

For a conventional loan that requires a down payment of 20 percent, the leverage will equal five, which is substantially greater. To put it in perspective, recall that the historical average appreciation rate for single-family rentals in the United States is 3.5 percent. The leveraged ROI for a lever of two and five is then 7 and 17.5 percent, respectively:

$$2 \times 3.5\% = 7\%;$$

$$5 \times 3.5\% = 17.5\%.$$

My personal preference is to make more money, meaning, I want access to better loan products. Further, by not using better loan products, you will not achieve the scaling indicated in **Example 25.4 Financial Performance and Scaling for Cash Flow and Appreciation Properties**. Moreover, my preference is to maintain as large of a hedge as possible against inflation, and that requires access to larger loan-to-value ratios.

Rental Property Tax Advantages are Nullified.

Another big disadvantage of holding investment property in a self-directed IRA is that the rental property tax benefits become nullified. The reason is simple: One requirement for using the retirement account is that all profits (cash flow and capital gains) must flow back into the retirement account. Since the funds in the retirement account grow tax-free, you do not file a tax return; hence, you do not pay taxes on the profits. This, in turn, makes you ineligible for those favorable real estate tax laws I mentioned.

Remember, if you are a real estate professional for taxation purposes, it is possible to reduce your W-2 income taxes. In this scenario, by using a self-directed IRA, you could actually INCREASE your tax bill. For non-real estate professionals, it is possible to earn cash flow and reduce the effective tax rate of your rental profits to $0. You cannot receive these funds. They will be restricted since they would go back into that retirement account. Even worse, you will pay tax on these funds when you begin taking contributions when you retire. These are taxes you would never have had to pay.

Lastly, you do not pay tax on the money received from a cash-out refinance. Unfortunately, a cash-out refinance would likely not even be possible. If you can manage it, it will be for a smaller dollar amount, and the funds will, again, be restricted by going into the retirement account. Again, you will pay tax on these funds when you take contributions during retirement, which you would not have had to pay to begin with.

From a logistical standpoint, the contribution limits are small. This will likely result in two pools of money to invest – your money in the self-directed IRA and your money not in your retirement account. You are forced to operate two different investment funds independently where one funding source (the retirement account), has built-in tax benefits and the second funding source has no built-in tax benefits.

Since I already have to work with two different pools of money, my personal preference is to use the tax benefits provided by a self-directed IRA for investments that do not have tax benefits such as stocks and options. I choose to invest in real estate using the funds outside of the retirement account where I can take advantage of the tax and lending-related benefits. An investor could choose to invest in real estate for both funding sources, but my preference is to diversify over multiple asset classes. Again, this is my personal investment criterion and may or may not be applicable to your goals and objectives.

Expenses Must be Paid from the IRA

All expenses must be paid from the IRA. With this restriction, you cannot easily contribute funds to replace a roof or some other large capital expenditure. Remember, the annual contribution limits are small and not likely to cover an unexpected, large capital expense. The only real solution is to maintain a large reserve fund within your IRA. The end result is a much lower ROI because you will have money in the account that is not performing.

Other disadvantages to this strategy include complications with selling and buying the property and executing your succession plans. You are also not allowed to use the property for anything outside of investment purposes.

To summarize, the only reason I would choose to use a self-directed IRA is to

1. lower my taxable income by making a contribution, and
2. take advantage of option trading and stocks that have no tax benefits.

In general, I do not recommend building a turnkey rental portfolio using a self-directed retirement account. I prefer to maintain as much control as possible over my assets, a hard thing to do with all the regulations in place and even more so since they are constantly changing.

401k Retirement Account Plan

A 401k can be broken into

1. a 401k with your employer's company and
2. a 401k with your own company.

401k from Your Employer

Your employer puts a lot of restrictions on this type of account, including the investment choices available to you. The returns tend to be low at 2 to 7 percent (with low-return investment options and high management fees). The best approach for this type of account is to contribute only the match because that way, there is a guaranteed ROI of 100 percent. You can then put some percentage of the funds to use with a better-performing investment vehicle. What I have done in the past is borrow such funds to buy turnkey properties.

401k from Your Own Company

As your turnkey rental business matures, the profits should increase and thus, at some point, it might be advantageous to change how the business is taxed from a sole proprietor to an s-corporation. Many serious tax considerations are beyond the scope of this book, so be certain to discuss this option with your CPA.

At any rate, if you choose to tax your business as an s-corporation, you will be treated as an employee of the business and can thus give yourself a salary. An option that then presents itself is you can then set up a 401k retirement account plan for the business. As an employee, you can participate in this retirement account. Because it is your business, you set up how the 401k account functions, granting you a lot more control over any potential restrictions. For this option, the only restrictions to consider are those that are government-mandated.

At the time of this writing, regulations allowed for a match of up to 25 percent. How the match works is fairly simple; for example, if your salary is set at $100,000, you have the option to contribute up to 25 percent of your salary to your 401k, which corresponds to $25,000:

$$25\% \times \$100{,}000 = \$25{,}000.$$

Your business would then match the contributed amount, resulting in a $50,000 yearly contribution to your 401k.

Furthermore, your tax liability on your salary is reduced from $100,000 to $75,000. You can make additional contributions beyond the 25 percent match as long as the total contribution (the contribution from the employer and the employee) doesn't exceed 100 percent of the employee's salary or is capped at $61,000 for people under fifty years old and at $67,500 for people fifty years old and older. Again, the regulations change on a yearly basis. The information provided here will certainly grow outdated quickly, so seek professional guidance.

Moreover, you can take a loan from your retirement account in the amount of 50 percent or $50,000, whichever is smaller. The interest paid for the loan is deposited into your retirement account. The borrowed funds can be used to purchase investment properties or be put to any other use. Again, many regulations and tax implications may apply. If you choose to utilize a retirement account in this capacity, it is crucial that you speak with your CPA.

Putting it All Together

When it comes to investing using retirement accounts, my general approach is to

- build my turnkey rental business outside of a retirement account so that I can take advantage of leverage, maintain a larger hedge against inflation, and capitalize on the many real estate-specific tax benefits available such as depreciation, a cash-out refinance, and a 1031 tax exchange;
- use a self-directed IRA for investment vehicles that do not have tax benefits such as stock and option trading;
- choose how to manage my accounts based on (1) the ROI, (2) the risk, and (3) my portfolio's needs and diversification; and
- listen to my CPA—if your CPA recommends it, set up a 401k if you change the taxation of your business from a sole proprietor to an s-corp.

Now that we've discussed this element of the turnkey rental business, let's move on to Part Nine, a short section dedicated to exploring other real estate investment strategies that are complementary to what you will experience while operating a turnkey rental business.

PART NINE:
BEYOND TURNKEY RENTAL INVESTING

CHAPTER 33

COMPLEMENTARY REAL ESTATE INVESTING STRATEGIES

Turnkey rental investing can, if properly implemented, be considered a low-risk investment strategy that builds your experience in the real estate investment industry. The experience you gain while operating your turnkey rental business will significantly reduce the risks involved with other, more complex real estate investment strategies.

Operating a turnkey rental business allows you to establish connections with real estate professionals, not to mention add to your experience regarding such business processes as selecting property management and insurance providers. In this regard, turnkey rental investing could easily be a gateway to more involved real estate investments such as:

- Converting Personal Residences into Rentals
- Buying, Renovating, and Leveraging Your Network

Converting Personal Residences into Rentals

You will find many lucrative reasons to convert your personal residence into a rental. Numerous investors have built their entire rental businesses using this strategy, which can be complementary to your turnkey rental business. For example, the profits from converting a personal residence can be used to scale up your turnkey rental business.

Converting your property into a rental offers many advantages, including

- a loan with potentially a lower down payment—as low as 5 percent at the time of this writing,
- a lower interest rate, and
- a tax advantage if you sell when it is still considered a personal residence.

The conversion requires some planning such as

- hiring a property management company,
- renovating the property into rent-ready condition,
- making sure the property is compliant with the local legal requirements for rentals such as having enough smoke detectors,
- maintaining compliance with the loan requirements, and
- maintaining compliance with your property insurance provider.

To date, I have converted two personal residences into rental properties. One property was recently sold; the other is still in my portfolio and now operates very much like one of my turnkey rental properties. That is, I manage the property once per month just as I do my other properties. The biggest difference: A converted personal residence has the potential to be far more profitable than a turnkey property.

The following quick example illustrates the advantages listed above to help you understand why this strategy might be attractive. Let's assume you buy a personal residence for $210,000 with a minimum down payment of 5 percent. If the closing costs are 3 percent, the invested funds will be small at approximately $16,800:

$$(5\% + 3\%) \times \$210{,}000 = \$16{,}800.$$

Because the down payment is below 20 percent, the lender will require that you pay private mortgage insurance (PMI).

Further assumptions include:

1. You have lived in the property for three years.
2. The loan balance details are: The balance equals $187,601 at a 3.5 percent interest rate with a thirty-year term.
3. The appreciation rate is 3.8 percent.
4. At the end of the three-year mark, interest rates are lower. So, at that point, you can refinance at a lower rate of 3.25 percent. This changes your LTV so that it is less than 80 percent, eliminating the need to pay PMI.

The fixed annual expenses after refinancing are shown below in Table 42.

Table 42. Fixed annual expenses for a personal residence conversion.

Fixed Expenses	Cost
Mortgage Interest	$6,041
Property Tax	$3,000
Property Insurance	$900
Property Management	$1,872
Depreciation	$7,185
HOA	$350
Total	**$19,348**

For the purposes of this example, the property tax and insurance were rounded up. Once the property is in service as a rental, the insurance will likely increase. The property insurance in Table 42 reflects the increased rate.

To turn a personal property into a rental property, some renovations must be done so that the home meets the proper requirements. For this example, let's assume $12,000 was spent renovating the property. Renovation can then be viewed as an expense and used to reduce the cost basis. Since the appraised value was approximately $235,000 at the time the property was placed into service, your CPA can then adjust the cost basis to $247,000 because of the renovation, which enhanced the depreciation expense.

The Year 1 rental rate was $1,950 per month, and the property was leased using a two-year lease in which the Year 2 rental rate was $2,000 per month. The four profit returns for the property are shown below in Table 43.

Table 43. Year 1 profits.

Four Profit Returns	Dollars
Cash flow, Annual	$7,480
Loan Paydown, Annual	$3,756
Appreciation	$8,930
Depreciation	$1,437
Total	$20,166*
The total does not include depreciation.	

As shown, the total return after Year 1 was $20,166. The results shown are clearly superior to the performance of a typical turnkey rental property. To further reinforce the performance, the cash ROI is given as 44.5 percent:

$$7{,}480 / \$16{,}800 = 44.5\%.$$

The annual cash flow of $7,480 is $623 per month, which is significantly more than the turnkey property with the caveat that it is an appreciation property. Lastly, the effective tax rate for the property was 7.2 percent. Revenue of $623 per month while only paying 7.2 percent in income tax is a very good outcome.

There is more to think about: Remember that the property is a personal residence for tax purposes. Let's assume you sold the property to your tenant at the end of the third year in which the property is leased. Though this is extremely difficult to accomplish, I want to illustrate the best-case scenario. At any rate, assume the property continues to appreciate at 3.8 percent, resulting in a value of approximately $253,000 when you sell it. The outstanding mortgage balance is $175,956, and your gross profit is $77,044:

$$\$253{,}000 - \$175{,}956 = \$77{,}044.$$

Assuming the closing costs are 3 percent of the purchase price puts the closing expenses at $7,590. The net profit is then $69,453, and *no capital gain taxes are owed*. The total return is approximately $91,895:

$$\$69{,}453 + \$7{,}480 \times 3 \text{ years} = \$91{,}895.$$

To further reinforce the power of the result, the ROI over three years is 547 percent and 182 percent per year:

$$\$91{,}895 / \$16{,}800 = 547\%;$$
$$547\% / 3 \text{ years} = 182\%/\text{year}.$$

If you decide not to sell early, your basis is $247,000, which will help reduce the capital gain tax. More importantly, you can use a 1031 tax exchange and defer the taxes.

For the purposes of transparency, the example provided is very similar to the property I sold. Hence, the numbers presented are accurate, with the exception that I used a lower appreciation rate for the example to illustrate a more typical result.

Many people use this strategy to build their portfolios. The plan is fairly simple: Purchase a property and live in it for at least two years and one day. At the end of two years, convert the property into a rental property. Prior to choosing this path, make sure that you check with the neighborhood HOA (if there is one). Some HOAs will not allow a personal residence to be converted into a rental property. If they do, they may have stipulations regarding this change.

If you choose to implement this strategy, be certain to review the loan documents; there may be specific requirements that must be met. For example, you may be required to live in the property for at least one or two years. You may also need to notify your lender.

Remember to also notify your property insurance company or your insurance broker when

- you move from the property,
- you put the property into service as a rental, and
- when the property is vacant between tenants.

The insurance company will need to update the insurance coverage to reflect that the property is now considered a rental property. Lastly, you are setting up a business. Speak with your estate and asset protection attorney on how to structure the business to reduce liability risk and protect your assets.

Buying, Renovating, and Leveraging Your Network

Recall that one of the benefits of renovating a property is the increase in equity from forced appreciation, which represents the gains from the renovation. The plan presented in this section is about identifying excellent buying opportunities for below-market deals in neighborhoods your turnkey providers operate in, and then renovate the property. Once the property is in move-in-ready condition, have your already proven management company handle property management.

Not all turnkey rental companies manage properties from outside sources. Understand, this is not a small step concerning your potential risk and time requirements. Success will hinge on your ability to market consistently for below-market deals and manage the contractors you hire to complete the renovations. Detailed instructions concerning these tasks are outside the scope of this book; however, many excellent resources are available on the topic. Look for books dedicated to wholesaling and house flipping, which will reference various systems you can use to find below-market deals and manage the renovation.

You can put to good use the two real estate investing strategies presented in this chapter by leveraging your turnkey rental experience. Do not limit yourself to only these two strategies as your experience will allow you to use many others. Regarding the latter strategy—operating as a more traditional rental investor—the risks are real, and you will need to carefully craft a plan to minimize those risks. Obviously, I would advocate that you develop a business checklist for each process.

WRAPPING UP

Before finishing, I want to dedicate a section toward wishing the best of luck to anyone who has read or even skimmed this book. I sincerely hope the information presented in these pages was helpful and that those who choose to take action will have success with their turnkey rental businesses. Remember, you are not alone. Many real estate investment organizations are out there and easy to join. These organizations can provide a wealth of information and, more importantly, a network of professionals you can connect with.

Lastly, you are always welcome to email me at:

scott@scottastanfield.com.

I do not have all the answers but am more than willing to help if I can. Do not hesitate to send comments or questions regarding this book as well. The feedback will certainly help me grow. Who knows? If the demand is there, I will likely release a new, up-to-date edition, or at the very least, can provide up-to-date information on my website at:

https://scottastanfield.com.

That said, the plan going forward is to keep building and adding tools for turnkey rental investing, which I will continue to make available for free on my website. Some examples in this book may have been challenging to follow, and it is my intent to incorporate those onto my website as well. My plan is to use pre-populated Google Sheet documents, which will be listed on my website so that those in need can adjust the values as necessary to model their unique scenarios. Lastly, please provide feedback about any topics you found difficult to understand. I will include instructional videos to help clarify topics based on the feedback I receive on my YouTube channel (TheTurnkeyRentalGuide). Sometimes a written document does not convey information as well as a video. With that, I wish everyone great success in their investment careers. Thank you for reading.

APPENDIX A: CHECKLISTS

Master Checklist

Objective: Provide a logical order for the action items and day-to-day tasks required to execute and manage the business plan for a turnkey rental business. Note: These are the action items for the turnkey rental business plan.

References: **Chapter 2 The Master Checklist for Turnkey Investing**

- ☐ Set up the initial business processes using the **New Business Setup Checklist**.
- ☐ Select a metropolitan area using the **Market Evaluation Checklist**.
- ☐ Select a turnkey provider using the **Questionnaire for Finding Good Turnkey Partners**.
- ☐ Establish your purchase criteria using the **Establish a Purchase Criteria Checklist**.
- ☐ Interview and select a property inspector using the **Inspector Questionnaire**.
- ☐ Complete the preapproval process with a lender using the **Loan Preapproval Checklist**.
- ☐ Evaluate properties using the **Property Evaluation Checklist**
- ☐ Put a property under contract using the **Purchase and Sales Agreement Checklist**
- ☐ Use the **Due Diligence Checklist** to complete the due diligence process.
- ☐ Use the **Post-Purchase Checklist** to set up a new property purchase.
- ☐ Use the **Monthly Business Management Checklist** to manage your ongoing business.

APPENDIX A: CHECKLISTS

Due Diligence Checklist

Objective: Complete the action items listed as soon as a property is under contract and before closing. The action items will help reduce risk and seamlessly move the process to closing.

Reference Section(s): **Chapter 21 Due Diligence and the Inspection Process**

- ☐ Order property insurance.
- ☐ Schedule the property inspection.
- ☐ Provide all the documentation requested by the lender.
- ☐ If buying in cash, schedule an appraiser; the lender will order the appraisal otherwise.
- ☐ Confirm that the appraised value matches the purchase price.
  - ◊ If the price is below the appraisal, do not sign the addendum sent to you by the turnkey provider until you have a chance to confirm the property still meets your criteria.
  - ◊ Absolutely negotiate for reduced or zero closing costs and a reduced price. Follow the four steps below:
    1. Determine the difference between the price and appraisal (appraisal gap).
    2. Start by reducing the closing costs and then reduce the price until the total reduction is equal to the appraisal gap.
    3. Terminate the contract if the turnkey provider is unwilling to negotiate.
    4. Have them begin sending new property brochures.
- ☐ If you are planning to title the property in a land trust or LLC, have your attorney prepare the documents and inform the closing attorney or title company.

- ◊ The closing attorney or title company might be able to title the property in your name to satisfy the mortgage requirements and then transfer the title to your LLC or trust.

Title Inspection:

- ☐ Order title insurance.

Documentation Inspection

- ☐ Ask for a copy of the current lease agreement.
    - ◊ Verify the rental rate.
    - ◊ Verify when the lease expires.
- ☐ Verify the security deposit.
    - ☐ Receive, review, and verify the Homeowners Association (HOA) documents if applicable.
        - ◊ Confirm the HOA expense.

Physical Inspection:

Before the inspection:
- ☐ Provide your property inspector with the scope of work.
    - ◊ Have the inspector verify the scope of work.
        - Were permits pulled?
        - Were the renovations done to code?
        - Were the renovations done with quality materials?
- ☐ Give the property disclosure to your property inspector.
    - ◊ Have the inspector verify the information in the property disclosure.
- ☐ Emphasize your desire for them to verify the age of the roof (as best they can), along with the age of the hot water tank and the HVAC system.

After the inspection:

- ☐ Follow up with the inspector as soon as possible while the property is still fresh in their memory—immediately after the inspection is best.
- ☐ Confirm that they verified the scope of work and the property disclosure.
- ☐ Ask their opinion about the renovations.
- ☐ Ask about the ages of the roof, the hot water tank, and the HVAC.

Review the Inspection Report:

- ☐ Read the entire inspection report.
- ☐ Follow up with the inspector on all of your questions.
- ☐ Make the report available to the turnkey provider so that they can fix any problems identified.
- ☐ Terminate the purchase and sales agreement if there are any major issues that cannot be addressed.
- ☐ Schedule the closing with the turnkey liaison.
    - ◊ Make sure you schedule according to the date provided in the purchase and sales agreement.
    - ◊ Make sure to schedule during the first week of the month; do not let the bank move the date to the end of the month.
    - ◊ Review the loan disclosure and confirm the loan terms are as expected.
- ☐ Have a copy of your driver's license for the closing.
- ☐ Send the required funds using a wire transfer before closing.
    - ◊ The funds required will be listed in the settlement statement.

Establish a Purchase Criteria Checklist

Objective: Establish your purchase criteria for buying properties.

Instructions: Evaluate the property brochure examples you received from the turnkey provider. Establish your property requirements and financial requirements. My requirements are provided for reference. Bold criteria can be skipped as they are more advanced.

Reference Sections: **Part 2, Chapter 12 Personal Financials, Objectives, and Goals**

- ☐ How many years have passed since the start of the last real estate recession?
    - ◊ The last recession started in 2007. The current date is September 2022. Fifteen years have passed since the last bottom.
- ☐ What is the likely phase of the real estate market?
    - ◊ Beginning of the recession phase
        - Recession phase: Buy properties only after the bottom of the market. Look for cash flow or appreciation properties tenanted with two-year leases.
        - Recovery phase: Buy cash flow and appreciation properties with two-year leases.
        - Early expansion phase: Buy appreciation and cash flow properties.
        - Middle expansion phase: Buy cash flow properties with two-year leases.
        - Last quarter of the expansion phase—Consider waiting to buy. Only buy cash flow properties with two-year leases that are producing $300 per month or greater than 20 percent (preferably closer to 30 percent) of the gross rent. Use the current cash flow as a

bellwether indicator for the market. Instead, focus on financing options that increase cash flow, reduce debt, and/or increase reserve fund.
- Hyper supply phase: Wait to buy properties. Instead, focus on increasing the cash flow, reducing debt, and/or increasing the reserve fund.

☐ Is it a buyer's market or seller's market?
  ◊ I will purchase turnkey properties in both markets, but I will not buy in an extreme seller's market.
☐ Cash flow property or appreciation property?
  ◊ Buy cash flow property for the first property or if you are unsure (Greater than $300 per month in cash flow or greater than 20 percent of the gross rent).
☐ Cash flow requirement?
  ◊ Greater than $300 per month or
  ◊ Greater than 20 percent of the gross rent, preferably closer to 30 percent
☐ Number of bedrooms?
  ◊ Three to four bedrooms
☐ Number of full bathrooms?
  ◊ Two full bathrooms
☐ Exterior finish?
  ◊ Brick
☐ Age of roof?
  ◊ Less than four years; new is preferred.
☐ Age of HVAC?
  ◊ Less than two years; new is preferred.
☐ Age of hot water tank?
  ◊ Less than two years; new is preferred.
☐ Interior renovation requirements?

- ◊ Fully renovated.
- ☐ Sewer system?
  - ◊ No septic system.
- ☐ Size requirement?
  - ◊ I do not have a size requirement. I evaluate size during the property evaluation process.
- ☐ Target purchase price?
  - ◊ At the time of this writing, my target prices were between the $150,000 to $220,000 range for a single-family turnkey rental property.

APPENDIX A: CHECKLISTS

Loan Preapproval Checklist

Objective: Select a lender and obtain preapproval for a mortgage.
Reference Section(s): **Chapter 16 The Preapproval Process**

- ☐ Do you have a lender or are you in the process of evaluating many lenders?
    - ◊ If you are evaluating lenders, complete the Prequalification Process.
    - ◊ If you have selected a lender, complete the Preapproval Process.

Prequalification Process:

- ☐ Select candidate lenders and make sure to include the lenders the turnkey provider recommends.
    - ◊ Make sure your lenders have online tools to process payments and download statements.
    - ◊ Make sure your lenders can accommodate remote closings using a traveling notary.
- ☐ Begin the prequalification process.
    - ◊ Make sure the lender understands that this is a prequalification and doesn't pull your credit report.
    - ◊ Lenders will ask for an estimate of the money you have available in bank accounts and retirement accounts.
    - ◊ Lenders may ask for a list of assets, a list of debts, your employment status and salary, and a list of income sources.
- ☐ Review the estimated mortgage terms provided by lenders and select the lender with the best option.

Preapproval Process:

- ☐ Select a lender.

- ☐ Complete the mortgage application.
  - ◊ The lender will want your social security number, the last two months of bank account statements, a list of assets, a list of debts, a list of income sources, your employment status, your past addresses, and your last two employment payment stubs. They may also request other documents.
- ☐ Review the loan estimate and confirm:
  - ◊ The type of loan
  - ◊ The interest rate
    - I use fixed-rate loans.
  - ◊ The mortgage term (fifteen-, twenty-, or thirty-year)
  - ◊ The principal and interest payment
  - ◊ The estimated closing costs
  - ◊ Whether there is a prepayment penalty:
    - I do not use loans with a prepayment penalty.
- ☐ Notify the turnkey provider with proof of preapproval.

Market Evaluation Checklist

Objective: Identify metropolitan areas to invest in.

Reference Section(s): **Chapter 17 How to Evaluate Properties**

- ☐ Put together a list of candidate metropolitan areas with a population greater than 500,000.
- ☐ Is the population of the city growing faster than 7 percent?
  - ◊ https://www.bestplaces.net
- ☐ Has the population of the city been growing for multiple years?
- ☐ Is the population of the city projected to continue growing?
- ☐ What is the rent-to-price ratio? Acceptable range: 6.4 to 8.2 percent.
- ☐ What is the housing affordability index? Acceptable range: 11 to 30 percent.
  - ◊ https://www.bestplaces.net
- ☐ What is the percentage of renters? Acceptable range: 25 to 40 percent.
  - ◊ http://www.deptofnumbers.com
- ☐ Is the city's job market growing above the national average?
- ☐ Is the projected job growth greater than the national average (33.5 percent)?
- ☐ Is the city's gross domestic product growing at a higher rate than the national average (11.8 percent)?
  - ◊ https://www.bea.gov
- ☐ Has the city's gross domestic product been growing for multiple years?
- ☐ Which companies are the biggest employers in the city?
- ☐ Which sectors do these companies operate in?

At the time of this writing, metropolitan areas that have satisfied the market evaluation criteria listed above include (1) Atlanta-Sandy Springs-Alpharetta, GA; (2) Augusta-Richmond County, GA; (3) Dallas-Fort Worth-Arlington, TX; (4) Indianapolis-Carmel-Anderson, IN; (5) Jacksonville, FL; (6) San Antonio-New Braunfels, TX; and (7) Tampa-St. Petersburg-Clearwater, FL. Additional markets to evaluate are Little Rock, AR; Oklahoma City, OK; and Tulsa, OK. Treat this list as a starting point only.

APPENDIX A: CHECKLISTS

Monthly Business Management Checklist

Objective: A monthly routine to manage business (financial tracking) and identify opportunities to scale business (business scaling).

Reference Sections: **Chapter 5 Financial Bookkeeping, Chapter 29 Turnkey Business Scaling**

Financial Tracking:

- ☐ Block a two-hour window at the end of each month to handle financial bookkeeping and financial monitoring.
- ☐ Download financial statements from turnkey providers and mortgage statements from lenders.
- ☐ Log in to the business checking account and confirm receipt of funds.
- ☐ Confirm that the scheduled mortgage payment(s) matches the mortgage statements from the mortgage lender(s).
- ☐ Confirm that the business credit card has been paid.
- ☐ In a separate spreadsheet dedicated to business accounting, input the revenue (rent) and expenses for each property.
- ☐ Make sure the business accounting spreadsheet ties to the business checking account.

Business Scaling:

- ☐ Estimate the cash funds available in the business account to reinvest.
- ☐ Estimate the cash funds available in your personal account to reinvest.
- ☐ Estimate the equity in your properties by subtracting the Zestimate from the current loan balance.
- ☐ Estimate the loan-to-value ratio for each property.
- ☐ For each property with a loan-to-value less than 75 percent:

Estimate the funds available from the different loan products and from selling.
- [ ] Estimate the funds available for investing by summing the business cash, personal cash, and funds from the loan products.
- [ ] Determine how many properties can be purchased.
- [ ] Determine the total ROI and financial impact for each loan product.
- [ ] Determine how many years have passed since the beginning of the last real estate recession.
- [ ] Determine if it is a buyer's or a seller's market.
- [ ] Estimate the likely phase for the real estate market. The phases are recession, recovery, expansion, and hyper supply.
- [ ] Build a plan based on market-generated data and take action (my generalized plan is below).
    - ◊ Recession Phase: Buy property only after the market hits bottom. Look for cash flow or appreciation properties tenanted with two-year leases.
    - ◊ Recovery Phase: Buy cash flow or appreciation properties with two-year leases.
    - ◊ Expansion Phase:
        - Early in the expansion phase—buy appreciation or cash flow properties.
        - Middle of the expansion phase—buy cash flow properties with two-year leases.
        - Last quarter of the expansion phase—consider waiting to buy. Only buy cash flow properties with two-year leases that are producing $300 per month or greater than 20 percent (preferably closer to 30 percent) of the gross rent. Use the current cash flow as a bellwether indicator for the market. Instead,

focus on financing options that increase cash flow, reduce debt, and/or increase reserve fund.
◊ Hyper supply phase—wait to buy properties. Instead, focus on financing options and strategies that increase cash flow, reduce debt, and increase the reserve fund.

New Business Setup Checklist

Objective: Set up your initial business structure.

Instructions: The steps below that are set in bold can be completed at a later time.

- ☐ Determine your maximum purchase price.
- ☐ Determine the total investment funds you will need, namely,
    - ◊ a 20 percent down payment,
    - ◊ closing costs at 3 percent of the purchase price, and
    - ◊ $5,000 for an initial reserve fund.
- ☐ **Determine a unique business name.**
    - ◊ **Do not use all or part of a personal name.**
- ☐ **Determine your business structure.**
    - ◊ **Title in your personal name, as a limited liability Company (LLC), or as a land trust.**
    - ◊ **Use the Lawyer Questionnaire to select an asset protection attorney.**
        - • A lawyer will complete the paperwork to create the LLC.
        - • Do not use your personal name as part of the naming convention for any trusts or LLCs.
    - ◊ Use the CPA Questionnaire to select a certified public accountant (CPA).
        - • A CPA will advise you on the best structure for your taxes.
        - • Make sure the lawyer and CPA communicate with each other.
- ☐ **Select a bank and open a business account using the Business Bank Account Questionnaire.**

Post-Purchase Checklist

Objective: The initial setup of business processes to manage properties.

References: **Chapter 23 What to Expect Going Forward**

- ☐ If this is your first property with this turnkey provider, set up the portal account by following the instructions your turnkey provider will send you.
- ☐ Set up automatic payment for the mortgage.
- ☐ Set up automated email or text messaging to alert you when a payment is due, paid, or returned.

Property Evaluation Checklist

Objective: Evaluate the property brochures sent by turnkey providers. Make sure to also receive corresponding scope of works. This checklist is used to select a suitable turnkey rental property to purchase using the purchase criteria established by my **Establish a Purchase Criteria Checklist**. Action items in bold can be skipped.

Reference Sections: **Chapter 17 How to Evaluate Properties**

- ☐ Evaluate the property's curb appeal.
    - ◊ Use the property photo included in the property brochure.
    - ◊ Use Google Maps.
        - Go to https://www.google.com/maps.
        - Enter the property address.
        - Click on the property photo, then use your cursor to zoom out and view the subject property and surrounding neighborhood.
- ☐ Note the amenities (cul-de-sac, walking distance to schools, parking, privacy fence, deck, etc.).
- ☐ What is the exterior finish type? _____
- ☐ What is the number of bedrooms? _____
    - ◊ Are any/all of these above average for the neighborhood?
- ☐ What is the number of full bathrooms? _____
- ☐ What is the square footage? _____
    - ◊ Are any/all of the above listings above average for the neighborhood?
    - ◊ What is the most desirable size for potential tenants?
- ☐ Estimate the appraised value of the property. _____
    - ◊ I use Zestimate (not the most accurate, but it is fast).
    - ◊ This step is crucial because of the Appraisal Problem (this occurs when the asking price is purposely too high, resulting in an appraisal gap).

APPENDIX A: CHECKLISTS

- ◊ If the appraised value is below the purchase price, do not eliminate the property yet; instead, go through the following action items:
    - Notify the turnkey provider of the problem.
    - If they disagree, ask for their comps.
    - Ask the turnkey provider what they can offer you if the property doesn't appraise at the asking price. Note: The Purchase Checklist includes action items to help you negotiate.
    - Either negotiate for a lower appraisal gap or, if possible, negotiate to remove all appraisal gap language from the purchase and sales agreement.
    - The last option: Understand how to profit from the Appraisal Problem. Refer to Chapter 15 How to Find Good Turnkey Operators for more information.
- ☐ Is the property tenanted with a two-year lease? _____
- ☐ What is the market rent? _____
    - ◊ If tenanted, confirm the market rental rate is similar to the rental rate in the property brochure.
    - ◊ Estimate the market rental rate using https://www.rentometer.com, https://www.zillow.com, or some other website.
    - ◊ If the property is currently vacant, are the rents in the brochure realistic or way above the market rents?
- ☐ Review the scope of work.
    - ◊ What is the age of the roof? _____ Is it older than four years? _____
    - ◊ What is the age of the HVAC? _____ Is it older than two years? _____
    - ◊ What is the age of the hot water tank? _____ Is it older than two years? _____
    - ◊ Is the interior fully renovated? _____
        - Make sure the interior is fully renovated.

- ◊ Does the property have a septic system? ____
  - Make sure the property's sewage system isn't a septic system.
- ☐ Estimate the property tax at the purchase price. _____
  - ◊ Call the county auditor and ask, or
  - ◊ use the tools on the county auditor's website.
  - ◊ Use estimated property tax to evaluate the property instead of the current rate.
- ☐ Determine the cash flow. _____ Is it less than $300 per month? ____
  - ◊ I require at least $300 per month or a cash flow greater than 20 to 30 percent of the gross rent.
  - ◊ Use the estimated property tax, not the current property tax.
- ☐ What is the property's appreciation rate? _____
  - ◊ Estimate this rate using https://www.zillow.com or some other website.
  - ◊ Note: I do not buy for appreciation, but I still estimate the rate to help guide my long-term plan.
- ☐ What is the property's closing date? _____
  - ◊ Only close during the first week of the month.
- ☐ Is there a Homeowners Association (HOA)?
  - ◊ I am less likely to purchase a property with an HOA, but I do not eliminate the option based on this.
- ☐ What is your exit plan for the property?
  - ◊ Review exit plans and determine the best strategy for that property for your needs. You can perform this step after purchasing the property. Note: Doing so means your plan for the property is as a long-term rental (which is what a turnkey rental is).
- ☐ Verbally commit to buying a property that satisfies this checklist.

APPENDIX A: CHECKLISTS

Purchase and Sales Agreement Checklist

Objective: Perform the recommended action items to highlight and address the important information in a purchase and sales agreement.

Instructions: Read and review the purchase and sales agreement. Never sign anything without reading first and only sign if you agree with the requirements. ALL requirements and dates in the purchase and sales agreement are negotiable.

Reference Sections: **Chapter 18 Purchase and Sales Agreement**

- ☐ Read the complete purchase and sales agreement before signing.
- ☐ Read the property disclosure.
- ☐ Confirm and record the crucial information.
    - ◊ Confirm the price. _____
        - Was a leasing fee included? If so, ask to have it waived.
        - Make sure the property tax is prorated based on the settlement date.
        - Confirm who is paying for the closing costs.
    - ◊ What is the settlement date (closing date)? _____ Is it set during the first week of the month?
    - ◊ What is the earnest deposit amount _____? Note: The buyer usually sets the amount. In turnkey transactions, the purchase and sales agreement will usually list the amount.
    - ◊ Determine the delivery instructions and deadline for the earnest deposit.
    - ◊ List all the dates for the due diligence period. _____
    - ◊ Is there a financing contingency? Make certain there is one.
    - ◊ Is there an inspection contingency?

- ◊ Record all the dates associated with the inspection.
- ◊ Review and understand all the contingencies.
- ◊ Look for appraisal gap language.
  - Make sure you can terminate the agreement if the appraisal is well below the purchase price.
- ☐ If you fully understand the agreement, sign the purchase and sales agreement.
  - ◊ Signing will occur through a signing portal such as DocuSign.
- ☐ Send the earnest deposit exactly as instructed.

APPENDIX B: QUESTIONNAIRES

Business Bank Account Questionnaire

Objective: Find a bank that offers the banking systems required to streamline your turnkey rental business and open a business account.

Reference Sections: **Chapter 5 Financial Bookkeeping**

Selecting a Bank:

- ☐ Start with your personal bank because it will offer a convenient method with which to link the business account to your personal account but remember not to comingle funds.
- ☐ Is the bank insured by the Federal Deposit Insurance Corporation (FDIC)?
- ☐ Are there any recurring fees or initial fees, and if so, are the fees waived if the account balance is above a certain value?
- ☐ Are there any fees for too many monthly transactions, and if so, what is the threshold?
- ☐ Does the bank have any promotional offers?
- ☐ Does the bank offer a credit card that can be linked to the business account?
- ☐ Does the bank offer online wire transfer options, and if so, what is the dollar limit?
    - ◊ You will want at least $5,000 for the earnest deposit.
    - ◊ If possible, look for a higher wire transfer limit to enable wiring down payments.
- ☐ Are any physical locations nearby?
    - ◊ This facilitates large wire transfers (down payments).
- ☐ What online services does the bank offer?
    - ◊ You will want automatic bill payment.
    - ◊ You will want automated email or text messaging that informs you whenever an automatic payment is scheduled, processed, or returned.

- [ ] What mobile apps does the bank offer?
  - ◊ Find out if the bank offers apps that allow you to check your balance and cash flow, pay bills, and transfer funds.
- [ ] Can the account transaction history be downloaded in Excel or whatever software package you've chosen for the financial monitoring of your business?
- [ ] What services or other options are available?

Opening the Account:

- [ ] Go to the bank, open the account, and deposit your reserve fund.
- [ ] Bring in your business documents, including a record of the EIN number.
- [ ] Bring two photo IDs.
- [ ] Provide the legal name of the business.
- [ ] Provide your business address.
  - ◊ Consider using a PO box if the business address is also your personal residence.
- [ ] When the business account is opened, simultaneously open a credit card.
  - ◊ Make sure the card is linked to that business account.
- [ ] Ask for instructions to set up automatic bill payment and email and/or text message notifications.
- [ ] Deposit your reserve fund.

Certified Public Accountant Questionnaire

Objective: Find a good certified public accountant (CPA) who can minimize your tax bill, give excellent tax-related advice, and provide a long-term plan that will help your business and personal financials.

Instructions: Compile a list of at least four potential candidates and perform the steps listed below. You can perform a quick internet search, collect referrals, or visit the American Institute of Certified Public Accounts (AICPA) to compile your list. The website for the AICPA society can be found at:

www.aicpa.org/research/externallinks/associationsstatecpalinks

Before the Meeting With the CPA:

1. Verify each candidate's Preparer Tax Identification Number (PTIN) by visiting the IRS website: https://irs.treasury.gov/rpo/rpo.jsf. Note: The IRS requires CPAs who prepare taxes to register and have a PTIN.
2. Look up the candidate's state license on the website: https://nasba.org/stateboards. Take note of their license status, issue date, expiration date, and most importantly, any disciplinary actions or suspensions. The issue date gives you some indication of the candidate's experience.
3. Continue steps 1 and 2 until you have your four candidates. Contact each candidate and ask the questions in the next section.

During the Meeting:

1. Ask the candidate about their specialization. Remember, you are looking for a CPA who has an excellent understanding of real estate taxes.
2. Ask the candidate "Will you sign my return, and will you represent me before the IRS?" Move on to the next

candidate if they are unwilling to support their work.
3. Determine the candidate's experience by asking whether they file returns electronically. Note: The IRS requires tax preparers who file eleven or more tax returns per year to file electronically.
4. Ask the candidate if they offer year-round tax planning.
5. Determine the candidate's fees, and make sure it includes both federal and state returns. Note: CPAs are not allowed to charge a percentage of your return.

Inspector Questionnaire

Objective: Select a property inspector with the help of the list below.

Instructions: Compile a list of at least four potential candidates and perform the steps listed below. To find candidates, you can perform a quick internet search, collect referrals, or visit the American Society of Home Inspectors (ASHI). The website for the ASHI: http://www.ashi.org. The International Association of Certified Home Inspectors (InterNACHI), another good resource, can be found online at: https://www.nachi.org.

Before the Meeting:

1. Check online reviews at Angi (https://www.angi.com), HomeAdvisor (https://www.homeadvisor.com), Google (https://www.google.com), and Yelp (https://www.yelp.com).
2. Research the company. You want a company that only does inspections and not repair work. Check the Better Business Bureau (https://www.bbb.org).
3. Make sure the company is licensed and insured. If it isn't, eliminate it from your list of potential candidates.
4. Do not use an inspector who was recommended by the seller.
5. If applicable within the state in which you are working, check for records of complaints and verify the inspector's license with the state agency.

Questions to Ask During the Meeting:

1. Are you a full-time inspector?
2. What did you do before becoming an inspector?
3. Are you or does your company carry errors and omissions insurance?
4. Are you licensed? What are your certifications? The

inspector should be licensed with the state and have certifications with ASHI or InterNACHI.
5. What will the inspection cover?
6. What won't the inspection cover? Make sure to ask how to determine the condition of anything not included in the inspection.
7. Do you use advanced measurement equipment such as infrared detectors, water pressure gauges, water test strips, moisture meters, and gas leak detectors?
8. Can you send me an example of a past report?

While considering inspectors, look for one with broad knowledge. Comparing reports will provide a lot of insight into which inspector to hire. Look at the detail provided. The report should include the issue, a description of the issue, why the issue matters, pictures of the issue, and suggested maintenance for the issue.

After the Inspection:

Set up a follow-up meeting with the inspector immediately after the inspection. You want the inspector to describe the condition of the property while it is fresh in their mind. The information they will provide will be in the report, but it is beneficial to discuss it over the phone as that will provide you with a clearer picture of the property.

Insurance Broker Questionnaire

Objective: Select an insurance broker using the list of questions below.
Reference Sections: **Chapter 20 Property Insurance**

- ☐ Are you an insurance broker or an insurance agent?
- ☐ Are you independent or owned by an insurance company?
- ☐ What is your experience?
- ☐ Are you a national firm?
- ☐ Do you reevaluate my coverage annually prior to renewing to find the lowest premiums?
- ☐ Do you handle notifying the lenders if the insurance provider changes?
- ☐ Do you have references from clients?
- ☐ Can you provide a personalized policy for my business?
- ☐ What does my policy include?
- ☐ How much will it cost?
- ☐ Do I need an umbrella policy?

APPENDIX B: QUESTIONNAIRES

Lawyer Questionnaire

Please note: The demand for asset protection has grown substantially in recent years, and many law firms that did not specialize in asset protection are now advertising asset protection services. Unfortunately, such services are expensive and often inadequate. Even worse, the saturation of so-called asset protection attorneys and the misinformation from their rebranded websites have made it difficult to find good legal services. I have gone through multiple legal teams and, as a result, have learned a lot about what to look for and the questions to ask when interviewing law firms.

Instructions: To begin the process, compile a list of at least four potential law firms and perform the steps listed below. To find candidates, you can perform a quick internet search, collect referrals, or visit the American Bar Association (ABA) at: https://www.americanbar.org.

Before the meeting:

1. Look up the attorneys on your list at the ABA and note how many years they have been practicing. Sometimes the ABA will list their specializations. Make sure asset protection is included.
2. Research each law firm and read their reviews. Make sure to note the types of legal services listed in those reviews. Again, asset protection needs to be the primary service.
3. Review their website and determine whether that law firm specializes in asset protection or it is a rebranded law firm looking to take your money.

During the meeting, ask the following questions:

1. Will you keep our discussion privileged?
    ◊ Make sure to ask this question at the beginning before

you do anything else. Move on to the next attorney on your list if that attorney cannot.
2. Does your law firm work nationally?
    ◊ Remember, your turnkey rental business has the flexibility to purchase properties in any state, and the business can be performed from anywhere. The asset protection plan needs to work regardless of where you choose to live and own property.
3. Which areas of law do you specialize in?
4. How many years have you practiced asset protection?
5. How many clients have you set up an asset protection plan for?
6. Can you provide referrals from your clients?
    ◊ This is a trick question because they shouldn't be able to do this; discussions with their clients should be confidential.
7. Can you provide professional referrals from professionals outside of your practice or outside of the law firm you work at?
    ◊ Make sure to:
        a. call their referrals and
        b. ensure that those referrals can describe them as a law firm that specializes in asset protection.
8. How many clients have you worked with that owned rental properties in multiple states?
9. Can you provide me with what you have written about asset protection?
    ◊ They will have documents that outline their strategy if they specialize in asset protection.
10. Can you provide a written plan specific to my needs and include the costs, results, and requirements?
    ◊ They absolutely should be able to include a specific price.

11. What educational materials do you provide?
    ◊ No matter how much support they offer, they cannot be with you at all times, so they should be able to provide you with some sort of training.
12. How much does the educational materials cost?
13. What kind of support does your firm provide after the plan is set up?
    ◊ Make sure there is ongoing support to add and remove properties.
14. What are the costs for ongoing support?
    ◊ Ask about accounting, reports, compliance, and tax status, and again, verify the costs for these services.

Property Management Questionnaire

Objective: Find quality property management with the help of the questionnaire below.

Reference Sections: **Chapter 24 Replacing or Finding Property Management**

General Questions to Ask:

- ☐ How long has your company been in business?
- ☐ How many employees does your company have?
- ☐ Have you done business under other company names? If so, what are the names of those companies?
- ☐ What type of properties will your company not manage?
- ☐ How many properties does your company manage?

Communication Questions:

- ☐ Does your company have an online system that I can use to access copies of my monthly financial statements, the property's lease, and the property management agreement?
- ☐ How will your company communicate with me, and how often will I hear from your team?
- ☐ How and when are maintenance and vacancy issues communicated to me?
- ☐ Who will be my main point of contact? How long has this person been with the company?

Statistical Performance Questions:

- ☐ What is the occupancy rate for the properties under management for the last three months?
- ☐ What is the average length of stay for a tenant?

APPENDIX B: QUESTIONNAIRES

- [ ] What percentage of the rent is collected?
- [ ] Is your company able to complete a full rehab if needed? If so, what is the average time and cost of a rehab?
- [ ] What is the average length of time for tenant turnover?
- [ ] What is the average cost of tenant turnover?
- [ ] What is the average percentage of the gross rents used toward maintenance?
- [ ] How many evictions has your company dealt with in the past year?
- [ ] What is the average length of time for an eviction?

Marketing Questions:

- [ ] What is your company's marketing strategy for finding tenants?
- [ ] Does your company handle the marketing in-house or is it outsourced?
- [ ] What are the processes and screening criteria your company uses to screen potential tenants?

Fee Structure Questions:

- [ ] What is your monthly management fee?
- [ ] What is your tenant placement fee?
- [ ] What is your maintenance fee?
- [ ] Are there any other fees that I haven't asked about, and if so, what are they and what are the associated costs?

Questionnaire for Finding Good Turnkey Partners

Objective: Find quality turnkey rental partners with the help of the questionnaire below.

Instructions: Interview at least two but preferably three turnkey rental providers. Compare each. Hire the one best suited to your needs.

Reference Sections: **Chapter 15 How to Find Good Turnkey Operators**

Questions to Ask During the Meeting:

- ☐ How many properties have you sold to investors?
- ☐ Can you provide referrals from your investor clients?
- ☐ Do you own the properties you sell?
- ☐ Do you own the management company that manages the properties you sell?
- ☐ Do you own the construction company that performs the renovations?
- ☐ What is the average length of time for a tenant?
- ☐ Do you use chargebacks?
- ☐ What is the average collected rent? 90 percent? 95 percent? Etc.?
- ☐ What is your current vacancy rate?
- ☐ How long does it take to clean, repair, and place a new tenant for tenant turnover?
- ☐ How much does the average tenant turnover cost?
- ☐ Can you provide the financial models for properties you've recently sold?
- ☐ What percent of the properties you sell appraise at the asking price?

APPENDIX B: QUESTIONNAIRES

- ☐ What will you offer if the property does not appraise at the asking price?
- ☐ Do you offer any warranties on the renovations for the property?
- ☐ Do you offer rental guarantees?
- ☐ How many evictions have you had to handle in the last year?
- ☐ How much are the maintenance costs on average per month per property?
- ☐ Can you provide a detailed scope of work and a list of materials used for your average renovation?
- ☐ What are your management fees?
- ☐ Can you send me example property brochures and the corresponding scope of works?
  - ◊ Make sure the brochures cover the different price points offered by the turnkey provider in your target metropolitan area.
  - ◊ Make sure the brochures include the property address, number of bedrooms, number of bathrooms, square footage, asking price, estimated property tax, estimated property insurance, and rental rate.

After the Meeting, Ask the Following Questions/Perform the Following Tasks:

- ☐ Were the properties in the property brochures recently sold?
  - ◊ You want recently sold examples because they provide more meaningful information.
- ☐ Perform a quick appraisal for each subject property in the property brochures.
  - ◊ Use the Zestimate or some other quick method to estimate the property value.

- To get a Zestimate, go to https://www.zillow.com and enter the property address, and the Zestimate should be displayed in the upper right corner of the page.
- A Zestimate is not likely to be overly accurate, but it will be sufficient for your immediate needs.
  ◊ Are the asking prices well above the Zestimate?
☐ Use the appropriate county auditor's website to determine whether the sold price was less than, more than, or the same as the asking price shown on the property brochures. This:
  ◊ Provides an idea of how much room there is for negotiating.
  ◊ Provides an idea as to whether the appraisal will be a problem.
☐ How does the rental rate compare to the market rental rate?
  ◊ Are the rents advertised realistic? Are they above or below market rates?
    - I use https://www.RentOMeter.com to determine rental rates. Other available sources to find this information include https://www.zillow.com.
☐ Review the scope of works provided.
  ◊ Was the roof replaced? If not, is it less than four years old?
  ◊ Was the HVAC replaced? If not, is it less than two years old?
  ◊ Was the hot water tank replaced? If not, is it less than two years old?
  ◊ Was the interior fully renovated?
  ◊ What is the quality of the materials used in the renovation?
    - Follow up with questions if needed but make

certain all the above questions have been answered to your satisfaction.
- ☐ Compute the four profit returns of a property.
  - ◊ Are there example properties with a cash flow greater than $300 per month or greater than 20 percent of gross rent?
- ☐ After comparing each turnkey provider, hire a company or reopen the search.

Real Estate Agent Questionnaire

Objective: Identify and hire a good seller's agent using the questionnaire included below. Remember that real estate agents do not work for you; they work for their commission. Always prepare for the worst case.

Before the Meeting:

- ☐ Identify four candidates to interview using:
    - ◊ An internet search
    - ◊ Referrals
    - ◊ Recommendations from your turnkey provider
        - You are looking for agents who have sold a fair number of properties in the area where your property is located.
- ☐ Pull comparable properties and determine the value of your property.
    - ◊ I like estimating the value before talking with an agent. Some agents like to provide a target price that is higher than the market to influence you to hire them over other agents.
- ☐ Determine if it's a buyer's market or a seller's market.
    - ◊ I try to only sell during a seller's market. During a seller's market, it is much easier to negotiate for lower agent commissions.
    - ◊ I find that my ability to negotiate improves significantly if I am prepared.
- ☐ Look at some of the past listings for each candidate.
    - ◊ Were the photos professionally taken?
    - ◊ If not, were those photos of good quality, or were they out of focus?
        - I have seen many listings with blurry photos. This represents an agent who doesn't take

pride in their work. Remember, if they are willing to be sloppy with someone else's property, they may also treat your property the same way.
- ☐ Were the descriptions for their listings well written?
  - ◊ Again, you are looking for someone who takes the time needed to put together a quality listing.
- ☐ Go to each agent's website. Does it look as if the agent is actually running a business? Does the website look professional?
  - ◊ An agent's business is all about marketing. If their marketing is poor, I would move on to the next agent.
- ☐ Call each candidate; schedule a walkthrough of the property you plan to sell and a follow-up meeting.
  - ◊ I tend to not ask many questions during the initial phone call.
  - ◊ Provide the property address and other property-specific information they request.
  - ◊ Make sure they understand that you are interviewing multiple agents and will hire one after the interviews are completed.
  - ◊ Make sure they have an opportunity to visit the property you're selling and to assemble their plan for selling it for you.
  - ◊ You will need to coordinate with the turnkey provider to give the agents access to the property.
  - ◊ Schedule a teleconference to take place after they visit the property.

During the Teleconference, Determine the Following Information/Ask the Following Questions:

- ☐ Was the agent on time?

- ◊ The agent should call you in a timely manner. It is a red flag if the agent is significantly late. In general, I am not interested in working with someone who does not respect my or their own time.
- ☐ Was the agent's presentation professional?
  - ◊ The materials they present as part of the teleconference should be of professional quality. An agent with experience knows how to deliver powerful presentation instead of relying on a cheesy elevator pitch that is clearly memorized. Again, you want an experienced agent.
- ☐ Do you use a professional photographer?
  - ◊ A professional photographer is a must. The small optics in camera phones are not great for low-light situations or for putting together a professional-looking portfolio.
- ☐ Do you recommend staging?
  - ◊ Note: Staging is an excellent strategy for selling houses but isn't necessary when the market is really hot. The agent should have a good recommendation about staging.
- ☐ How many people are on your team?
  - ◊ In general, I do not want an agent who performs all the different tasks required for selling the property. Established agents will have a team. Again, you are looking for an experienced agent.
- ☐ Will you be or will someone else on your team be selling my house?
  - ◊ I want the person I interviewed to sell my house, not an unknown individual whom I did not vet during the interview process.
- ☐ Do you plan to have an open house? Tell me more about how you plan to market my property.

- ◊ An open house is a must. Understanding each candidate's marketing plan will quickly help you narrow down the search to one agent.
- ☐ How many houses have you sold in the last two months? How many have you sold in the past year?
  - ◊ Remember, experience matters.
- ☐ What were the days-on-market for the properties you sold?
  - ◊ I like to get an idea of how well their listing has performed with respect to other listings.
- ☐ What was the initial listed price, and what was the sale price for your last five transactions?
  - ◊ Again, some agents like to recommend a higher sale price so that you will hire them. If the recommended price is much higher than your estimated value and the recommended prices from the other candidates, there is a good chance the agent is using this tactic. If so, eliminate the agent from contention.
- ☐ Can you tell me more about your network of lenders, contractors, and other real estate professionals?
  - ◊ A good agent with lots of experience will have plumbers, inspectors, lenders, roofers, and other real estate-related professionals. Surprises can come up during the inspection; you want an agent who can take care of the problem quickly.

After the meeting, do the following:

- ☐ Review the materials each agent provided during their meeting.
- ☐ Were any of their promises too good to be true? If so, eliminate the candidate.

APPENDIX C: MATHEMATICS FOR LOAN PRODUCTS

Building financial models for different financial situations and scenarios can help you garner a solid understanding of the processes involved. The results can help you form a strong foundation from which to make informed decisions. The discussion in this section will

- introduce definitions for the different terminology used regarding mortgages,
- develop the mathematical equations to compute the amortization table,
- offer a quick introduction to the equivalent Excel functions,
- provide an example of how to use the equations to compute an amortization table,
- discuss how the different dependent variables of a loan affect the ROI of the loan paydown, and
- go into a little more detail about what all this means.

To begin, there is a lot of terminology that an investor should be familiar with, including:

◊ Adjustable-Rate Mortgage: A loan with an adjustable interest rate. Typically designated as a 5/1 ARM (adjustable-rate mortgage) in which the "5" is the number of years the initial interest remains fixed, and the "1" is the number of years the rate will adjust. There are other ARM products besides the 5/1 type. The specific details of ARMs are outside of the scope of this book, but in general, ARMs offer lower interest rates than fixed-rate mortgages. ARMs also carry more risk than a fixed-rate mortgage, so please exercise caution if you are considering this option.

◊ Margin: The number of percentage points used to determine the interest rate for an ARM after the initial fixed-interest rate period. The number of percentage points added to the mortgage interest rate is the sum of the margin and the index.

◊ Index: An interest rate that represents the general health or

APPENDIX C: MATHEMATICS FOR LOAN PRODUCTS

condition of the market. There are different indexes that can be used by the lender.

- ◊ Fully Indexed Rate: The sum of the margin and the index.
- ◊ Closing Costs: The total costs incurred from the lender to receive the loan. The costs will include title fees, origination fees, and any other fees required by the lender.
- ◊ Closing Disclosure: A summary of the mortgage and will include all the terms involved such as the interest rate, mortgage term, borrowed amount, and closing fees. The lender is required to send the closing disclosure prior to closing.
- ◊ Down Payment: The monetary difference between the purchase price and the loan amount. The down payment is the money required from the buyer at closing. Other required funds include the closing costs.
- ◊ Earnest Money: A deposit from the buyer to the seller at the execution of the purchase and sales contract. The money is typically held in escrow and is usually applied at closing.
- ◊ Escrow: A separate account set up by the lender. The account is used to hold the property tax and property insurance funds. The lender receives these funds when the borrower pays their mortgage. Note: The monthly mortgage payment can adjust due to a shortage whereby the escrow funds were insufficient to cover the costs of the property tax and insurance. The typical cause for this is an increase in property tax due to a reassessment.
- ◊ HUD-1 Statement: A statement that summarizes the charges and credits to the buyer and the seller for the purchase. This document is needed for tax purposes.
- ◊ Loan-to-Value Ratio: The ratio of the loan amount and the appraised value of the property. Banks will loan up to some specified loan-to-value ratio, typically 75 or 80 percent for a rental property. Personal homes tend to allow for higher loan-to-value ratios, for example, 95 percent.

- ◊ **Mortgage Term:** The maximum time allotted to pay the loan off. Typically, the mortgage term is fifteen, twenty, and thirty years.
- ◊ **Origination Fees:** A fee the lender charges the borrower for the loan. Note: Consult with your tax professional as some of the fees associated with loans are not considered business expenses for taxes.
- ◊ **Prepayment Penalty:** A fee lenders will charge if you pay the mortgage off early. Many loans do not have a prepayment penalty.
- ◊ **Mortgage Points:** Fees the investor can choose to pay to reduce the mortgage interest rate. Typically, one mortgage point costs 1 percent of the mortgage balance and lowers the interest rate by 0.25 percent, or 25 basis points.
- ◊ **Balloon Mortgage:** A mortgage for real estate purchases with an initial period during which there are no payments or small payments, followed by a one-time payment in the amount of the borrowed balance plus interest. The mortgage term is typically less than ten years with a standard term of five years.

The principal and interest payment, designated as P, is given as:

$$P = \frac{B_0 R}{1 - (1 + R)^{-n}} = PMT(R, n, B_0). \qquad \text{A.1}$$

In Eq. A.1, B_0 is the initial balance of the mortgage, n is the number of payments during the amortization, and R is the periodic interest rate given as:

$$R = \frac{\delta}{T}. \qquad \text{A.2}$$

In the above equation, T is the number of interest periods per year, and δ is the annualized percentage rate. The equivalent function in

APPENDIX C: MATHEMATICS FOR LOAN PRODUCTS

Excel and Google Sheets is PMI, which can be used to compute the principal and interest payment. The interest payment, designated as I, is given as:

$$I_t = RB_{t-1} \text{ for } i = 0, 1, 2 \ldots n. \quad\quad \text{A.3}$$

In Eq. A.3, B_i is the mortgage balance for payment number i. The principal component of P is given as:

$$G_i = P - I_i. \quad\quad \text{A.4}$$

Note: The mortgage payment P is the same for every payment, but the interest and principal vary for each payment. Specifically, the interest component of the mortgage payment will decrease while the principal will increase; hence, the ROI from the loan paydown will increase a little each month. The loan paydown accrued over N-months is given as:

$$\sum_{i=1}^{N} G_i = \sum_{i=1}^{N} (P = I_I) = CUMPRNC. \quad\quad \text{A.5}$$

Let's discuss how to set up Excel or Google Sheets to compute the amortization table. A screenshot of the amortization table, inputted into Excel, is shown in Figure 11.

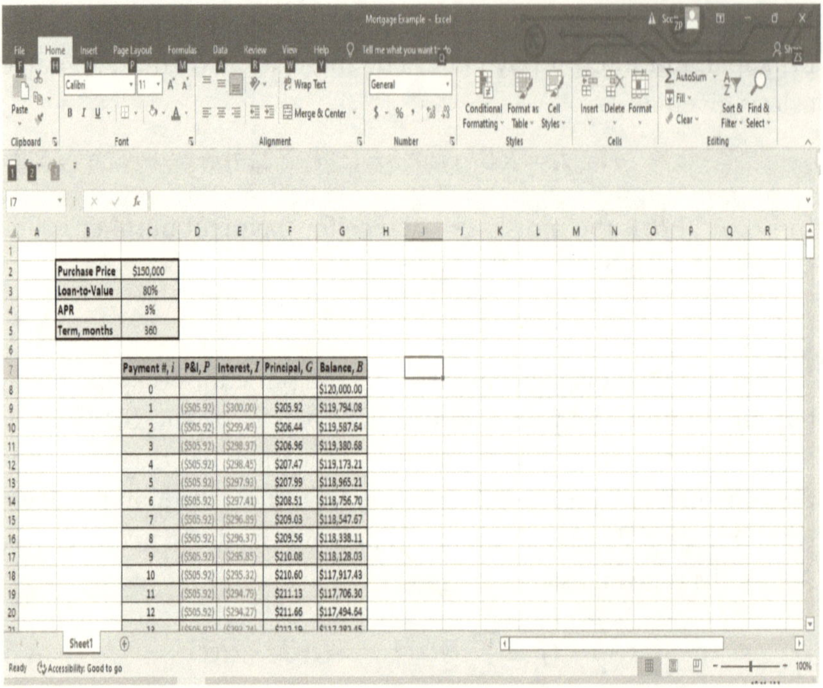

Figure 11. Set up for an amortization table in Excel or Google Sheets.

To begin, Excel and Google Sheets are spreadsheet programs organized into columns. The columns are designated as capital letters, and the rows are designated as numbers, as can be seen in the figure.

In Figure 11, the spreadsheet is set up with the label Purchase Price in column B, row 2. The value of $150,000, indicated for the Purchase Price, is in column C, row 2. Similarly, the other dependent variables for the amortization table are Loan-to-Value, APR, and Term, located in column C and rows 3, 4, and 5, respectively. These values are inputted by the user.

The next step is to define names and assign them to these dependent variables. For example, to define the name of the Purchase Price, right-click on the numerical value in column C, row 2 and select Define Name. In the popup window titled New Name, enter the desired name in the field Name and click the OK button. I chose to define the name as PurPrice. Similarly, define names for

APPENDIX C: MATHEMATICS FOR LOAN PRODUCTS

the Loan-to-Value, APR, and Term. I named these parameters as L2V, APR, and term, respectively.

Now it is time to begin the process of building the amortization table by computing the values shown underneath the labels P&I, P; Interest, I; Principal, G; and Balance, B. I have broken this into the following steps.

Step 1. In column C, row 7, enter the label Payment #. Similarly, enter the labels P&I, Interest, Principal, and Balance.

Step 2. Enter the payment numbers under the label Payment # starting with 0 and 1 in rows 8 and 9, respectively. The last payment number entered is 360, which corresponds to thirty years (twelve months x thirty years). Manually inputting these numbers would take a long time. There are multiple ways to automate this process. You can use the Fill function in Excel, or (the way I usually do it) you can highlight the numbers, left click and hold while the cursor is on the box in the lower right corner, and then drag the mouse down until you reach 360. The box on the lower right-hand box (after highlighting the numbers) is shown in Figure 12.

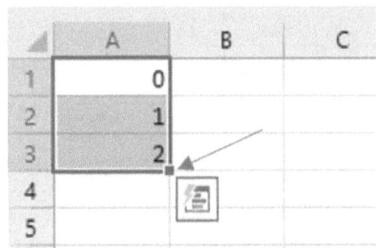

Figure 12. Excel example.

Step 3. Use the PMT function to determine the mortgage payment as shown in Figure 13.

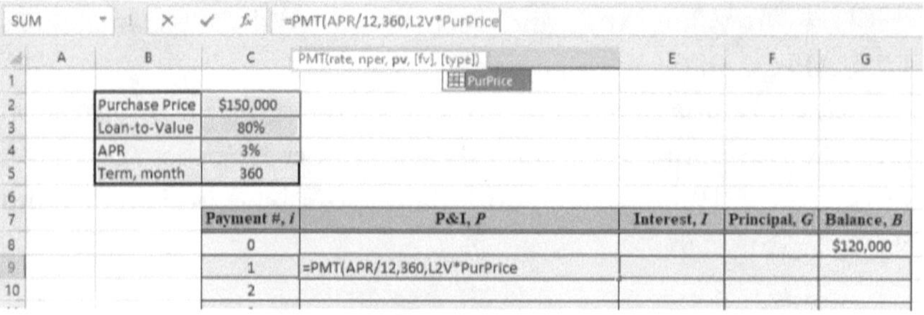

PASSIVE PROFITS: THE TURNKEY RENTAL INVESTOR'S GUIDE

	A	B	C	D	E	F	G
1				PMT(rate, nper, pv, [fv], [type])			
2		Purchase Price	$150,000				
3		Loan-to-Value	80%				
4		APR	3%				
5		Term, month	360				
6							
7			Payment #, i	P&I, P	Interest, I	Principal, G	Balance, B
8			0				$120,000
9			1	=PMT(APR/12,360,L2V*PurPrice)			
10			2				

(Formula bar: =PMT(APR/12,360,L2V*PurPrice))

Figure 13. How to use the PMT function in Excel.

As shown, in column D, row 9, type the following and hit enter.

=pmt(APR/12,360,L2V*PurPrice)

All functions in Excel are inputted by beginning with the equal sign, whereas numbers can be typed in without an equal sign.

Step 4. Calculate the interest component of the first payment, as shown in Figure 14.

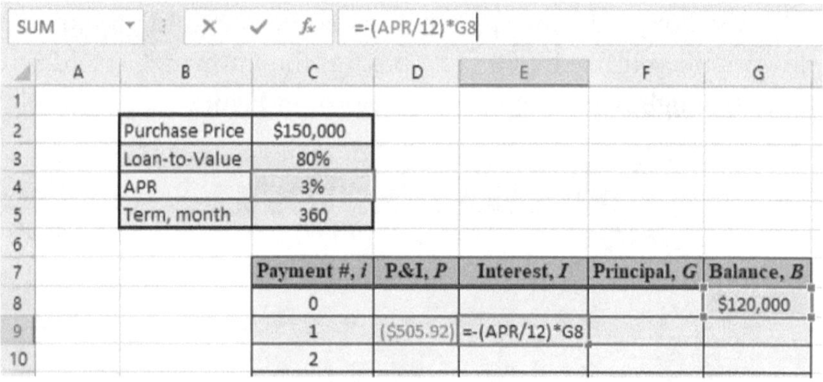

	A	B	C	D	E	F	G
1							
2		Purchase Price	$150,000				
3		Loan-to-Value	80%				
4		APR	3%				
5		Term, month	360				
6							
7			Payment #, i	P&I, P	Interest, I	Principal, G	Balance, B
8			0				$120,000
9			1	($505.92)	=-(APR/12)*G8		
10			2				

(Formula bar: =-(APR/12)*G8)

Figure 14. How to enter the Interest, I.

As shown, in column E, row 9, type the following and hit enter.

=-(APR/12)*G8

Step 5. Calculate the principal component of the first payment as shown in Figure 15.

APPENDIX C: MATHEMATICS FOR LOAN PRODUCTS

	A	B	C	D	E	F	G	H
1								
2		Purchase Price	$150,000					
3		Loan-to-Value	80%					
4		APR	3%					
5		Term, month	360					
6								
7			Payment #, i	P&I, P	Interest, I	Principal, G	Balance, B	
8			0				$120,000	
9			1	($505.92)	($300)	=E9-D9		
10			2					

Figure 15. How to enter the Principal, G.

As shown, type the following in column F, row 9, and hit enter.

$$=E9-D9$$

Step 6. Calculate the mortgage balance as shown in Figure 16.

	A	B	C	D	E	F	G
1							
2		Purchase Price	$150,000				
3		Loan-to-Value	80%				
4		APR	3%				
5		Term, month	360				
6							
7			Payment #, i	P&I, P	Interest, I	Principal, G	Balance, B
8			0				$120,000
9			1	($505.92)	($300)	$205.92	=G8-F9
10			2				

Figure 16. How to enter the Balance, B.

As shown, type the following in column G, row 9.

$$=G8-F9$$

Step 7. The last step is to autofill the table using a similar approach for auto-filling the payment numbers. Highlight the row with the

P&I, Interest, Principal, and Balance, as shown in Figure 17.

	A	B	C	D	E	F	G	H
1								
2		Purchase Price	$150,000					
3		Loan-to-Value	80%					
4		APR	3%					Double Click
5		Term, month	360					
6								
7			Payment #, i	P&I, P		Interest, I	Principal, G	Balance, B
8			0					$120,000
9			1		($505.92)	($300)	$205.92	$119,794.08
10			2					

Figure 17. How to auto-populate the amortization table.

Next, double-click the box located on the lower right corner of the highlighted box. The values will automatically populate down to the last payment (payment 360). Scroll down to payment number 360 and confirm the loan balance is $0.00.

The discussion thus far has

- provided definitions for mortgages,
- introduced the equations, and
- demonstrated how to use a spreadsheet to compute an amortization table.

Two additional Excel functions that are useful for mortgages, the CUMPRINC and CUMIPMT functions, provide the sum principal or interest over a specified timeframe.

The principal and interest payments for the 360 mortgage payments are shown in Figure 18.

APPENDIX C: MATHEMATICS FOR LOAN PRODUCTS

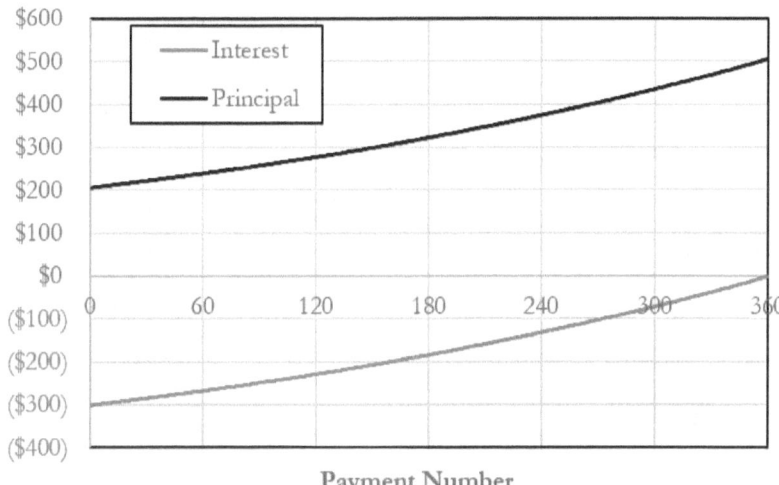

Figure 18. Interest and principal vs the payment number.

As shown, the interest payment is at a maximum value of $300.00 for the first payment and then slowly goes to a minimum value of $1.26 at payment number 360. Similarly, the principal is a minimum ($205.92) for the first payment and then slowly increases to a maximum value of $504.66 at payment number 360. Hence, the return from the loan paydown (principal) increases steadily over time.

The total interest paid is simply the sum of the monthly interest. The SUM function or the CUMIPRINC can be used to determine the total interest; for this loan, the total interest paid after thirty years is $62,132.94. Note: A lower interest rate results in a larger return from the loan paydown (less interest paid).

Another interesting fact about mortgages is that the repayment period can be reduced by exactly one month if an additional payment is made that is equal to the principal of the next payment. For example, at the top of Figure 19, an additional payment is added by reducing the mortgage balance by $206.44, which is the principal of the next payment.

PASSIVE PROFITS: THE TURNKEY RENTAL INVESTOR'S GUIDE

Top table (formula bar: =G8-F9-206.44)

	A	B	C	D	E	F	G	H
1								
2		Purchase Price	$150,000					
3		Loan-to-Value	80%					
4		APR	3%					
5		Term, month	360					
6								
7			Payment #, i	P&I, P	Interest, I	Principal, G	Balance, B	
8			0				$120,000	
9			1	($505.92)	($300.00)	$205.92	=G8-F9-206.44	
10			2	($505.92)	($299.49)	$206.44	$119,587.64	
11			3	($505.92)	($298.97)	$206.96	$119,380.68	

Bottom table

	A	B	C	D	E	F	G	H
1								
2		Purchase Price	$150,000					
3		Loan-to-Value	80%					
4		APR	3%					
5		Term, month	360					
6								
7			Payment #, i	P&I, P	Interest, I	Principal, G	Balance, B	
365			357	($505.92)	($3.78)	$502.15	$1,008.07	
366			358	($505.92)	($2.52)	$503.40	$504.66	
367			359	($505.92)	($1.26)	$504.66	($0.00)	
368			360	($505.92)	$0.00	$505.92	($505.93)	
369								

Figure 19. Top: An additional payment of $206.44 is applied; and Bottom: The resulting mortgage balance from the additional payment.

The resulting mortgage balance is shown at the bottom of Figure 19. Note: Payment number 359 equals $0.00. The corresponding ROI of 245 percent is given as the return divided by the invested funds:

$$\$505.92 \ / \ \$206.44 = 2.45 \ (245\%).$$

The annualized return can be calculated by first determining the monthly return and then multiplying it by twelve months. The result is 8.19:

$$12 \times 2.45 \ / \ 359 \text{ times} = 0.0819 \ (8.19\%).$$

To summarize, this section in the appendix was dedicated to mortgages with a focus on

- introducing mortgage terminology and definitions,

- introducing the mathematical equations to compute amortization tables,
- introducing some of the mortgage-related Excel functions,
- Showing, by example, how to compute an amortization table.

APPENDIX D: MATHEMATICS FOR THE EXAMPLES

The format adopted within this appendix will partition the problem into four defined components:

- Revenue
- Expenses
- Debt
- Assets

The mathematical analysis in each of these sections will seek to adequately describe

- all the revenue streams in the revenue section,
- all the expenses in the expenses section,
- all the various sources of debt in the debt section, and
- all the assets in the asset section.

The underlying assumption is that the financial state of most financial instruments, or at least those evaluated in this book, are completely defined once these four components are understood.

The purpose of providing a systematic approach is simple; this book covers many scenarios, but it is impossible to cover every situation that could arise. Thus, the examples and the format adopted are meant to

(1) illustrate the methodology for a specific scenario,
(2) quantify specific financials that are pertinent to turnkey rentals,
(3) introduce key concepts, and
(4) provide a framework that can be extended to scenarios not covered in this book.

Lastly, the mathematical equations provided in the examples below were placed here in the appendix to improve the readability of this book.

Example 3.1 Turnkey Investor versus Turnkey Provider

The results from Example 3.1 are summarized in **Chapter 3 Turnkey Investor vs Turnkey Providers**. The full treatment of this example is provided here.

Objective:

1. Quantify the difference in profit and working hours for (a) the turnkey rental investor, (b) the turnkey provider, and (c) the traditional rental investor.
2. Provide a reasonable description of the efforts of (a) the turnkey rental investor, (b) the turnkey provider, and (c) the traditional rental investor.

Note: The estimates that follow utilize a simplistic approach. There are many factors that could change the results. Regardless, it is still worth developing a model to gain insight into how the business plan for each investor functions.

Scenario:

Example 3.1 is a case study using the first turnkey property I purchased. Not all the financial values used in this example are known, and hence, some of the values are approximate. The timeline in this example is straightforward: The turnkey provider or the traditional rental investor purchased the property, renovated the property, and found a tenant. It is assumed that this process took three months.

At the three-month mark, the turnkey provider sold the property to the turnkey investor, whereas the traditional rental investor continued to self-manage the property. It is assumed the turnkey provider and traditional rental investor purchased the subject property using cash, whereas the turnkey investor purchased the property using a mortgage.

The turnkey provider or traditional rental investor could have purchased using a mortgage. However, many active real estate investment deals are cash purchases; this allows the buyer to purchase at as low a price as possible. Additionally, some of the best deals have significant deferred maintenance, and such properties would not qualify for a bank-issued mortgage.

Analysis:

An itemized breakdown of the investment funds for the turnkey investor, turnkey provider, and traditional rental investor is shown in Table 44.

Table 44. Itemized list of investment funds needed to secure an investment property.

	Turnkey Rental Investor	Turnkey Provider	Traditional Rental Investor
Purchase Price	$119,000	$64,000	$64,000
Down Payment	$23,980	$64,000	$64,000
Closing Costs	$5,000	$3,000*	$3,000*
Renovation	$0	$32,000	$32,000
Holding Costs	$0	$700*	$700*
Total Investment Funds	$28,980	$99,700	$99,700

The purchase prices shown in the table ($119,000 and $64,000) were the actual purchase prices. Information about the past sales history can be found by visiting the county auditor's website, which is where I was able to determine how much the turnkey provider paid for the property. All approximated values within Table 44 have an * next to them. Remember, the values can be adjusted to model other scenarios.

The three investors all require some initial funds, labeled Total Investment Funds. The investment funds for the turnkey rental investor included the down payment and the closing costs for a total of $28,980. For simplicity, other smaller expenses have been lumped together with the closing costs.

The investment funds required for the turnkey provider and the traditional rental investor are identical at $99,700. This total includes purchasing the property, funds to renovate the property, and service utilities. The property tax and insurance have been lumped together in the holding costs. The equations required to model this example are given in **Appendix C: Mathematics for Loan Products**.

Revenue:

The revenue sources for the turnkey investor and the traditional rental investor are the rent collected. Similarly, the revenue sources for the turnkey provider are the gross proceeds from selling the property and the property management fees collected (typically, the turnkey provider offers property management services).

In this example, the rent is $1,025 per month or $12,300 per year. Therefore, the revenue of the turnkey investor and the traditional rental investor are $12,300 and $9,225, respectively. Remember, once the turnkey investor purchased the property from the turnkey provider, they were able to collect rent for the full twelve months during the first year of ownership. The traditional rental investor started to collect rent in the fourth month because the property was under renovation for the first three months.

The turnkey provider sold the property for $119,000, which is the gross proceeds. In addition to the sale proceeds, the turnkey provider collected a management fee of $738 from the turnkey investor. The management fee was 8 percent of the rent, which gives $738:

$1,025 / month x 8% x 9 months = $738.

Hence, the total Year 1 revenue for the turnkey provider was $119,738:

$119,000 + $738 = $119,738.

An itemized description of the annual gross revenue for each investor is summarized in Table 45.

Table 45. Annual gross revenue comparison of Year 1.

	Turnkey Rental Investor	Turnkey Provider/ Property Manager	Traditional Rental Investor
Rent	$12,300	$0	$9,225
Sale Proceeds	$0	$119,000	$0
Management Fee	$0	$738 (8%)	$0
Total Revenue	**$12,300**	**$119,738**	**$9,225**

Expenses:

The expenses for the turnkey provider include

- the acquisition cost of $64,000,
- the closing costs of $3,000,
- the holding costs of $700,
- the capital gains tax for a capital gain of $19,300 ($119,900 - $99,700),
- insurance, and
- the renovation costs for the property of $32,000.

The capital gain is treated in this example as ordinary income (owned for less than one year) and, assuming the tax bracket is 37 percent,

APPENDIX D: MATHEMATICS FOR THE EXAMPLES

results in a tax liability of $7,141:

$$0.37 \times \$19{,}300 = \$7{,}141.$$

The total expenses for the first year are $106,841:

$$\$64{,}000 + \$3{,}000 + \$700 + \$7{,}141 + \$32{,}000 = \$106{,}841.$$

Note: For simplicity, the expenses do not include insurance or income taxes for the property management fees collected as revenue by the turnkey provider. It is worth pointing out that the turnkey provider no longer has expenses associated with the property after it is sold to the turnkey investor, though some business expenses will continue such as insurance, traveling expenses, and office-related expenses. These expenses have not been included for simplicity. Lastly, the cost of the materials was confirmed because this turnkey provider made available the scope of work, which included the skew numbers for the different materials and the total costs of $32,000 for materials and labor.

The expenses for the turnkey investor can be broken into several categories, which include

- acquisition expenses,
- fixed expenses,
- variable expenses, and
- depreciation.
- The acquisition expense includes the down payment of $23,980 and closing costs of $5,000. Note: The acquisition expenses will show on the turnkey investor's balance sheet but are not used to determine profit as they are startup funds.

The fixed expenses include

- the mortgage of $5,918,
- the property tax of $1,379,
- the property insurance of $434, and
- the property management fee of $984.

The mortgage was computed using Eq. A.1. My preference is to separate the fixed expenses from other expenses as it greatly simplifies the process of evaluating potential properties during the purchasing process.

It must be mentioned that the mortgage payment can be broken into an interest and principal component of $4,380 and $1,538, respectively. The principal component is how much the borrowed balance is reduced and is determined using Eq. A.4. The interest component is an allowable expense; however, the principal portion is not. The principal component is included in the fixed expenses because it affects monthly profit. Remember, when reporting to the IRS, only the interest portion is an expense.

The variable expense includes a maintenance cost of $0, a vacancy cost of $0, and an income tax equal to approximately $303. The depreciation (assuming a full year of service) was $3,607:

$$80\% \times \$124{,}000 / 27.5 = \$3{,}607.$$

When calculating depreciation, first determine the cost basis, which, for this example, is given by summing the purchase price and the closing costs together, resulting in a cost basis of $124,000:

$$\$119{,}000 + \$5{,}000 = \$124{,}000.$$

Next, separate the cost basis into the building and land values. Here, it is assumed that 80 percent of the cost basis is the value of the building. Lastly, divide by 27.5 years, the number of years the building is depreciated. Note: It is assumed the property is in service for the entire year (thus, depreciation for the entire year is appropriate instead of using a prorated figure).

The tax expense was calculated as follows:

- Compute the gross income.
- Compute the total allowable expenses.
- Determine the taxable income by subtracting the result from Step 2 from the result derived from Step 1.

APPENDIX D: MATHEMATICS FOR THE EXAMPLES

- Multiple the result from Step 3 by the appropriate tax bracket.

For Step 1, the gross income is shown in Table 45. For Step 2, the total tax-deductible expense is determined by summing the allowable expenses listed in Table 46.

Table 46. Annual expenses comparison of Year 1.

Expenses	Turnkey Rental Investor	Turnkey Provider	Traditional Rental Investor
Mortgage Interest	$4,380	$0	$0
Property Tax	$1,379	n/a	$1,379
Insurance	$434	n/a	$434
Management	$984	$0	$0
Maintenance	$0	$0	$0
Vacancy	$0	$0	$0
Depreciation	$3,607	$0	$2,880
Taxes	$365	$7,141	$1,088
Total Expenses	**$11,149**	**$7,141**	**$5,781**

The result is $10,784, which includes all the listed expenses except the taxes. The taxable income is $1,516:

$$\$12,300 - \$10,784 = \$1,516.$$

Assuming a tax bracket of 24 percent results in a tax expense (liability) of $365:

$$0.24 \times \$1,516 = \$365.$$

The expenses for the traditional rental investor include most of the considerations for the turnkey provider and turnkey rental investor. The acquisition expense includes the cash purchase of $64,000 and the closing costs of $3,000. The renovation expense for the property was $32,000, and the holding costs were $700.

The cost basis is the sum of the cash purchase, the renovation expense, and closing costs, as shown below:

$$\$64,000 + \$32,000 + \$3,000 = \$99,000.$$

The fixed expenses include

- the property tax of $1,379 and
- the property insurance of $434.

The variable expenses include

- a maintenance cost of $0,
- a vacancy cost of $0, and
- income tax equal to approximately $766.

The depreciation (assuming a full year of service) was $2,880:

$$80\% \times \$99,000 / 27.5 = \$2,880.$$

The tax expense was calculated using the same procedure. For comparison purposes, the tax bracket used was 24 percent. The taxable income is $4,532:

$$\$9,225 - \$4,693 = \$4,532.$$

The tax liability is $1,088:

$$0.24 \times \$4,532 = \$1,088.$$

The annual expenses for the turnkey investor, turnkey provider, and traditional rental investor are summarized above in Table 46. Note: The acquisition expenses are listed in Table 44. As shown, the ongoing expenses are greatest for the turnkey rental investor because of the mortgage interest and depreciation.

Debt:

The turnkey provider and the traditional rental investor purchased the property using cash; therefore, they do not have any debt. Note: The traditional rental investor will almost certainly refinance as soon as the property is eligible. For simplicity, the example assumes the refinance does not occur during the first year of operating the property.

The turnkey investor purchased the property with a mortgage and will have debt. The debt is initially the borrowed balance of $95,200:

$$80\% \times \$119,000 = \$95,200.$$

The debt decreases each month by the principal component of the mortgage payment, resulting in a debt at the end of the year of $93,662:

$$\$95,200 - \$1,538 = \$93,662.$$

The principal of $1,538 is computed using Eq. A.5. The debt for the three investors is summarized in Table 47.

Table 47. Debt comparison and summary.

	Initial Debt	Year 1 Debt
Turnkey Provider	$0	$0
Turnkey Investor	$95,200	$93,662
Traditional Rental Investor	$0	$0

Assets:

The assets category is simply the monetary value of the property at the end of the first year. The appraised value of the property after renovations is $119,000. For the purposes of this example, the appreciation rate is assumed to be 3 percent. For reference, the historical appreciation rate is between 3.5 and 3.8 percent, so a 3-percent appreciation rate is a reasonable rate to use. After one year, the property value has increased from $119,000 to $122,570:

$$\$119,000 * 1.03 = \$122,570.$$

The property value is assumed to be $64,000 before the renovations.

The asset category for the turnkey provider changed during ownership. At the time of purchase, the asset value for the turnkey provider was $64,000. The turnkey provider spent $32,000 to renovate the property resulting in an after-repair value (ARV) of $119,000 (assets). Once renovated and tenanted, the turnkey provider decided to sell the property, resulting in $0 in assets. Note that the turnkey provider's assets began at $64,000, went to $119,000, and then went to $0. Technically, the year-end profits for each investor should be listed as a cash asset. For simplicity, the evolution of the property is the only listed asset.

Similarly, the traditional rental investor had an initial asset value of $64,000 and spent $32,000 in renovations, resulting in an asset value of $119,000 that increased to $122,570 at the end of the first year. Lastly, the turnkey rental investor purchased the property for $119,000 (initial asset value), which increased to $122,570 at the end of the first year. A summary of the assets for the three investors is given in Table 48.

Table 48. Asset comparison and summary.

	Initial Assets	ARV, Assets	Year 1 Assets
Turnkey Provider	$64,000	$119,000	$0
Turnkey Investor	$0	$119,000	$122,570
Traditional Rental Investor	$64,000	$119,000	$122,570

APPENDIX D: MATHEMATICS FOR THE EXAMPLES

Discussion:

An itemized summary of the total profits for the turnkey investor, turnkey provider, and traditional rental investor for the first year is shown below in Table 49.

Table 49. Annual net profit comparison after the first year.

Profit	Turnkey Rental Investor	Turnkey Provider	Traditional Rental Investor
Cash flow (Gross / Net)	$3,585 / $3,220	$738	$7,412 / $6,234
Loan Paydown	$1,538	$0	$0
Appreciation @ 3%	$3,570	$0	$3,570
Forced Appreciation	$0	$22,300	$22,300
Depreciation	$721	$00	$576
Total Profit (Gross / Net)	$8,693 / $8,325	$23,038 / $15,897	$33,282 / $32,194

The total profits are broken into various profit sources, which include cash flow, loan paydown, appreciation, forced appreciation, and depreciation. These metrics are computed from the revenue, expenses, debt, and assets.

The cash flow is the money remaining after the revenue reported in Table 45 is used to pay the operational expenses listed in Table 46. Note: The cash flow is the monthly profit, and while the principal component of the mortgage is not an expense, it certainly reduces the monthly profit. Remember, too, the depreciation is a paper loss and does not lower the cash flow. The cash flow can be computed as:

Revenue - Total Expenses - Loan Paydown + Depreciation.

In Table 49, the cash flow is given as the gross cash flow and net cash flow. The net cash flow is the cash remaining after paying income tax.

The loan paydown is equal to how much the borrowed balance of the mortgage decreased after one year of debt service. Hence, the loan paydown is nothing more than the difference between the initial debt and the debt after one year; in other words, it is identical to the total principal payment.

Appreciation is the change in the value of the property with respect to the purchase price, which is nothing more than how much the asset value increases after one year. The forced appreciation is the value added to the property by renovating it and is the increase in the monetary value of the asset.

As shown in Table 49, the turnkey provider and the traditional rental investor see a profit from forced appreciation within the first year. This forced appreciation (renovation) is seen by the turnkey provider with the sale of the property to the turnkey rental investor. The forced appreciation is one of the key advantages for the turnkey provider and the traditional rental investor.

Note, too, the turnkey rental investor paid income tax on the cash flow and the loan paydown. The sum of the cash flow and loan paydown is $5,113. The effective tax rate is given as the income tax paid divided by the earnings taxed:

$$\$365 / \$5,113 = 7.1\%.$$

Thus, depreciation reduced the tax rate of the turnkey rental investor from 24 to 7.1 percent.

Again, this reduction in tax is the return from depreciation. The effective tax rates for the turnkey provider and the traditional rental investor are 37 and 14.7 percent. Hence, the effective tax rate for the turnkey provider was unchanged, whereas the tax rate for the traditional rental investor decreased from 24 to 14.7 percent. Lastly,

APPENDIX D: MATHEMATICS FOR THE EXAMPLES

note that the total profit included in Table 49 does not include the return from depreciation. This return was included by accounting for taxes in the other profit returns and by computing the effective tax rate.

The return on investment (ROI) is shown for each investor below in Table 50.

Table 50. Comparison of the performance of each investor.

Performance Comparison	Turnkey Rental Investor	Turnkey Provider	Traditional Rental Investor
Total Investment	$28,980	$99,700	$99,700
Total Profit (Gross / Net)	$8,693 / $8,325	$23,038 / $15,897	$33,282 / $32,194
ROI	32.5%	23.1%	33.4%
Hours Worked	20	480	480
Hourly Rate	$471	$48	$69

The Total Net Profit was used for the ROI calculation. For the turnkey investor, the ROI is 28.7 percent, which is greater than the 15.9 percent return for the turnkey provider and very similar to the traditional rental investor's return. The ROI for the traditional rental investor is similar to the turnkey investor's but will likely be much greater than the turnkey investor's in Year 2. Note: Most of the returns for the turnkey provider occurred after only three months. Hence, a more accurate ROI would be 61.6 percent:

$$4 \times \frac{\$15,897 - \$738}{\$99,700} + \frac{\$738}{\$99,700} = 61.6\%,$$

in which the first term is the annualized ROI for selling the property, and the second term is the annualized ROI for the property management income.

What is even more telling is the hourly rate. The turnkey investor worked for approximately three hours to purchase the property (two hours and fifteen minutes spent providing documents to the bank, with an additional forty-five minutes spent signing documents at the closing), twelve hours of reviewing monthly statements (one hour per month), and one hour to gather and send documents to a CPA for taxes, for a total of sixteen hours. This estimate was rounded to twenty hours (includes an extra four hours for contingencies).

To determine the total hours worked by the turnkey provider, it was assumed they put in a full-time effort (forty hours per week) for three months until the property was sold. This estimate does not include operating the asset for nine months. At any rate, the total time worked was estimated at 480 hours:

$$3 \text{ months} * 4 \text{ weeks} * 40 \text{ hours} = 480 \text{ hours}.$$

As shown, the turnkey investor's hourly rate is calculated as $495, significantly higher than the $48 made by the turnkey provider.

Conclusions:

The relevant results are summarized in Table 50. Again, the turnkey provider and traditional rental investor are both working full-time positions that assume more risk. The ROI for the traditional rental investor is slightly better than the turnkey rental investor. The ROI for the turnkey provider, at 15.9 percent, is deceiving because the funds received at the three-month mark could be used to acquire another property. Assuming the turnkey provider could operate at an efficiency of 100 percent, their ROI would then be 61.6 percent.

Example 10.2 Market Cycle Analysis for Atlanta, GA

The results from Example 10.2 are summarized in the section **Chapter 10 The Real Estate Market Cycle**. The full treatment of this example is provided below.

The objective of Example 10.2 is to demonstrate how some of the various dependent variables, such as property value, rental rates, and gross domestic product, fluctuate with the real estate market cycle. To begin, consider the following case study for the Atlanta metropolitan area. Note: The following analysis can be used for any metropolitan area.

The average home price and number of building permits, as a function of time, are shown in Figure 20 for the Atlanta metropolitan area.

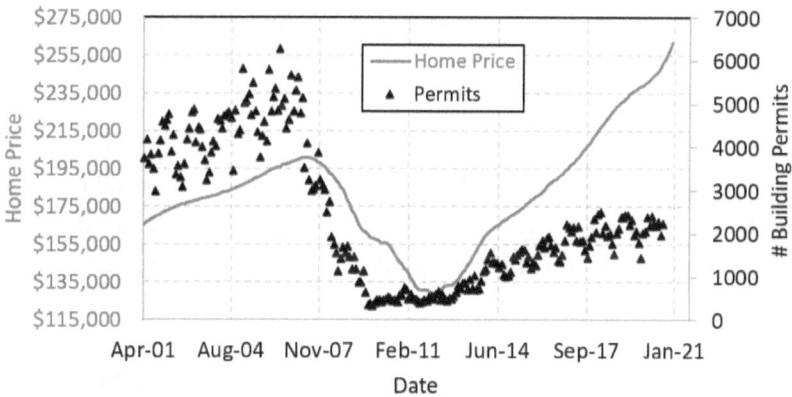

Figure 20. Home price and number of building permits versus the time for the Atlanta metropolitan area.

As shown, the most recent bust occurred around December 2007, which corresponds to the point in the figure where you can see the housing prices starting to decrease. Note: The number of new building permits issued each month is a reasonable indicator of how much new construction is being commissioned.

As shown in the figure, the number of permits was around 3,500 per month in the spring of 2001 and increased to a maximum of 6,000 per month in June 2006. You will notice, however, that the number of new permits dropped drastically in June 2010 to a localized minimum. Also, note that the number of permits has been increasing almost linearly since early 2021.

The beginning of this chart shows an expansion, leading to hyper supply and a recession. Recovery began roughly in 2010, followed by the expansion. Now, take note of how much the property values fluctuate. The average property price at the beginning of the expansion phase in 2012 was around $130,000 and then grew rapidly. The average home price increased from $130,000 in 2012 to $250,000 in 2020, which is a 7.5 percent compounding rate.

During the recession, the average home price peaked at $200,000 in December 2007, then decreased to $130,000 at the start of the recovery in 2012. While the domain in the figure is not sufficient to show the full timeline, the average home price at the beginning of the recovery (the local minimum) and the peak at the end of the expansion (local maximum) are greater than the corresponding values from the previous cycle. This trend, when averaged over all markets, i.e., the national average, has held true since the eighteen hundreds, which means that, during a long enough time scale, property values will increase. The national average for the appreciation rate is around 3.5 percent.

The gross domestic product (GDP) is the estimated monetary value of a metropolitan area. The GDP and change in percentage for the GDP versus time for the Atlanta metropolitan area are shown below in Figure 21.

APPENDIX D: MATHEMATICS FOR THE EXAMPLES

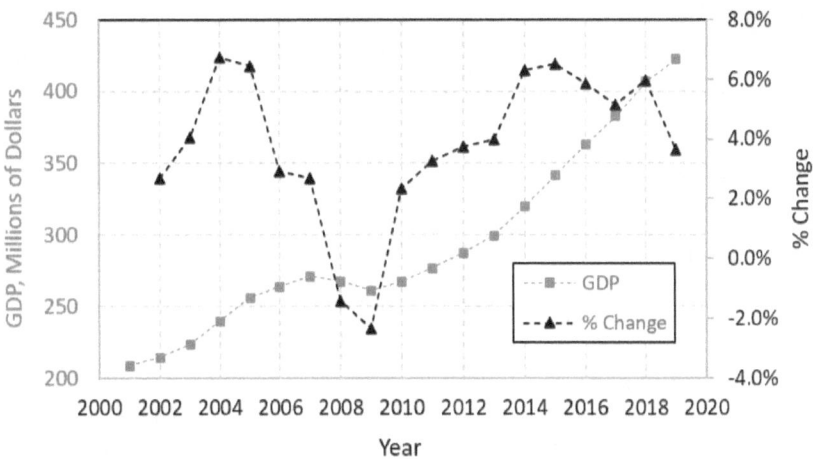

Figure 21. The gross domestic product versus time for the Atlanta metropolitan area.

As shown, the GDP for the Atlanta metropolitan area grew rapidly from 2002 to 2004. This growth continued but slowed as the years passed until the GDP peaked at $270 million in 2007. The GDP decreased to a local minimum in 2009 before beginning to grow rapidly during the expansion phase. While the different market phases are not as clear in the raw GDP numbers, plotting the GDP as the percent change in GDP helps to highlight the market cycles (black line).

Another interesting plot is given in Figure 22.

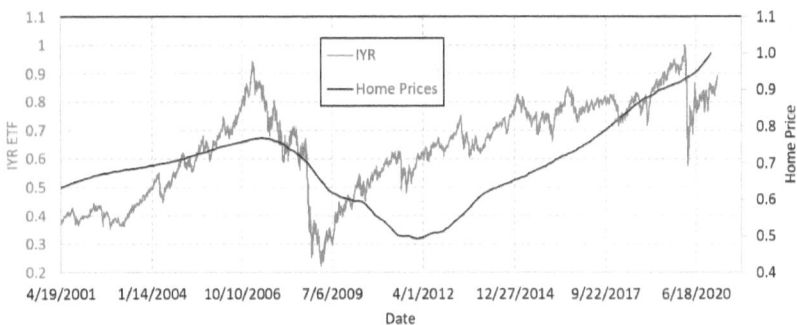

Figure 22. The IYR ETF and average home price versus time for the Atlanta metropolitan area.

The red line depicts the daily price chart for the IYR, the symbol (ticker symbol) for an equity traded fund that some stock traders use as an indicator for the housing sector. The prices shown are the closing prices. Note: There are multiple index funds for different types of real estate. For this analysis, I used IYR, but other index funds may be more suitable for your specific research. As shown, the price for the IYR peaked in February 2007, about ten months prior to the beginning of the recession phase. The average home price peaked in July 2007. Again, the IYR is shown to lead the average home price.

Note: This plot shows the range for the IYR and average home price between 0 and 1. The data was purposely collapsed for display purposes. This plot is a classic illustration of how normalizing data can help collapse different data sets on the same range. In this case, each time series was normalized by using the largest value in the series, which is why each time series has a maximum value of 1. While using the maximum value is a simple normalization parameter, many of the parameters used to nondimensionalize data are not simple, and some do not have a range between 0 and 1.

The rental rate and vacancy versus time for the Atlanta metropolitan area are shown in Figure 23.

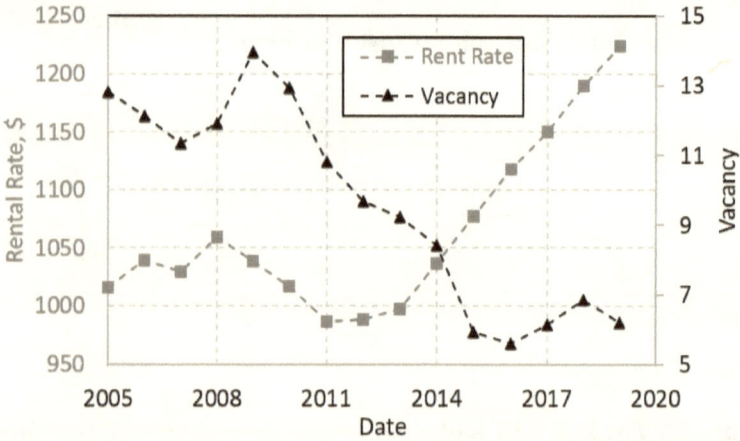

Figure 23. The rental rate and vacancy versus time for the Atlanta metropolitan area.

As shown, the vacancy decreased from 2005 to a local minimum of 11 percent in 2007. The vacancy rate then increased to 13 percent by 2009 and then decreased steadily to around 6 percent by 2015. The rental rate increased to just over $1,050 per month in 2008 and then decreased during the recession to a minimum of around $975 per month in 2011. The rate remained low during the recovery period and then began to increase after 2013.

The housing supply, another indicator of note, is usually reported in months and represents how many months of inventory are listed. To calculate supply, determine the number of houses listed for sale (existing inventory or supply) and the number of houses that sold (demand) over a specified time period. Usually, one month is used as the time period. Next, divide the existing inventory by the number of sold properties (inventory divided by demand).

The result is a value in months during which a housing supply below six months results in appreciating home prices, a housing supply above six months results in negative appreciating home prices, and a balanced supply of six months results in slight appreciation. In general, a six-month supply supposedly represents a healthy real estate market.

Multiple factors influence the housing supply such as, but not limited to,

- population growth,
- interest rates,
- employment,
- weather,
- government policy, and
- crowd psychology.

An example of how housing supply fluctuates with time and the corresponding change in home value is shown in Figure 24.

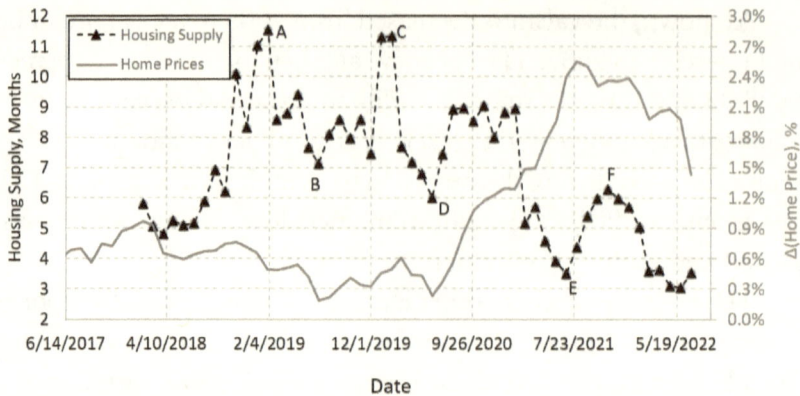

Figure 24. Housing supply vs time on the left axis is compared with the % change in home price on the right axis.

Cold weather tends to increase the housing supply, as shown by labels A and C, whereas warm weather tends to result in a decreasing housing supply (labels B, D, E, and F). The corresponding home prices are not overly sensitive to seasonal fluctuations. Note: For dates before label D, the housing supply is mostly above six months, and the corresponding changes in house prices are lower than those at the dates after label D, at which point, the housing supply drops well below six months. While not shown in this figure, the housing supply tends to be at all-time highs during the recession phase and at values below six months during the expansion phase.

While many other parameters could also be analyzed, this section has purposely kept to only some key parameters. To summarize, the different variables that are dependent on the real estate market cycle are shown to fluctuate significantly with respect to the different market cycle phases. Some of these parameters, such as house value, illustrate why it is useful to include the market cycle in the purchase criteria. Other parameters, such as the number of permits, are variables that can be used to help estimate the phase of the market cycle.

APPENDIX D: MATHEMATICS FOR THE EXAMPLES

Example 13.3 Cash Flow Properties vs Appreciation Properties

The results from Example 13.3 are summarized in **Chapter 13 Cash Flow vs Appreciation Properties**. The full treatment of this example is provided here.

The objective of Example 13.3 is to show the financial differences in purchasing and operating a cash flow property and an appreciation property. To begin, consider the two involved properties; the financials are shown below in Table 51.

Table 51. Comparison of financials for a cash flow property and an appreciation property.

	Cash Flow Property	Appreciation Property
Purchase Price	$150,000	$350,000
Rental Rate	$1,300	$2,300
Appreciation Rate	2%	5%

As shown, the purchase prices for the cash flow and appreciation properties are $150,000 and $350,000, respectively. The corresponding rental rates are $1,300 and $2,300 per month. Real properties were used to set the purchase price and rental rate, as well as some of the other financials.

The appreciation rates were selected to represent a rate below and above the national average. These rates are similar to the anticipated appreciation rates for the respective properties. As shown, the two properties under consideration have very different purchase prices, appreciation rates, and rental rates.

Revenue

The annual revenue for the cash flow and appreciation properties are $15,600 and $27,600, respectively:

$$12 \text{ months} * \$1,300 = \$15,600;$$
$$12 \text{ months} * \$2,300 = \$27,600.$$

Table 52. Revenue for the cash flow and appreciation properties.

	Cash Flow Property	Appreciation Property
Revenue	$15,600	$27,600

Debt

For this example, funds were borrowed from a bank to purchase the properties. A loan-to-value ratio of 80 percent was used, resulting in initial loan balances of

$$0.8 * \$150,000 = \$120,000$$

and

$$0.8 * \$350,000 = \$280,000$$

for the cash flow and appreciation properties, respectively.

The interest rate and term used to compute the mortgages were 5 percent and 360 months, respectively. The total principal after one year of service is given using Eq. A.5 and is $1,770 and $4,131 for the cash flow and appreciation properties, respectively. The debt for each property after one year of service is given as:

$$\$120,000 - \$1,770 = \$118,230$$

and

$$\$280,000 - \$4,131 = \$275,869.$$

APPENDIX D: MATHEMATICS FOR THE EXAMPLES

Table 53. *Summary of debt for the cash flow and appreciation properties.*

	Cash Flow Property	Appreciation Property
Initial Debt	$120,000	$280,000
End of Year 1 Debt	$118,230	$275,869

Expenses

The expenses for the cash flow and appreciation properties can be broken into the startup funds and operational expenses. The startup funds include the down payment and closing costs. The down payment is given as the difference between the purchase price and the initial loan balance.

The closing costs were estimated at 3 percent of the purchase price. For the cash flow property, the down payment and closing costs are estimated at:

$$\$150,000 - \$120,000 = \$30,000$$

and

$$3\% * \$150,000 = \$4,500.$$

Similarly, for the appreciation property, the down payment and closing costs are estimated at:

$$\$350,000 - \$280,000 = \$70,000$$

and

$$3\% * \$350,000 = \$10,500.$$

As for the closing costs for the appreciation property, the estimated value used is likely too high. Also, the closing costs are usually a percentage multiplied by the borrowed balance. This estimate, however, is below the actual closing costs for all the properties I have purchased. For this reason, I estimated using the appraised value. The result is much closer to the closing costs I have paid for the properties in my portfolio.

The other expenses included in this example are the

- mortgage interest,
- property insurance,
- property tax,
- management fee, and
- depreciation.

Other, more detailed examples will include vacancy and maintenance, which are omitted here. Also, overhead costs for professionals such as lawyers and CPAs, along with the costs for limited liability companies, trusts, and umbrella insurance, are not included for simplicity.

The mortgage interest is determined using Eq. A.3. The mortgage interest paid after one year of service for the cash flow and appreciation property is given as $5,960 and $13,906, respectively. The property insurance was estimated at $780 and $1,540, respectively.

These estimates were based on premiums for similarly priced properties. The property taxes for the cash flow and appreciation properties were $2,400 and $6,160, respectively, and were again estimated from similarly priced properties.

The management fee is determined by multiplying the annual rent collected by the property management fee. For this example, the management fee was 8 percent, and the corresponding property management expenses are:

$$8\% * \$15,600 = \$1,248$$

and

$$8\% * \$27,600 = \$2,208.$$

Depreciation is determined by multiplying the cost basis for each property by 80 percent and then dividing by 27.5 years. The cost basis was adjusted to $154,500 and $360,500, respectively, by adding the closing costs to the purchase price. The depreciation is:

APPENDIX D: MATHEMATICS FOR THE EXAMPLES

$$0.8 * \$154{,}500 / 27.5 = \$4{,}495$$

and

$$0.8 * \$360{,}500 / 27.5 = \$10{,}487$$

for the cash flow and appreciation properties, respectively.

The taxable income was determined by subtracting the revenue from the total expenses, which included mortgage interest, property insurance, property tax, management fee, and depreciation. The income tax expense was estimated at:

$$\$15{,}600 - \$14{,}882 = \$718$$

and

$$\$27{,}600 - \$34{,}302 = -\$6{,}701.$$

The income tax expense or tax liability is determined by multiplying the taxable income by the appropriate tax bracket. For the purposes of this example, it is assumed that the earnings are treated as passive income and taxed at a tax bracket of 24 percent. The income tax owed by the cash flow and appreciation properties are:

$$24\% * \$718 = \$172.$$

The income tax for the appreciation property is $0 since the reported taxable income is negative. Note: The expenses that were not used to offset taxes are carryover losses. The total expenses, including income tax, are $15,054 and $34,301 for the cash flow and appreciation properties, respectively.

Table 54. Summary of expenses for the cash flow and appreciation properties.

	Cash Flow Property	Appreciation Property
Mortgage Interest	$5,960	$13,906
Property Tax	$2,400	$6,160
Property Insurance	$780	$1,540
Property Management	$1,248	$2,208
Depreciation	$4,495	$10,487
Income Tax	$172	$0
Total Expense	$15,054	$34,302
Total expense includes the income tax.		

Assets

The assets for the investor will be the monetary value of the properties and the year-end cash profits. The asset value will increase from appreciation. The value after the first year of service for the cash flow and appreciation properties are:

$$1.03 * \$150,000 = \$153,000$$

and

$$1.05 * \$350,000 = \$367,500.$$

The year-end profit is determined by summing the monthly cash flow, to be determined below, and is $3,298 and -$345, respectively. The total assets include the property value and the cash generated, as shown:

$$\$153,000 + \$3,298 = \$156,298$$

and

APPENDIX D: MATHEMATICS FOR THE EXAMPLES

$$\$367{,}500 - \$345 = \$367{,}155.$$

Table 55. *Summary of assets for the cash flow and appreciation properties.*

	Cash Flow Property	Appreciation Property
Assets, Beginning	$150,000	$350,000
Asset, Year 1 Property Value	$153,000	$367,500
Assets, Cash	$3,298	-$345
Total Assets	$156,298	$367,155

The Four Returns

We will now compute the four returns for the cash flow and appreciation properties. The cash flow is determined by subtracting the total expenses from the revenue in which the expenses include income tax but exclude depreciation. Remember, depreciation is a paper expense only, and the cash flow represents the actual cash asset in the business account. Lastly, the loan paydown (principal) needs to be excluded. Also, the actual cash assets accumulate after paying the mortgage.

The expenses include the mortgage interest but are missing the principal component; hence, the principal is included too. After the first year of service, the cash flow is given as:

$$\$15{,}600 - \$15{,}026 + \$4{,}495 - \$1{,}770 = \$3{,}299$$

and

$$\$27{,}600 - \$34{,}301 + \$10{,}487 - \$4{,}131 = -\$345.$$

The corresponding monthly cash flow is:

$$\$3{,}299 / 12 = \$275$$

and

$$-\$345 / 12 = -\$29.$$

The loan paydown is determined by subtracting the debt from the beginning of ownership by the debt at the end of the first year of service. The loan paydown is $1,770 and $4,131, respectively. Note: The loan paydown can also be calculated using Eq. A.5.

The return from depreciation for the cash flow property is $1,079 and is determined by multiplying the depreciation listed in the expenses by the tax bracket (24 percent). The appreciation property was taxed as passive income; hence, the tax return is $0. There would have been some income tax if depreciation was not claimed; however, not all the depreciation expense was used immediately to lower income tax as some of the depreciation expenses are carryover losses.

The immediate return from depreciation for the appreciation property is the tax bracket times the difference between the depreciation and the carryover losses, or

$$0.24 \times (\$10,487 - \$6,701) = \$909.$$

The rest of the return from depreciation will have to wait until the carryover losses are eligible to offset the taxes. Note: The carryover losses are at risk of inflation. For real estate professionals, the carryover losses can be applied the year they occur, thus making appreciation properties an excellent option for real estate professionals who earn enough revenue to handle the risks for the monthly losses in cash flow.

The ROI for each of the four returns is determined by dividing the annualized return by the startup funds or invested funds. For the cash flow property, the ROI for the different returns is given as:

Cash-on-cash ROI = 12 months x $275 / ($30,000 + $4,500)
= 9.6%;

Loan Paydown ROI = $1,770 / ($30,000 + $4,500) = 5.1%;

Depreciation ROI = $909 / ($30,000 + $4,500) = 2.6%;

Appreciation ROI = $3,000 / ($30,000 + $4,500) = 8.7%.

The total ROI is determined by summing the cash-on-cash ROI, loan paydown ROI, and the appreciation ROI, or, alternatively, it can be calculated as the total monetary return divided by the invested funds in which the total monetary return is the increase in assets plus the loan paydown. At any rate, the total return is given as:

Total ROI = 9.6% + 5.1% + 8.7% = 23.4%

or

$8,070 / $34,500 = 23.4%.

Similarly, for the appreciation property, the ROI for the different returns is given as:

Cash-on-cash ROI = -$29 x 12 / $80,500 = -0.4%;

Loan Paydown ROI = $4,131 / $80,500 = 5.1%;

Depreciation ROI = $2,036 / $80,500 = 2.5%;

Appreciation ROI = $17,500 / $80,500 = 21.7%.

The total ROI is:

-0.4% + 5.1% + 21.7% = 26.4%.

The percentage of tax paid, which is the effective tax rate, for the cash flow property is given as the taxes paid divided by the sum of the cash flow and the principal. The reason: Taxes were paid for the cash flow and principal (the principal component is not an expense).

The effective tax rate for the cash flow and appreciation properties are:

$172 / $5,069 = 3.4%

and 0%, respectively. Note: For the cash flow property, the return from depreciation reduced the tax rate from 24 to 3.4 percent; for the appreciation property, it was reduced from 24 to 0 percent.

Table 56. Summary of the four returns for the cash flow and appreciation properties.

	Cash Flow Property	Appreciation Property
Cash Flow	$3,299 / 9.6%	-$345 / -0.4%
Loan Paydown	$1,770 / 5.1%	$4,131 / 5.1%
Appreciation	$3,000 / 8.7%	$17,500 / 21.7%
Depreciation	$909 / 2.6%	$2,036 / 2.5%
Effective Tax Rate	3.4%	0%
Total Return	$8,069 / 23.4%	$21,286 / 26.4%

The returns are listed as monetary return / ROI.

Example 25.4 Projected Financial Performance and Scaling for Cash Flow and Appreciation Properties

The results from Example 25.4 are summarized in the section **Example 25.4 Financial Performance and Scaling for Cash Flow and Appreciation Properties**. The full treatment of this example is provided here.

The objective of Example 25.4 is to determine how the returns for one cash flow or one appreciation property can be used to purchase more properties. The returns from the additional properties will then speed up the rate of new acquisitions. Specifically, this example seeks to determine when new properties can be added over a twenty-year period using only the returns included in the portfolio. The property financials and loan terms are shown below in Table 57.

APPENDIX D: MATHEMATICS FOR THE EXAMPLES

Table 57. Property parameters.

Property Parameters	Cash flow Property	Appreciation Property
Purchase Price	$119,900	$250,000
Loan-to-Value Ratio	80%	80%
Mortgage Interest Rate	4.625%	4.625%
Mortgage Term	30 years	30 years
Year 1 Rental Rate	$1,025	$1,700

Revenue

The Year 1 rental rate for the cash flow and appreciation properties were set at $1,025 and $1,700 per month, respectively. The rental rate growth used for the cash flow properties was 1.823 percent per year.

An initial guess for the rental rate growth was used and then iteratively changed until the ROI for the first-year returns of each property was constant, regardless of when the property was purchased. The assumption is that, by averaging all the quantities so that there are no fluctuations associated with the market cycle, the total ROI for all the properties in the portfolio should be constant, regardless of when the property was purchased.

The total ROI for the properties in the portfolio varied by only 0.2 percent for a rental rate growth of 1.823 percent, which demonstrates that the fit is decent. Moreover, the rental growth rate of 1.823 percent falls within the range of historical rental rate growth. The rental rate growth used for the appreciation properties was 4.320 percent. The corresponding increase in rent for Year 2 is $18.7 and $73.4 per month for the cash flow and appreciation properties, respectively.

The Year 1 revenue for the cash flow and appreciation properties are $12,300 and $20,400, respectively. The Year 2 revenue is $12,524 and $21,281, respectively. The annual revenue for each property would continue to grow slowly for the twenty years represented in this simulation, again, at the same constant rates. The values used for the rental rate growth, appreciation rate, and maintenance and vacancy expense are shown in Table 58.

Table 58. Property assumption for growth in expenses, growth in revenue, and maintenance and vacancy expenses.

Property Performance Metrics	Cash flow Property	Appreciation Property
Average Annual Appreciation Rate	2%	5%
Average Monthly Rental Rate Increase per Year	2%	2%
Maintenance Rate	5%	5%
Vacancy Rate	4%	4%

Expenses

The operational expenses included in this example were the

- mortgage interest,
- property tax,
- property insurance,
- property management fee,
- maintenance and repairs,
- vacancy,
- depreciation, and
- income tax.

APPENDIX D: MATHEMATICS FOR THE EXAMPLES

The startup expenses were the downpayment and closing costs of the properties. Note: The only out-of-pocket funds were the down payment and closing costs for the first property. The additional properties were purchased from the total return of the portfolio. The investment funds required to purchase a property is given as:

Purchase Price = (Initial Value)(1 + Appreciation Rate)^{Year}

in which the initial value is the value of the first property purchased.

As for the mortgage interest, the simulation uses a single snapshot in time; hence, the loan parameters remain constant for the twenty-year period. The interest rate used was 4.625 percent, the loan-to-value ratio for all purchases was 0.8, the loan-to-value ratio for cash-out refinances was 0.75, and the term for all the loans was thirty years (360 months). The closing costs for all the loans was 3 percent of the appraised value.

The initial property tax and property insurance for the cash flow property were $1,469 and $478, respectively. The initial property tax and property insurance for the appreciation property were $3,756 and $1,513, respectively. The initial property tax and property insurance were determined using real properties. Starting in Year 2, the property tax and property insurance expenses were increased by 1 percent every year.

The annual maintenance and repairs expense is given as 5 percent of the annual revenue. The vacancy expense was calculated as 4 percent of the annual revenue, and the property management expense is 8 percent of the collected rent. Lastly, the tax bracket used to determine the income tax expense was 24 percent. All income is treated as passive income for tax purposes.

Note: When a new property is purchased, the other properties in the portfolio are refinanced so that the equity can partially fund the purchase of the new property. This results in the mortgage interest changing for the new borrowed balance, which modifies the total expenses and income tax. The expenses for the initial cash flow property in years one through four are tabulated below in Table

59. The expenses for the initial appreciation property in years one through four are tabulated below in Table 60.

Table 59. Expenses for the initial cash flow property for years 1, 2, 3, and 4.

	YR 1	YR 2	YR 3	YR 4
Total Expenses	**$12,087**	**$12,121**	**$12,154**	**$12,185**
Mortgage Interest	$4,404	$4,333	$4,258	$4,180
Property Tax	$1,469	$1,483	$1,498	$1,513
Insurance	$478	$482	$487	$492
Management	$984	$1,002	$1,020	$1,039
Repairs	$615	$626	$638	$649
Vacancy	$492	$501	$510	$519
Depreciation	$3,593	$3,593	$3,593	$3,593
Income Tax	$64	$121	$180	$240

Table 60. Expenses for the initial appreciation property for years 1, 2, 3, and 4.

	YR 1	YR 2	YR 3	YR 4
Total Expenses	**$25,411**	**$25,465**	**$25,518**	**$25,571**
Mortgage Interest	$9,184	$9,035	$8,878	$8,715
Property Tax	$3,756	$3,794	$3,832	$3,870
Insurance	$1,513	$1,528	$1,543	$1,559
Management	$1,632	$1,703	$1,776	$1,853
Repairs	$1,020	$1,064	$1,110	$1,158

APPENDIX D: MATHEMATICS FOR THE EXAMPLES

	YR 1	YR 2	YR 3	YR 4
Vacancy	$816	$851	$888	$926
Depreciation	$7,491	$7,491	$7,491	$7,491
Income Tax	$0	($0	$0	$0

Debt and Assets

The debt is given as the sum of the mortgage balances of the properties in the portfolio. The total assets in the portfolio include the monetary value of the properties and the sum of the cash returns.

A new property is purchased as soon as the returns from appreciation, loan paydown, and cash flow are sufficient to purchase a new property and cover the closing costs for the cash-out refinance and the purchase. New cash flow properties are purchased in years 7, 11, 14, 16, 18, 20, and 20. Note: Two properties were purchased in Year 20. The performance of the portfolio with the cash flow properties (which includes all the properties in the portfolio) one year after each new purchase is shown below in Table 61.

Table 61. Cash flow properties.

Year	Revenue	Expenses	Assets	Debt
1	$12,300	$12,087	$137,727	$94,407
8	$27,916	$26,736	$280,964	$210,109
12	$45,012	$42,681	$456,187	$337,475
15	$63,359	$59,714	$645,478	$479,631
17	$82,113	$77,181	$839,445	$615,600
19	$102,160	$95,714	$1,048,030	$766,878
21	$141,225	$132,706	$1,453,827	$1,065,161

New appreciation properties are purchased in years 7, 11, 14, 16, 18, and 20. The performance of the portfolio with the appreciation properties (which includes all the properties in the portfolio) one year after each new purchase is shown below in Table 62.

Table 62. Appreciation properties.

Year	Revenue	Expenses	Assets	Debt
1	$20,400	$25,411	$262,500	$196,844
8	$54,857	$63,692	$738,728	$536,648
12	$97,453	$94,496	$1,346,892	$967,928
15	$147,515	$101,916	$2,078,928	$1,485,877
17	$195,866	$106,904	$2,864,023	$2,041,011
19	$243,687	$111,904	$3,790,425	$2,694,335
21	$294,762	$117,293	$4,875,435	$3,460,149

Example 29.5 Executing the Business Scaling Action Items

The results from Example 29.5 are summarized in **Example 29.5 Executing the Business Scaling Action Items**. The full treatment of this example is provided here. The objective of Example 29.5 is to illustrate how to use the action items listed in the checklist **Monthly Business Management Checklist** in the subsection Business Scaling.

To begin, the financial model developed for **Example 25.4 Projected Financial Performance and Scaling for Cash Flow and Appreciation Properties** is used to model the financial state of Example 29.5. The portfolio for Example 29.5 includes three hypothetical properties: 123 Main Street, 456 Cemetery Road, and

APPENDIX D: MATHEMATICS FOR THE EXAMPLES

789 High Street. These properties were purchased nine, six, and three years ago, respectively.

The financial performance for 123 Main Street for the first ten years of ownership is shown in Table 63.

Table 63. Financials for 123 Main Street for the first 10 years of ownership.

Financials for 123 Main Street					
Year	1	2	3	4	5
Revenue	$12,300	$12,524	$12,753	$12,985	$13,222
Mort. Interest	$4,404	$4,333	$4,258	$4,180	$4,098
Prop. Tax	$1,469	$1,483	$1,498	$1,513	$1,528
Insurance	$478	$482	$487	$492	$497
Management	$984	$1,002	$1,020	$1,039	$1,058
Repairs	$615	$626	$638	$649	$661
Vacancy	$492	$501	$510	$519	$529
Depreciation	$3,593	$3,593	$3,593	$3,593	$3,593
Income Tax	$64	$121	$180	$240	$302
Total Expenses	$12,098	$12,141	$12,184	$12,225	$12,265
Cash Flow	$2,281	$2,391	$2,502	$2,615	$2,729
Loan Paydown	$1,513	$1,585	$1,660	$1,738	$1,820
Appreciation	$2,398	$2,446	$2,495	$2,545	$2,596

Year	6	7	8	9	10
Revenue	$13,463	$13,708	$13,958	$14,213	$14,472
Mort. Interest	$4,012	$3,922	$3,827	$3,728	$3,625
Prop. Tax	$1,54	$1,559	$1,574	$1,590	$1,606
Insurance	$502)	$507	$512	$517	$522
Management	$1,077	$1,097	$1,117	$1,137	$1,157
Repairs	$673	$685	$698	$711	$724
Vacancy	$539	$548	$558	$569	$579
Depreciation	$3,593	$3,593	$3,593	$3,593	$3,593
Income Tax	$366	$431	$499	$568	$640
Total Expenses	$12,304	$12,342	$12,37	$12,413	$12,446
Cash Flow	$2,845	$2,963	$3,082	$3,203	$3,325
Loan Paydown	$1,906	$1,996	$2,091	$2,190	$2,293
Appreciation	$2,648	$2,701	$2,755	$2,810	$2,866

The performances for 456 Cemetery Road and 789 High Street after six and three years of service are shown in Table 64 and Table 65, respectively. Again, the steps listed below are required to execute the Business Scaling action items.

APPENDIX D: MATHEMATICS FOR THE EXAMPLES

Table 64. Financials for 456 Cemetery Road for the first 10 years of ownership.

Financials for 456 Cemetery Road					
Year	4	5	6	7	8
Revenue	$12,753	$12,985	$13,222	$13,463	$13,708
Mort. Interest	$4,674	$4,598	$4,519	$4,436	$4,348
Prop. Tax	$1,543	$1,559	$1,574	$1,590	$1,606
Insurance	$502	$507	$512	$517	$527
Management	$1,020	$1,039	$1,058	$1,077	$1,097
Repairs	$638	$649	$661	$673	$685
Vacancy	$510	$519	$529	$539	$548
Depreciation	$3,701	$3,701	$3,701	$3,701	$3,701
Income Tax	$39	$100	$160	$223	$288
Total Expenses	$12,628	$12,672	$12,715	$12,756	$12,797
Cash Flow	$2,281	$2,333	$2,447	$2,563	$2,681
Loan Paydown	$1,606	$1,682	$1,761	$1,845	$1,932
Appreciation	$2,545	$2,596	$2,648	$2,701	$2,755

Year	9	10
Revenue	$13,958	$14,213
Mort. Interest	$4,257	$4,162
Prop. Tax	$1,622	$1,638
Insurance	$527	$533
Management	$1,117	$1,137
Repairs	$698	$711
Vacancy	$558	$569
Depreciation	$3,701	$3,701
Income Tax	$354	$423
Total Expenses	$12,836	$12,873
Cash Flow	**$2,801**	**$2,922**
Loan Paydown	$2,023	$2,119
Appreciation	$2,810	$2,866

Table 65. *Financials for 456 Cemetery Road for the first 10 years of ownership.*

Financials for 789 High Street				
Year	7	8	9	10
Revenue	$13,463	$13,708	$13,958	$14,213
Mort. Interest	$4,960	$4,880	$4,795	$4,707
Prop. Tax	$1,543	$1,559	$1,574	$1,590
Insurance	$502	$507	$512	$517
Management	$1,077	$1,097	$1,117	$1,137

APPENDIX D: MATHEMATICS FOR THE EXAMPLES

Financials for 789 High Street				
Repairs	$673	$685	$698	$711
Vacancy	$539	$548	$558	$569
Depreciation	$3,928	$3,928	$3,928	$3,928
Income Tax	$58	$121	$186	$253
Total Expenses	$13,280	$13,325	$13,369	$13,411
Cash Flow	$2,406	$2,526	$2,648	$2,772
Loan Paydown	$1,704	$1,785	$1,869	$1,958
Appreciation	$2,701	$2,755	$2,810	$2,866

Step 1. Determine the cash funds in the business account.

These cash funds would normally be determined by checking the account balance. For this example, the yearly profits of each property in the portfolio were summed together to determine the balance.

The reasons I've utilized a hypothetical portfolio are

1. to provide realistic numbers to the best of my ability, and
2. to properly execute later action items that require the financial performance of a portfolio.

At any rate, the property expenses included in the analysis are the

- mortgage interest,
- property tax,
- property insurance,
- property management fees,
- maintenance and repairs,
- vacancy,
- depreciation, and
- income tax.

The expenses and revenue were modeled to grow each year, again, using the same model developed in Example 25.4. The resulting cash from the accumulated cash flow is $47,236.

Step 2. Determine how much cash is in your personal account for investing.

The funds in your personal account for investing is assumed to be $0.

Step 3. Estimate the equity for the properties in the portfolio.

The equity is determined using the appraised value and the current mortgage balance of the properties. The mortgage balance at the end of each year for the three properties in the portfolio is given in Table 66.

Table 66. Mortgage balance by year for a hypothetical portfolio.

Year	123 Main	456 Cemetery	789 High
Initial Balance	$95,920	$101,791	$108,021
1	$94,407		
2	$92,822		
3	$91,162		
4	$89,423	$100,185	
5	$87,603	$98,503	
6	$85,697	$96,742	
7	$83,700	$94,897	$106,317
8	$81,609	$92,965	$104,532
9	$79,420	$90,942	$102,663
10	$77,127	$88,823	$100,705

APPENDIX D: MATHEMATICS FOR THE EXAMPLES

As shown, the initial balance, which corresponds to the borrowed funds from the bank, is greater for the newer properties because the purchase price was higher due to appreciation. The purchase prices for 123 Main Street, 456 Cemetery Road, and 789 High Street were $119,900, $127,239, and $135.027, respectively. The corresponding mortgage balances at the end of Year 9 are $79,420, $90,942, and $102,663, respectively.

The appraised value does not need to be professionally determined. At this stage, a simple estimate, such as the Zestimate through https://www.zillow.com, is sufficient. For this example, the value of $143,213 was determined using an annual appreciation rate of 2 percent. The corresponding equity is given as the property value minus the mortgage balance. The equity for 123 Main Street, 456 Cemetery Road, and 789 High Street are $63,872, $52,350, and $40,629, respectively.

Step 4. Estimate the loan-to-value ratio for each property in the portfolio.

The loan-to-value ratio is given as the mortgage balance divided by the property value. The loan-to-value ratio for 123 Main Street, 456 Cemetery Road, and 789 High Street is 55.4 percent, 63.5 percent, and 71.8 percent, respectively.

Step 5. Estimate the funds from the different loan products and selling options for each property with a loan-to-value ratio of less than 0.75.

For simplicity, the different selling options are not analyzed. The four loan products we are comparing are a refinance, a cash-out refinance, a home equity loan (HEL), and a home equity line of credit (HELOC). The funds available will depend on the closing costs and the loan-to-value ratio offered by the lending institution. The closing costs for the refinance and cash-out refinance are assumed to be 3 percent of the appraised value. The closing costs for the HEL is assumed to be 3 percent of the borrowed funds, and the closing costs for the HELOC is assumed to be $500. The loan-to-value ratio for the cash-out refinance, HEL, and HELOC are 0.75, 0.75, and 0.80, respectively.

The funds from refinancing are $0. The funds from the cash-out refinance are given as:

*L2V * Appraised Value - Mortgage Balance - Closing Costs*

For 123 Main Street, the estimated funds from refinancing are given as:

0.75 * $143,292 - $79,420 - 0.03 * $143,292 = $23,750

Similarly, the estimated funds for 456 Cemetery Road and 789 High Street are $12,228 and $507, respectively.

The funds available from the HEL is determined using the same calculation as the cash-out refinance. For 123 Main Street, 456 Cemetery Road, and 789 High Street, the estimated funds from the HEL are $27,297, $16,527, and $4,806, respectively.

The HELOC balances, which would be the maximum funds available, are also estimated using the same equation as the cash-out refinance. For 123 Main Street, 456 Cemetery Road, and 789 High Street, the estimated HELOC balances are $34,713, $23,191, and $11,470, respectively. The estimated funds available from each loan product are summarized below in Table 67.

Table 67. Estimated from the four loan products for a hypothetical portfolio.

	Refi	Cash-Out Refi	HEL	HELOC
123 Main	$0	$23,750	$27,207	$34,713
456 Cemetery	$0	$12,228	$16,527	$23,191
789 High	$0	$507	$4,806	$11,470

APPENDIX D: MATHEMATICS FOR THE EXAMPLES

Step 6. Estimate the total investment funds.

The total funds available is the sum of the funds derived from steps 1, 2, and 5. The sum of steps 1, 2, and 5 for a refinance, cash-out refinance, home equity loan, and a home equity line of credit are $48,201, $84,686, $96,741, and $117,576, respectively. Note: Refinancing does not provide additional funds.

Step 7. Determine how many properties can be purchased with the total funds derived in Step 6.

It is assumed that the turnkey provider has properties for sale for $170,000, with the financials shown in Table 68.

Table 68. Financials for purchasing a new property.

Purchase Price	$170,000
Interest Rate	3.5%
Rental Rate	$1,400
Investment Funds	$39,100

Note: The property shown in Table 68 satisfies the purchase criteria for the cash flow. It is assumed that the property also satisfies the other purchase criteria. The financial state and four returns for the property are shown in Table 69. The expenses for the property are shown in Table 70.

Table 69. The portfolio's financial state and the four returns for a new purchase.

Revenue	$16,800
Total Allowable Expenses	$15,775
Assets	$170,000
Debt	$136,000
Cash flow	$3,341
Year 1 Loan Paydown	$2,610
Appreciation @ 2%	$3,400
Depreciation @ 24% Tax Bracket	$1,231

Table 70. Expense categories for a new purchase.

Expense Category	
Mortgage Interest	$4,718
Property Tax	$1,739
Property Insurance	$1,338
Property Management Fee	$1,344
Maintenance and Repairs	$836
Vacancy	$669
Depreciation	$5,131
Income Tax	$205
Total Allowable Expenses	$15,775

The required funds to purchase the property are the down payment and the closing costs. It is assumed the bank requires a

APPENDIX D: MATHEMATICS FOR THE EXAMPLES

loan-to-value ratio of 80 percent, and the closing costs are estimated at 3 percent of the appraised value. The required funds to purchase the property is given as:

$$(1 - 0.8) * \$170{,}000 + 0.03 * 170{,}000 = \$39{,}100$$

The maximum number of properties that can be purchased for each lending option is given as the total funds from Step 6 divided by the funds required to purchase a new property. The number of properties and the remaining cash is given in Table 71. The number of new purchases ranges from one to three properties, depending on the loan product.

Table 71. Maximum number of properties that can be purchased and the remaining cash in the portfolio.

	# Properties	Cash Remaining
Refinance	1	$9,101
Cash-Out Refinance	2	$6,486
HEL	2	$18,541
HELOC	3	$276

Step 8. Determine the total ROI and the financial impact of each loan product.

The different options are evaluated as part of Step 8. The revenue, expenses, assets, debt, cash flow, loan paydown, appreciation, and effective tax rate are determined for each option. The baseline corresponds to the projected performance of the portfolio without any changes. The profit returns and the financial state at the end of Year 10 for 123 Main Street, 456 Cemetery Road, and 789 High Street are given in Table 63, Table 64, and Table 65, respectively.

Baseline:

The financial state of the baseline is determined by summing the revenue, expenses, assets, and debt of the three properties. The portfolio is projected to produce $42,638 in revenue, with $38,731 in expenses. The total asset value of the portfolio is $485,798, which is the sum of the value of the three properties and the cash in the business account. The debt of the portfolio is $266,656. The next step is to determine the cash flow, loan paydown, and appreciation of the portfolio. The cash flow is given as:

$$Cash\ Flow = Revenue - Expenses + Depreciation - Loan\ Paydown \quad \text{D.1}$$

in which the revenue, expenses, depreciation, and loan paydown are the sums of the three properties, which can again be found in Table 65, Table 66, and Table 67. The cash flow is $8,760 per year. The loan paydown and appreciation are $6,369 and $8,598 per year, respectively. The invested funds for each property are the sum of the down payment and the closing cost for the appraised value at the time of purchase. The equation for the investment funds is given as:

$$Investment\ Funds = (1-L2V) * Appraised\ Value + 0.03 * Appraised\ Value \quad \text{D.2}$$

In Eq. D.2, $L2V$ is the loan-to-value ratio, which is assumed to be 0.8 when a property is purchased. The invested funds for 123 Main Street, 456 Cemetery Road, and 789 High Street are $27,577, $29,265, and $31,056, respectively, for a total of $87,898.

For this example, it is assumed the funds used to purchase the three properties were from personal savings. The ROI of the portfolio is the total return divided by the total investment from personal savings. The ROI for the baseline case is given as:

$$ROI = \frac{\$8,760 + \$6,369 + \$8,598}{\$87,898} = 27.0\%$$

APPENDIX D: MATHEMATICS FOR THE EXAMPLES

The last metric to determine is the effective income tax rate. The effective tax rate was determined by (1) calculating the income tax and (2) dividing the income tax expense by the sum of the cash flow and loan paydown. For (1), the taxable income is determined by subtracting the total allowable expenses from the revenue and then multiplying by the appropriate tax bracket. The equation for the effective tax rate is given as:

$$\textit{Effective Tax rate} = \frac{\textit{Income Tax Expense}}{\textit{Cash Flow} + \textit{Loan Paydown}} \qquad \text{D.3}$$

in which

$$\textit{Income Tax Expenses} = \textit{Tax Bracket} * (\textit{Revenue} - \textit{Allowable Expenses}) \qquad \text{D.4}$$

For this example, the tax bracket used is the 24 percent bracket, and the portfolio is treated as passive income for tax purposes. The projected total income tax expense for the portfolio is $1,316. The sum of the cash flow and loan paydown is $14,967. The effective tax rate is 8.8 percent ($1,316 / $14,967); hence, the return from depreciation reduced the tax rate from 24 to 8.8 percent.

Refinance, No Additional Properties:

Refinancing replaces the original loan with a new loan. The borrowed balance of the new loan is given as the mortgage balance for each property at the end of the ninth year of the original mortgage, plus the closing costs. The closing costs are given as 3 percent of the appraised value of the property. The borrowed balance for the new mortgages for 123 Main, 456 Cemetery, and 789 High are $83,805, $95,241, and $106,962, respectively.

Note: The only expenses that change because of refinancing are the mortgage interest and income tax. The mortgage interest expense and loan paydown are determined using Eq. A.3 and Eq. A.5, respectively.

The corresponding total allowable expenses for 123 Main, 456 Cemetery, and 789 High are $11,089, $11,593, and $12,162, respectively. The revenue is unchanged; however, the income tax expense for the portfolio is $1,584. The assets are unchanged from the baseline.

The cash flow is $11,943 and was determined using Eq. D.1. Lastly, the effective tax rate and ROI are 9.1 percent ($1,584 / $17,432) and 29.6 percent ($26,029 / $87,898), respectively. The results are summarized below.

Table 72. Summary of refinancing without purchasing a new property.

Profit Returns		Financial State	
Cash Flow	$11,943	Revenue	$42,638
Loan Paydown	$5,489	Expenses	$36,428
Appreciation	$8,598	Assets (Prop. | Cash)	$438,472 | $48,201
Total	$26,029	Debt	$280,518
ROI	29.6%	Effective Tax Rate	9.1%

Refinance with One New Purchase:

Refinancing 123 Main, 456 Cemetery, and 789 High and purchasing one new property increases the revenue to $59,438, which is determined by summing the revenue in Table 72 with the revenue in Table 69. Similarly, the debt, total allowable expenses, and property value were determined to be $416,518, $52,408, and $608,472, respectively.

The remaining cash assets total $9,101 after purchasing the new property. The cash flow and loan paydown of $15,284 and $8,099, respectively, were determined from Eq. D.1 and Eq. A.5. The effective tax rate and ROI are 7.7 percent ($1,789 / $20,096)

APPENDIX D: MATHEMATICS FOR THE EXAMPLES

and 40.3 percent ($35,380 / $87,898), respectively. The results are summarized below in Table 73.

Table 73. Summary of refinancing without purchasing a new property.

Profit Returns		Financial State	
Cash Flow	$15,284	Revenue	$59,438
Loan Paydown	$8,099	Expenses	$52,408
Appreciation	$11,997	Assets (Prop. | Cash)	$608,472 | $9,101
Total	$35,380	Debt	$416,518
ROI	**40.3%**	Effective Tax Rate	7.7%

Cash-Out Refinance, No New Properties

The cash-out refinance replaces the original loans with a new loan. The value of 123 Main, 456 Cemetery, and 789 High at the end of the ninth year is $143,292. The mortgage balance for the new mortgage is $107,469 (0.75 * $143,292). The debt at the end of the tenth year is the sum of the debt (3 * $107,469) minus the sum of the loan paydown ($6,187) or $316,219.

The revenue and property values are unchanged. The cash assets will increase to $83,721, which was determined by summing the business account balance with the cash received from the cash-out refinance. The allowable expenses will change because the mortgage interest changes with the new loans; hence, the income tax expense will change too.

The income tax expense of $1,331 was determined using Eq. D.4. The cash flow of $10,234 was determined from Eq. D.1. The loan paydown of $6,187 was determined using Eq. D.1. Lastly, the effective tax rate of 8.1 percent was determined using Eq. D.3. The results are summarized below in Table 74.

Table 74. *Summary of the cash-out refinance without purchasing a new property.*

Profit Returns		Financial State	
Cash Flow	$10,234	Revenue	$42,638
Loan Paydown	$6,187	Expenses	$37,438
Appreciation	$8,598	Assets (Prop. | Cash)	$438,472 | $83,721
Total	$25,019	Debt	$316,219
ROI	**28.5%**	Effective Tax Rate	8.1%

Cash-Out Refinance, Two New Properties

The financial state and four returns for the cash-out refinance and the purchase of two new properties is similar to the analysis of the other options in this example. The cash assets of $83,721, which are given in Table 75, are used to purchase two new properties, with the financials, expenses, and projected returns shown in Table 68, Table 69, and Table 70, respectively. The cash remaining is $5,521 and was determined by subtracting the investment funds required to purchase the two properties from the $83,721 in cash assets.

The total property value at the end of the tenth year was $778,472 and was determined by summing the value of the five properties. The revenue, debt, and expenses of $76,238, $588,219, and $69,399 were determined by summing the results in Table 74 with the results in Table 69 and Table 70. The cash flow, loan paydown, income tax expense, and effective tax rate were determined using equations D.1, A.5, D.4, and D.3, respectively. The results are summarized below in Table 75.

Table 75. Summary of the cash-out refinance with purchasing two new properties.

Profit Returns		Financial State	
Cash Flow	$16,916	Revenue	$76,238
Loan Paydown	$11,407	Expenses	$69,399
Appreciation	$15,398	Assets (Props. | Cash)	$778,472 | $5,521
Total	$43,720	Debt	$588,219
ROI	**49.7%**	Effective Tax Rate	6.2%

HEL, No New Properties

The revenue and property value of the portfolio is the same as the baseline. The mortgage interest, debt, and cash assets change because of the second mortgage. The borrowed balance for the second mortgage (HEL) is determined by (1) determining the maximum allowable borrowed funds and (2) subtracting the maximum allowable borrowed funds from the outstanding balance of the first mortgage. The maximum allowable borrowed funds are given as:

$$\text{Max Borrowed Funds} = L2V * \text{Appraised Value} \qquad \text{D.5}$$

The maximum borrowed funds for each of the three existing properties in the portfolio is $107,469 (0.75 * $143,292). The outstanding balances for 123 Main, 456 Cemetery, and 789 High are $79,420, $90,942, and $102,663, respectively. The balance of the HEL is given as:

$$\text{HEL Balance} = \text{Max Borrowed Funds} - \text{Mortgage Balance} - \text{Closing Costs} \qquad \text{D.6}$$

The closing costs are estimated as 3 percent of the maximum borrowed funds, minus the mortgage balance of the first mortgage.

The HEL balance for 123 Main, 456 Cemetery, and 789 High are $27,208, $16,031, and $4,662, respectively.

The loan paydown and mortgage interest for the HEL were determined using Eq. A.5 and Eq. A.3, respectively. The total loan paydown and mortgage interest expense are determined by summing the respective components from the primary and HEL mortgages. A summary of the financial state and profit returns is shown in Table 76.

Table 76. Summary of the HEL without purchasing a new property.

Profit Returns		Financial State	
Cash Flow	$6,797	Revenue	$42,638
Loan Paydown	$7,286	Expenses	$39,777
Appreciation	$8,598	Assets (Props. | Cash)	$438,472 | $95,013
Total	$22,680	Debt	$328,854
ROI	**25.8%**	Effective Tax Rate	5.0%

HEL, Two New Properties

The financial state for the HEL with two new purchases is determined by first utilizing some of the cash assets shown in Table 76 to purchase those two new properties. The profit returns and financial state of the portfolio are determined by summing Table 68 and Table 69 with Table 76. A summary of the result is shown in Table 77.

APPENDIX D: MATHEMATICS FOR THE EXAMPLES

Table 77. Summary of the HEL with purchasing two new properties.

Profit Returns		Financial State	
Cash Flow	$13,337	Revenue	$76,238
Loan Paydown	$12,521	Expenses	$71,764
Appreciation	$15,398	Assets (Props. | Cash)	$778,472 | $17,576
Total	$41,355	Debt	$600,854
ROI	**47.0%**	Effective Tax Rate	4.3%

HELOC, No New Properties

Determining the portfolio's revised financial state and profit returns for the HELOC option with no new purchases is similar to the cash-out refinance option with no new purchases. For the HELOC option, the primary mortgage is unchanged, resulting in the financial state of the portfolio being nearly identical to the baseline. The cash assets of $116,111 include funds in the business account and the balance of the HELOCs. A summary of the results is below in Table 78.

Table 78. Summary of the HELOC without purchasing new properties.

Profit Returns		Financial State	
Cash Flow	$8,760	Revenue	$42,638
Loan Paydown	$6,369	Expenses	$38,731
Appreciation	$8,598	Assets (Props. | Assets)	$438,472 | $116,611
Total	$23,727	Debt	$266,656
ROI	**27.0%**	Effective Tax Rate	8.7%

HELOC, Three New Properties

The financial state for the HELOC option with three new purchases is determined by first utilizing most of the cash assets shown in Table 78 to purchase three new properties. The monthly HELOC payments are interest-only during the draw period; hence, there is no contribution to the loan paydown from the HELOC during the tenth year.

The interest expense from the HELOC is given as the monthly rate times the outstanding balance (the outstanding balance is computed using Eq. D.5 and Eq. D.6). The remaining financial parameters are determined by summing the baseline financials with the financials for the three new property purchases. The results are summarized below in Table 79.

Table 79. Summary of the HELOC with purchasing three new properties.

Profit Returns		Financial State	
Cash Flow	$16,855	Revenue	$93,038
Loan Paydown	$14,199	Expenses	$88,598
Appreciation	$18,798	Assets (Props. | Cash)	$948,472 | $276
Total	$49,852	Debt	$751,900
ROI	**56.7%**	Effective Tax Rate	3.7%

Step 8. Determine how many years have passed since the beginning of the last real estate recession.

The last real estate recession began in 2007 and bottomed out in 2009. For the purpose of this example, let's assume it is 2021. Let's also assume we were evaluating scaling options during the summer of 2021. The number of years from the beginning of the last real estate recession is fourteen (2021–2007).

APPENDIX D: MATHEMATICS FOR THE EXAMPLES

Step 9. Is it a buyer's market or a seller's market?

In the summer of 2021, it was very much a strong seller's market.

Step 10. Estimate the likely phase for the real estate market.

The market is likely in the last quarter of the expansion phase. Remember, the average period for the real estate market cycle is 18.6 years, and the cycle under consideration has lasted for fourteen years.

Step 11. Build a plan based on market-generated data and then take action. The plan from the checklist is summarized below.

- Recession Phase: Buy property only after the bottom of the market. Look for cash flow or appreciation properties tenanted with two-year leases.
- Recovery Phase: Buy cash flow or appreciation properties with two-year leases.
- Expansion Phase:
    ◊ Early in the expansion phase—buy appreciation or cash flow properties.
    ◊ Middle of the expansion phase—buy cash flow properties with two-year leases.
    ◊ Last quarter of the expansion phase—consider waiting to buy. Only buy cash flow properties with two-year leases that are producing $300 per month or greater than 20 percent (or preferably closer to 30 percent) of the gross rent. Use the current cash flow as a bellwether indicator for the market. Instead, focus on financing options that increase cash flow, reduce debt, and/or increase the reserve fund.
- Hyper Supply Phase—wait to buy properties. Instead, focus on financing options and strategies that increase cash flow, reduce debt, and increase the reserve fund.

GLOSSARY

The terms defined here pertain to turnkey rental investing and may have other definitions. Please refer to outside sources for these other definitions.

Accredited Investor: A person with a net worth greater than $1,000,000 or with annual W-2 earnings greater than $200,000 ($300,000 if married) for at least two years with the expectation of maintaining this rate.

Amortization Table: A table that shows how your mortgage payment breaks down to the principal paid and interest paid each month.

Appraisal Gap: The difference between the purchase price and the appraisal.

Appraisal Methods: The methodologies used by an appraiser to determine the appraised value of a property.

Appreciation: An increase in monetary value; the change in value of the property with respect to the purchase price.

Appreciation Market: A metropolitan area where above-average appreciation is expected.

Business System: A checklist ordered chronologically that lists all the actionable items required to complete a task.

Business Structure: A structure pertaining to different methods of titling rental properties such as using LLCs or trusts or listing the property in your personal name to provide asset protection.

Capital Gain: The profit from the sale of a property or an investment.

Cash Flow: The profit achieved when you operate a property and that is realized every month after all the operating expenses have been covered.

Cash Flow Market: A metropolitan area where rental properties produce above-average cash flow.

Cost Basis: The purchase price of a property.

Debt-to-Income Ratio (DTI): The ratio of all your monthly debts divided by your monthly income.

Depreciation: An IRS-allowed reduction in the value of an asset with the passage of time, due, in particular, to wear and tear; the replacement cost of the property spread out over 27.5 years for the building (land is considered to last forever).

Due Diligence: Reasonable steps taken by a person to satisfy a legal requirement, especially in buying or selling something; it is used to mitigate risk and includes verifying the information provided by the seller, inspecting the physical property, and verifying the title of the property.

Earnest Deposit: A good faith deposit paid by the buyer to the seller as a token of confirmation that they are seriously interested in buying a property.

Equity: the money value of a property in excess of any claims or liens against it.

Escrow: A system in which things of value such as a deed, a bond, money, or a piece of property are held in trust by a disinterested third party until specified conditions have been met.

Exiting: A two-component strategy designed to let you remove yourself from the business and that also involves your long-term plan for the property.

Expansion Phase: An economic phase during which the economy grows and jobs increase, resulting in a rise in the demand for housing.

Forced Appreciation: The value added to the property by renovating that property.

Gross Domestic Product (GDP): The estimated monetary value of a metropolitan area.

Home Equity Line of Credit (HELOC): A loan product that is similar to a credit card in which the balance is determined by the amount of equity.

Housing Affordability Index: A measure of the likelihood a household can afford to purchase a home.

Housing Supply: A representation of how many months of inventory is listed; usually reported in months.

Hyper Supply Phase: An economical phase during which developers and redevelopers flood the market with inventory and the demand for housing peaks, eventually causing the supply to exceed the demand.

Investment Funds: Funds to cover the down payment, closing costs, and reserve fund.

Lease Option: A rental lease with an included option for the tenant to purchase the property at the end of that lease.

Loan-to-Value Ratio: The ratio of the loan amount divided by the value of the property; a representation of the amount of risk for the lender.

Metropolitan Area: An area with a population of at least 500,000.

Preapproval Process: A process in which the lender verifies an individual's financials and runs their credit.

Prequalification Process: A process less rigorous than preapproval during which the lender reviews the provided financial information but does not run credit or verify financials.

Prorated: The amount that is divided or assessed proportionately (as to reflect an amount of time that is less than the full amount included in the initial arrangement).

Purchase and Sales Agreement: A legally binding contract that lists all the terms and conditions between the seller and the buyer of a property.

Real Estate Market Cycle: A cycle that consists of four phases, namely, recovery, expansion, hyper supply, and recession.

Recovery Period: The period during which the real estate market is at its lowest point (the end of a recession).

Reserve Fund: Funds for unexpected expenses that the monthly cash flow is unable to cover.

Return on Investment (ROI): A measurement of gain and loss generated on an investment relative to the amount of money invested; the annualized return divided by the funds invested.

Seller Financing: A financing process in which the landlord (seller) becomes the lender for the buyer.

Succession Plan: A plan to exit your business when you determine you are ready to retire.

Turnkey Provider: A company that specializes in selling turnkey rental properties to investor clients.

Turnkey Rentals: Single and multifamily rental properties that have been renovated and tenanted, with property management in place, and sold to an investor.

Umbrella Insurance: Insurance that provides additional liability coverage that exceeds and kicks in after the normal homeowner's insurance. It is coverage that gives extra security for those at risk of being sued. It can also protect against libel, vandalism, slander, and invasion of privacy.

Scott A. Stanfield purchased his first rental property in 2013 and has been a professional turnkey rental property investor since 2017. He has amassed a portfolio of $3 million and owns properties across seven states, including Tennessee, Arkansas, Oklahoma, Georgia, Missouri, Alabama and Ohio.

Scott also holds a PhD in Engineering and had a fifteen-year career as a Research Scientist with Innovation Scientific Solutions, Inc and the Air Force Research Laboratory in Dayton, Ohio. He has published articles in fourteen scientific journals and over thirty scientific conference papers. He is a multiple award-winning scientific presenter.

Scott makes his home in Ohio. This is his first book.

Learn more about Scott at www.scottastanfield.com.

www.ingramcontent.com/pod-product-compliance
Lightning Source LLC
LaVergne TN
LVHW091612070526
838199LV00044B/768